THE ART OF POLITICS

THE · ART · OF POLITICS

THE NEW BETRAYAL OF AMERICA
AND HOW TO RESIST IT

✦   ✦   ✦

JOHN KEKES

ENCOUNTER BOOKS NEW YORK · LONDON

First edition published in 2008 by Encounter Books, an activity of Encounter for Culture and Education, Inc., a nonprofit, tax exempt corporation. Encounter Books website address: www.encounterbooks.com

Manufactured in the United States and printed on acid-free paper. The paper used in this publication meets the minimum requirements of ANSI/NISO Z39.48–1992 (R 1997) (Permanence of Paper).

FIRST EDITION

LIBRARY OF CONGRESS
CATALOGING-IN-PUBLICATION DATA
Kekes, John.
The art of politics : the new betrayal of America and how to resist it / John Kekes.
p.   cm.
Includes bibliographical references and index.
ISBN-13: 978-1-59403-235-6 (hardcover : alk. paper)
ISBN-10: 1-59403-235-1 (hardcover : alk. paper)
1. United States—Politics and government.
2. Politics, Practical—United States.
3. Political culture—United States.
4. Political science—Philosophy. I. Title.
JK275.K44 2008
320.973—dc22
2008001929

10 9 8 7 6 5 4 3 2 1

CONTENTS

INTRODUCTION

✦　　✦　　✦

In political activity ... men sail a boundless and bottomless sea; there is neither harbour for shelter nor floor for anchorage, neither starting-place nor appointed destination. The enterprise is to keep afloat on an even keel.... A depressing doctrine, it will be said.... But in the main the depression springs from the exclusion of hopes that were false and the discovery that guides, reputed to be of superhuman wisdom and skill, are, in fact, of a somewhat different character. If the doctrine deprives us of a model laid up in heaven, at least it does not lead us into a morass where every choice is equally good or equally to be deplored.... It should depress only those who have lost their nerve.

MICHAEL OAKESHOTT
"Political Education"

AMERICAN CONSTITUTIONAL DEMOCRACY is far from perfect and our dissatisfactions with it are many. Nevertheless it is the envy of the world and perhaps the least bad approach to politics to have emerged in the course of human history. Its chief merit is that it provides the political goods—such as liberty, toleration, justice, property, and equality—we need for our well-being. Politics involves never-ending disagreements about how to resolve unavoidable conflicts among these and other goods, and the art of politics is to find, again and again, optimal resolutions. This is formidably difficult because even if we agree about the goods we need, we tend to disagree about their interpretation and respective importance, and because there is no law, principle, or natural order of priority to which we could appeal. No resolution is final and seeking it is futile. There are reasonable resolutions but they work only in particular contexts, the contexts continually change, and we must resolve disagreements about what resolutions are reasonable.

This approach to politics is betrayed by ideologues. The betrayal began about forty years ago with protests against the war in Vietnam but it soon changed into an attack against the rule of law, the universities, the military, the police, family life, and against accepted standards and conventions of morality, politics, education, journalism, civility, and decency. As a result, private relations between men and women, husbands and wives, parents and children, teachers and students have become politicized, and so have institutions, such as newspapers, television, radio, health care, charities, and churches. Ideologues aim to change the way Americans see the world, evaluate facts, and judge the significance of what happens in politics.

Societies and values continually change but the changes that have occurred since the '60s are unprecedented in American history. They are deeper than any before, they affect virtually all areas of life, and their cumulative effect is inescapable. The justification ideologues offer for the changes is strident, hypocritical, and specious moralizing. What they condemn is held to be immoral, unjust, exploitative, discriminatory, racist, sexist, imperialist, and the like. They divide Americans into the good, who agree with them, and the bad, who do not. Individuals are seen as selfless or self-serving; perpetrator or victim; one of the haves or of the have-nots; moral or immoral, and the condemnation of those who are accused of falling into the wrong category is vicious. Opponents are demonized, hounded, maligned, and abused. Ideologues have made "borking" a necessary term to describe what they do to those who dare to disagree with them.

Contrary to appearances, however, their vicious attacks are not directed against individuals as such but against them as defenders of the prevailing political system. What ideologues really care about is changing the country, not specific persons. They attack people because they see them as obstacles to changing the existing unjust system into the just one to which the ideologues claim to hold the key. Their vehemence, fervor, inflated rhetoric, and endless fund of indignation is fuelled by the passionate certainty that they are on a crusade against the injustice America has perpetrated on its own citizens who suffer because they are female, black, or poor. They want to save Americans from the capitalist, sexist, racist, imperialist system that the haves maintain to exploit the have-nots.

This grotesquely false view of the American past and present is the prevailing orthodoxy at universities that are supposed to prepare the next generation for responsible positions. But the preparation consists in the indoctrination of students by ideologues ensconced in tenured positions. They rely on the privilege of academic freedom to betray the society that makes their betrayal possible. And they have been remarkably successful because their visceral hatred and condemnation of American policies are widely parroted by their students who are beginning to occupy important positions. That these maligned policies have been formulated and adopted by politicians whom Americans, including women, blacks, and the poor, have freely elected to do just that makes no difference to the ideologues. If the policies have been produced by the time-honored political process, then the ideologues know that the policies serve immoral goals by unjust means.

The routinely employed technique of ideologues is the systematic falsification of the facts. It proceeds by the misinterpretation of complex political situations by ignoring the success of policies designed to cope with them, exaggerating their costs and failures, and charging policy-makers with stupidity, ignorance, malevolence, and often all three at once. This technique is much favored by academics who claim to be experts. Their expertise is then touted by their allies who control much of the media and who have often been students of the so-called experts. They then use the media to disseminate the falsifications as the objective judgments of respected authorities.

Here are some examples of how this technique is used. Ideologues condemn the immorality of the system that allows approximately 15 percent of the population to live in poverty. They ignore the historically unprecedented achievement that 85 percent of American citizens enjoy at least some measure of prosperity. Ideologues stress poverty but they do not mention that it is relative poverty; not the poverty of people whose basic needs are unsatisfied but of those who do not have as much as others. They do not mention that what counts as poverty here would count as affluence at many places in the world. Nor do they acknowledge that the poor are supported by welfare and many of them own a house, car, television, and much else.

Ideologues rail against the prevailing inequalities. They claim that justice requires the equal distribution of wealth and they advocate radical redistribution that involves taking from people much of what they have earned and giving it to those who have not earned it. And they claim this in the name of justice while refusing to ask whether people deserve what they have or are responsible for what they lack. If this is justice, then black is white.

Ideologues claim that American society is racist. They ignore the Civil War in which hundreds of thousands of white males gave their lives to liberate slaves; they ignore that white males in Congress made the Civil Rights Act into law; and that discrimination in housing, education, and employment has been outlawed and that these laws are enforced. Nor do they see fit to mention that billions of tax dollars paid by whites have been and are being spent to improve the welfare of blacks.

Ideologues condemn discrimination against blacks and women but they applaud affirmative action programs that discriminate in favor of blacks and women. They condemn hate speech against homosexuals but they routinely employ hate speech against the

Christian right. They urge the prosecution of lies about the Holocaust but they enthusiastically support lies about American imperialism. They hypocritically appeal to the sanctity of human lives in condemning capital punishment but they do not think it applies to abortion. They pose as civilized tolerant people who put up with obscenity in public places but they are neither civilized nor tolerant about cigarette smoking in public places. They condemn prayer in public schools as an unjustifiable intrusion into private beliefs but they urge sex education in public schools regardless of the private beliefs of parents. They see their innocent fellow-citizens murdered by terrorists but instead of blaming the terrorists they invent absurd reasons for blaming America. They condemn their country for failing to prevent mass murders in Africa but they condemn their country for preventing mass murders in Iraq.

Ideologues excoriate American economic policies even though much of the rest of the world has eagerly adopted them as the key to prosperity. They condemn affluent citizens for their indifference to the plight of the poor but they ignore that their taxes support the federal budget, approximately 60 percent of which is earmarked for social programs that largely benefit the poor. They condemn their country for dooming illegal immigrants to a desperate situation but they ignore the ceaseless flow of illegal immigrants who clamor to get into the very situation the ideologues see as desperate. They blame their country for not spending enough billions to cope with AIDS but they fail to mention that the funds would have to come from taxes paid by prudent citizens who would be forced to pay for the imprudent sexual practices of others.

Ideologues claim that they are in favor of individual liberty but what they in fact favor is intrusion into private lives and the imposition of their moral views on others. They tell people what food is right or wrong to eat; what clothing they should not wear; how they should spend their after-tax income; how precisely they should phrase invitations for sex; what kind of bags they should carry their groceries in; when and where they should pray or smoke;

what jokes they ought to tell; who should pick the fruit they buy at the supermarket; how they should invest their money; what chemicals they should use in their gardens; by what method of transportation they should go to work; how they should sort their garbage; what they ought to think about cross-dressing, sex-change operations, teenage sex, and pot smoking; they forbid people to inquire about the age, marital status, drug use, or alcoholism of job applicants; they accuse people of sexual abuse if they spank their children or hug their neighbor's; they permit 19- and 20-year-olds to fight wars but not to buy a beer; they condemn people who say that someone is crippled, stupid, mentally defective, fat, or ignorant; and they censor words like "mankind," "statesman," or "He" when referring to God.

The ideologues' view is a poisonous mixture of hypocrisy, specious moralizing, and abuse of America, the country that provides the benefits they enjoy, benefits they use to betray their benefactor. It is hard to know what is more repulsive: the hypocrisy of phony indignation at policies they have misrepresented, the absurd prejudices that underlie their specious moralizing, or the ingratitude of repaying the benefits by feigning outrage at the political process that provides them.

Reasonable observers of the American political scene will recognize the accuracy of these descriptions but they may not be alarmed by them. They may think that American politics has often gone through periods of rough-and-tumble and that those who cannot stand the heat should get out of the kitchen. Or they are put off by politics, get on with their lives, and shrug at the lies. Both attitudes are dangerous because they ignore that what is at stake is not this or that policy but the American political system. What is happening is not the usual conflict between conservatives and reformers but the betrayal of what is now the oldest continuous constitutional democracy in the world.

It goes without saying that reform is always needed, that there has always been much in American society that should be changed.

Introduction

There has been dire poverty and discrimination against blacks and women; education is in a terrible state; the cost of health care is disgraceful; drug addiction is rampant; the level of violent crime is unacceptable; many inner cities have become ghettos; popular entertainment is mindless; the welfare system is permeated with fraud and inefficiency; prison conditions are barbaric; and so on.

If ideologues merely pointed to these ills and demanded urgent redress, they would stand in a long line of American reformers. But this is not what they do. They attack the foundation of American society and claim that only by radically changing it can what they falsely decry as defects be remedied. Thus they attack the economic system, the source of our prosperity; they undermine family life, the key to the moral education of children; they deny that individuals are responsible for their own welfare; they reject the basic idea of justice that people should get what they deserve and should not get what they do not deserve; and they advocate drastic restrictions of the liberty to speak one's mind, associate with people of one's choice, and dispose of private property as one sees fit. Attacks on prosperity, the family, individual responsibility, private property, justice, and liberty do not lead to reform but to radical change for the worse. That is why ideologues have brought America to a very dangerous state.

Why are we in this dangerous state now? Because the winds of doctrine have reached our shores and have blown our way the malady that has for centuries plagued Europeans. We are now "tossed to and fro and carried about with every wind of doctrine, by the cunning of men, by their craftiness in deceitful wiles," as *Ephesians 4:14* presciently remarks. Before this ill wind blew our way, American politics was occupied with solving problems, coping with emergencies, remedying justified grievances, and reconciling conflicting interests. It was a practical enterprise whose aim was to find practical solutions to practical problems. The Constitution and subsequent legislation defined the limits and guided the ways politics was to be conducted. This worked very well most of the time, although not always, as shown by the Civil War, the Prohibition, and the Great Depression. On the whole, however, it proved remarkably successful and it has enjoyed the continued allegiance of the overwhelming majority of native born Americans and of the millions of immigrants who have been attracted by the opportunities the political system provides. Before the '60s America was the richest, freest, the most powerful, prosperous, and stable political system in the world. And then came the '60s and the winds of doctrine.

Those infected by the malady of doctrine uncritically and unreflectively adopted the much-discredited European view that politics ought to aim at an ideal derived from an ideology. They were no longer satisfied with solving problems, coping with emergencies, and reconciling interests. They had an ideology that had to be followed because its ideal defined what is good. The right policies aim at the achievement of the ideal and the wrong policies hinder it. Those who understood the ideology and accepted its ideal knew how politics ought to go were said to have a moral obligation to make it go that way. This led them to see their opponents as either ignorant or wicked. Morality compelled them to force the ignorant for their own good to follow the policies dictated by the ideology because that is what the ignorant would do if they were not ignorant. And the wicked, who understood but rejected the ideology, had to be removed as obstacles to the betterment of humanity. This is the thinking that motivated the Jacobins of the French Revolution, the Bolsheviks of the Russian Revolution, the Nazi elite of Hitler's Germany, the henchmen of Mao, the cadres of Pol Pot, and the countless other ideologically inspired regimes that broke endless eggs without making any omelets. And this is the thinking that motivates present-day American ideologues as well. Their efforts have not led to the crimes of these other regimes partly because their technique of misrepresentation has proved remarkably effective in a free society that allows its enemies to have their say. The explanation of why we have reached our present state now, rather than at some earlier time, is that it has taken ideologues this long to dupe a sufficient number of naive people to swallow their ruinous ideology and the so-called moral imperative to realize its ideal.

The ideologies pursued by these deplorable regimes were of course varied, but the assumption that politics must be driven by an ideology was shared by all of them, including their American brethren. The ideal of American ideologues is an egalitarian society in which everyone has equal worth and an equal share of resources. All other values must be subordinated to the pursuit of this ideal. If the ideal conflicts with liberty, justice, individual rights, private property, or whatever else, the ideal must prevail over them.

Egalitarian ideology involves the absurd extension of the legal and political equality guaranteed by the Constitution to aspects of life in which equality has no place. Human beings differ in their characters, circumstances, talents and weaknesses, capacities and incapacities, virtues and vices; in their moral standing, political views, religious convictions, aesthetic preferences, and personal projects; in how reasonable or unreasonable they are, how well or badly they develop their inborn endowments, how much they benefit or harm others, how hardworking or disciplined they were in the past and likely to be in the future, and so forth. How could anyone believe that moral and immoral, law-abiding and criminal, prudent and imprudent people have equal worth and should enjoy equal benefits? How could anyone believe that terrorists and their victims, homeowners and burglars, pedophiles and raped children, benefactors and scourges of humanity have or should have equal moral status? How could anyone regard it as an ideal that a substantial portion of people's earnings should be taken from them and given to those who could have but did not earn anything? How could it be accepted as an ideal that all should enjoy the same benefits regardless of how responsible or irresponsible they are, or how much or little they have contributed to producing those benefits? Yet it is to this absurd ideal that ideologues appeal in defining good and bad policies, criticizing existing values, identifying moral and immoral people, indoctrinating those who are willing to listen to them, and justifying their attempt to transform American politics from a practical enterprise to the dogmatic pursuit of an indefensible ideology.

What, then, should we do to resist ideologues? The first thing is not to be bamboozled or intimidated by their moralistic bullying and to point out as frequently as practicable the absurdity of their dogmatic pronouncements. The other is to reaffirm American politics as a practical enterprise and resist its corruption by egalitarian or any other ideology. The fundamental aim of American politics is to maintain a balance, not to pursue perfection dictated by an ideology. The balance is of the political values formulated by the Constitution and interpreted and re-interpreted to fit the ever-changing circumstances at home and in the world. These values have stood the test of time and have continued to attract the allegiance of the overwhelming majority of Americans. It is not hard to list them: democracy, equality, individual rights, justice, liberty, order, peace, private property, rule of law, security, and stability. They continually conflict, their interpretations and comparative importance in particular situations are often controversial, and it is difficult to know how they should be applied to cope with new problems, emergencies, and interests. The practical aim of American politics has been to cope with these difficulties guided by the laws and limits as defined by the Constitution. Doing so is rarely easy and it has often failed. But the well-being of Americans largely depends on continuing to do as well as possible what fallible politicians have managed to do since the founding of the Republic. We should continue this process and take to heart the splendid Arab proverb: the dogs bark but the caravan ambles on.

What follows is my attempt to make a case for non-ideological politics and against the ideological approach. I have become convinced that the basic political division in contemporary democracies is between ideologues and their opponents, not between the left and the right, nor between liberals and conservatives.

There are many specialist books on politics but this is not one of them. It is about the political goods we have reason to value, not a book about other books. Because this topic is of interest to thinking people and not the closed turf of specialists, I wrote it for literate general readers. I did not want to clutter the pages with footnotes and references, but as a guide to further reading and a way of acknowledging the sources of my ideas, I provided notes, which are collected at the end. The chapters, however, stand on their own and can be understood without the notes.

The structure of the book is simple. The first chapter sketches the balanced view I defend and the ideological approach I oppose. Each subsequent chapter has a critical and a constructive aim. The critical one is to give reasons for rejecting the ideological interpretation of the political good that is the subject of the chapter. The constructive one is to provide what I take to be the right interpretation and give reasons for accepting it. The subjects I consider are reason as prudence, the plurality of goods, necessary limits, limited liberty, toleration within reason, justice as having what one deserves, the right to private property, equality as the exclusion of arbitrariness, political democracy, legitimate authority, and civility as a social condition. The complete account of the balanced view emerges only at the end when I provide an overview of the preceding discussions.

Each chapter starts with an epigraph intended to express the central point of the discussion that follows. Readers wanting to form a preliminary idea of the bare conclusions I have reached, without a decent clothing of reasons, could do worse than read the epigraphs one after the other.

CHAPTER ONE

✦ ✦ ✦

THE BALANCED VIEW

Many social reformers have an idea that they would like to clean the canvas . . . of the social world . . . and starting from scratch with a brand new rational world. This idea is nonsense and impossible to realize. . . . If we wipe out the social world in which we live, wipe out its traditions and create a new world on the basis of blue-prints, then we shall very soon have to alter the new world, making little changes and adjustments. But if we are to make these little changes and adjustments, which will be needed in any case, why not start them here and now in the social world we have? . . . It is very much more sensible and reasonable to start with what happens to exist at the moment, because of these things . . . we at least know where the shoe pinches.

KARL R. POPPER
"Towards a Rational Theory of Tradition"

1.1 MY TOWN

I LIVE IN A SMALL TOWN of about 4,000 people. It is a mixed community. Some are farmers, others commute by car to work in the nearby city; some are retired, others are raising young children; there are physicians, lawyers, engineers; local builders; owners and employees of small businesses; welders, electricians, plumbers, and carpenters; school teachers and nurses. The town has one main street, and most people live on several-acre lots spread over the countryside within a radius of about one mile from the main street. The dwellings on these rural lots range from very modest to quite expensive. Some are old farmhouses, some trailers, and some recently built. There is virtually no crime; the police consists of a part-time officer who occasionally tickets people when they drive too fast on the main street; there is a volunteer fire department; and the mail lady knows everyone at least by sight. My town is a nice place.

The town hall is on the main street: that is where we vote, pay taxes, where the town council, whose elected members serve at nominal salaries, have their offices, and where the monthly town meetings are held. The town hall is old; when a meeting is well attended, not everyone can be seated; its parking space is limited, so that on busy days some cars have to park on the main street; and the offices are small. The town hall is not quite as convenient as it might be.

As a result of prudent management, the town has accumulated a surplus. The council decided to build a new town hall, and use the surplus and future tax revenues to pay for it. Plans were designed and displayed. Opinions in the town were sharply divided on two issues. One was procedural: many people thought that the town council lacked the authority to make such a decision without putting the question to a general vote. The bylaws were unfortunately imprecise on whether a general vote was required. The other issue was substantive: numerous people doubted that a new town hall was needed at all, and many found the plans seriously flawed. Several town meetings were held, both sides on both issues were challenged and defended. The uncommitted were canvassed and the usually uninvolved were mobilized.

The procedural arguments for putting the question to a general vote were that the authority for making a decision lay with the people of the town, not the council. The council was elected to execute the people's wishes, so the council should find out what their wish was on this question. The argument against the vote was that the council had the authority to make the decision because they were elected to do just that. By voting them into office, people showed that they trusted them to represent their interests. If the council made a decision, it should be accepted. If people thought that the council's decisions were bad, they could show their disapproval at the next election.

The council listened to both arguments and decided to call a general vote. They made it clear, however, that it was not the strength of the pro-vote argument that persuaded them. Rather, they did not want to ignore the wishes of those who wanted a vote. They were after all neighbors and friends, attended the same church, served on the same committee in the local school district, had business dealings with each other, they were jogging or walking partners, saw eye to eye on national or international political issues, served together as volunteer firemen, their children were best friends, or they had a few beers together in the local inn every week, and so forth. The council could have held out, but did not because its members thought that it was more important to avoid bad feelings than to stand fast on a principle that has been called into question.

The substantive issue was difficult because everyone agreed that the old town hall was occasionally cramped. The disagreement was not about facts but whether anything should be done to change the facts. Those who favored building a new town hall emphasized the inconveniences of the old one; stressed the benefits of a large enough hall, ample parking space, more spacious offices, and a better looking building; they said that the town has a surplus, so it might as well be used; they pointed out that the old town hall has no wheelchair access and State law requires that there should be one; they argued that the town must move with the times, as several neighboring towns have done; and they claimed that as the population of the town increases in the future, the old town hall will become even less serviceable.

The anti-building argument was that the inconveniences of the old town hall are minor and rarely felt; a new town hall will also

THE ART OF POLITICS

have as yet unforeseeable inconveniences; the surplus should be kept for emergencies; it is absurd to want wheelchair access because no one in the town is confined to a wheelchair; there is no need to plan for the growth of the population because zoning regulations prevent it; no building was ever built within the originally estimated cost and time frame; and it is unwise to incur a debt that would have to be paid by future tax revenues and likely to lead to increased tax rates affecting everyone. The vote came and the pro-building side won by a narrow margin. In my opinion this was a pity because the anti-building arguments were much stronger.

1.2 CAUTION AND MODERATE REFORM

What happened about the town hall is the very model of how politics goes when it is going well. Even if the particular decision reached was mistaken, what mattered was that it had been reached in a way that no one could reasonably fault. Those who wanted to say something said it, their opinions were heard, and they had a chance to influence others. The happy result was that after the vote had been taken and counted, there was no enmity left. The issue was settled, people went on to think about other matters, and life continued as before. This was important because people liked to live in the town. If they were unhappy, it was not because of the affairs of the town but because of their marriage, work, children, or health. The local political aspect of their lives was all right. Civility prevailed and that mattered more than the town hall. People had something to lose, and they would have lost it if instead of civility there had been enmity. The council avoided procedural wrangling, opinions were not ignored, and the town's congenial way of life could go on unaffected.

Civility could prevail, however, only because the town hall in particular and local politics in general played only a small part in people's lives. It did not seriously affect their economic interests and they were engaged with the affairs of their family, work, hobbies, and friendships.

If they were worried, it was about the national economy, their sex life, the fortunes of their favorite team, aging, and being overweight. They dreamt, planned, plotted, quarreled, had affairs, gossiped, and raised kids. Town politics was not a matter of life or death, not even of poverty or affluence; it was for them an activity of low importance that engaged their attention only occasionally. If a particular political decision did not go as they would have preferred, it really did not matter all that much so long as the political process itself remained unchanged. It is one of the great goods of life if politics in one's society is like that. For it allows people to get on with their lives and make of them what they can. And if politics is like that, then those who enjoy it have something they have good reason to protect.

The dispute between the pro- and anti-building sides is not a peculiarity of this particular issue in my town, but a standard feature of normal politics. There are cautious people who want to protect what they have so they can continue to enjoy it; there are also venturesome ones who want to improve what they have in order to enjoy it more fully. The first is the party of caution; the second the party of reform. Both caution and reform are necessary, of course. Without caution, a society would court disaster; without reform, it could not cope with the endlessly shifting contingencies of life. The question, therefore, is not whether a society should favor caution or reform, but whether, given the particular circumstances of a particular society at a particular time, caution or reform is more important for the protection of what people have and do not want to lose. The reasonable answer is that, depending on the contingencies, sometimes one, sometimes the other is more important.

The arguments of the party of caution form a predictable pattern: we have something to lose, let us not risk it by reforms unless they are strictly necessary. The present state of politics always has some inconveniences and reform always has unpredictable consequences. Let us put up with the inconveniences if we can. If we cannot and reform is forced on us, let us make it no more than what is required for coping with the problem at hand. The arguments of the party of reform depend on whether moderate or radical reform is thought to be desirable.

There is a large area within which advocates of caution and moderate reform agree: the aim of politics is to protect what we have and enjoy, and what makes it possible for people to concentrate on their private affairs and pursue whatever goals they may have. They also agree that what calls for political decision is a generally felt dissatisfaction with some particular aspect of the largely satisfactory political conditions, like the inconveniences of the old town hall. They agree, therefore, that the cause of political arguments is a particular dissatisfaction and their aim is to remove it.

Supporters of moderate reform and caution disagree about two kinds of judgment that politics requires making. The first is about the extent and seriousness of a felt dissatisfaction. Moderate reformers tend to be more easily alarmed by dissatisfactions than supporters of caution. Grumbling is normal and expectable even in the best of societies. It calls for good judgment to decide when grumbling is widespread and turns into something more serious. Making such judgments well depends on knowing the details of the circumstances, the people who grumble, and what counts as a reasonable expectation in those circumstances. An overweight couch potato complaining about the distance he has to walk to get from his car to the town hall is one thing. Retired people finding it hard to walk on the icy road during the winter is quite another. Moderate reformers tend to err on the side of treating mere grumblings as dissatisfactions, while cautious people tend to err on the other side and treat dissatisfactions as grumblings. Who is right is a matter of judgment and making it depends on local knowledge.

The other judgment about which moderate reformers and cautious ones disagree is the extent of the reform needed to remove the dissatisfaction. Advocates of caution want only as little change as possible; moderate reformers tend to want more. They tend to think that if reform is needed, it might as well be extensive enough to remove not only the immediate dissatisfaction but also some foreseeable dissatisfactions even if they are not yet felt. They think, for example, that a reason for building a new town hall is not just to remove the inconveniences of the old one, but also to accommodate the future growth of the town's population. Advocates of caution do not want to remove a dissatisfaction before it is felt.

Assume for the sake of argument that the moderate reformers and the advocates of caution in my town had agreed that the dissatisfactions with the old town hall were serious enough to warrant change. Moderate reformers, then, would have voted to have a new one built. Cautious ones would not have. They would have voted to build a modest addition to the old town hall and find some way of expanding the existing parking space. That would have removed the dissatisfaction, cost much less, and avoided a grandiose project with cost over-runs, interrupted traffic on the main street, and other unforeseeable consequences.

Notwithstanding the disagreements between these two parties, their agreement is much more important. For they see eye to eye on the aim of politics, namely, protecting what we have. They disagree only about means, not about ends. It is good for a society to have such disagreements because they guard against under- or over-estimating dissatisfactions and needed changes. The judgments of both cautious ones and moderate reformers are fallible and tend to err in predictable ways. As they challenge one another's judgments, they reduce the risk of making bad judgments. It is also important about the two parties' agreement that it rules out a blueprint for making good political judgments. Since such judgments are about means, not about ends, good judgments depend on finding the best available means. And that, in turn, depends on familiarity with the ever-changing contexts in which dissatisfactions occur and reform is needed. It is futile to search for a blueprint that would tell us, independently of contexts, what dissatisfaction is serious and what reform is more or less than what is needed.

1.3 RADICAL REFORM

It is just such a blueprint, however, that radical reformers believe themselves to have. In holding this belief, they basically disagree with the parties of both caution and moderate reform. For the radicals deny that the aim of politics is to protect what we have and do not want to lose. They believe that politics should aim to provide what we should have. Radical reformers start with an ideal and their aim is to change the existing political conditions so as to bring them ever closer to the ideal. They think that it is a mistake to be satisfied with existing conditions if they fall short of the ideal. People who make this mistake have settled for the wrong thing because they are motivated by self-interest, or lack imagination, or have been indoctrinated, manipulated, or cowed. Radical reformers work to free them from these handicaps, make them dissatisfied with what there is, and they do this by providing a moral vision of what there ought to be.

In the dispute about the town hall, radical reformers would begin by faulting the thinking of both sides. It is superficial, they would say, to worry about the inconveniences of the old town hall. People should ask instead what an ideal community would be like. Once they know that, they will know whether a town hall is at all needed, and if it is, what its purpose should be. Find the ideal to aim at, they would say, and then you have the principle that covers all contexts and dissatisfactions, and tells you what reforms are necessary. And, of course, the invariable claim of radical reformers is that they have found the ideal and have formulated the principle. Politics, then, no longer needs to be a struggle to make less fallible judgments. It becomes a simple matter of applying the principle in whatever the context happens to be.

The disagreement between radical reformers, on the one hand,

and advocates of caution and moderate reform, on the other, is deep. The first aim to achieve an ideal; the second aim to protect what we have and enjoy. The first are guided by a principle; the second by prudential judgments. The first evaluate political conditions on the basis of their ideal and principle; the second on the basis of people's satisfactions or dissatisfactions. These are two very different approaches to politics. Their difference is central to what this book is about.

My view is that the approach of radical reformers is indefensible in contemporary Western democracies. In our circumstances the approach of either the party of caution or of moderate reform should be followed. There are, of course, circumstances other than those we enjoy in affluent societies. The circumstances in Communist Russia, Nazi Germany, and Maoist China were horrible and warranted radical reform. But even there the reforms called for getting rid of evils, such as the murder, torture, and enslavement of those who were suspected of less than enthusiastic support of these vile regimes, rather than the dogmatic pursuit of an alternative ideal, as radical reformers tend to suppose. Radical reform is justified when the political conditions of human well-being are systematically violated. But radical reformers are committed to reforming all political conditions that fall short of the ideal they favor, regardless of whether people are satisfied with their political conditions. Radical reformers scorn what people think, if they do not think as radical reformers think they ought to think.

1.4 IDEOLOGICAL POLITICS

I will say that it is ideology that marks the difference between these two approaches to politics. But since ideology has been used in many different senses, I must begin by explaining how I understand it. An ideology, then, is a systematic way of thinking about politics. It has a theoretical and a practical component. The latter is an application of the former. The theoretical component is a set of beliefs about human nature and another set about an ideal system of political goods. The two sets are closely connected because the ideal system specifies what the political goods are, given that human beings have a certain nature. There are and have been many different ideologies, and they differ partly because they contain different beliefs about human nature and the ideal system of political goods.

Human nature may be thought of as basically rational, irrational, or non-rational; altruistic, selfish, or mixed; free, determined, or partly both; based largely on inherited genetic structure or formed by post-natal environmental causes; the same in all contexts or malleable and responsive to cultural, religious, moral, economic, and like influences; subject to the laws of history, sociology, psychology or it can be free of them; created by God, formed by evolution, or both; motivated primarily by reason, or emotion, or will; and so forth.

The ideal system of political goods identifies what things are good from a political point of view. These goods form a hierarchy. At the peak of the hierarchy there is a (or perhaps a few) highest good. The other goods occupy a place in the hierarchy depending on how much they further or hinder the achievement of the highest good. Contemporary Western ideologues differ about what the highest good is, but perhaps the most favored candidates are equality, justice, liberty, and rights. Once the highest good is specified, ideologues typically formulate a principle that prescribes what ought to be done to achieve it. Such principles, for instance, as the categorical imperative; the greatest happiness; liberty, equality, fraternity; life, liberty, and property; the Rights of Man; and so forth.

The two theoretical components of ideologies naturally lead to two practical components. The first is a diagnosis of the ways in which a particular society falls short of the goods specified by the ideal system of political goods. The diagnosis identifies the respects in which the prevailing political conditions are worse than they ought be, and, as a result, people's lives are worse than they could and should be. Ideologues thus offer diagnoses, such as that the ills of a society are the result of coercion, injustice, inequality, or rights being violated. The second practical component is a set of policies intended to close or reduce the gap between what the actual political conditions are and what they ought to be. If liberty or rights are curtailed, then a bill of rights ought to be enacted and enforced. If inequality is extensive, wealth ought to be redistributed. If injustice is prevalent, the legal system should be strengthened.

In this way the four components of ideologies—a view of human nature, an ideal system of political goods, a diagnosis, and policies—form an interlocking, reciprocally reinforcing, systematic and coherent approach to politics. The great strength and persuasive power of such an approach is that it offers clear policies and clear reasons why these policies should be followed. Some examples of ideologies in contemporary Western democracies are egalitarianism, feminism, libertarianism, Marxism, socialism, some versions of liberalism and conservatism, and utilitarianism. According to the ideological approach, then, political goods form a permanent hierarchy, there is a highest good, and the relative position of other goods can be determined, once and for all, on the basis of the highest good.

The political goods in the hierarchical system of ideologies routinely conflict because resources are limited and not all goods can be enjoyed, emergencies occur and hard choices between goods must be made, and countless other contingencies force us to forgo goods we should like to have. The nature of these conflicts is that having more of one of the conflicting goods means having less of the other. More liberty may result in less order; more equality in less prosperity; more justice in less happiness; more autonomy in less civility; and so on. These conflicts occur in particular contexts and their resolution depends, in part, on the particularities of the context. A resolution is needed because both goods are recognized as important to the well-being of individuals in that context, but they cannot have as much of both as would be good to have. They will have to give up part of a needed and valued good. The problem is to decide which that should be and how much of it they should give up. Making a reasonable decision depends on taking into account how much of each good is already enjoyed; how a decision would affect other goods; what would happen if nothing was done; how would possible decisions be regarded by public opinion; and so forth.

One difficulty with ideological politics is that a reasonable decision cannot be arrived at by following a principle that can be applied in all contexts. For even if all political contexts were alike in some ways—a very doubtful supposition—a reasonable decision would have to take into account the particularities of the context in which a conflict occurs, and the particularities are bound to differ from context to context. If this is right, then the ideological approach cannot lead to reasonable decisions.

Defenders of ideological politics may respond by saying that whatever defects their approach may have, at least it has a clear procedure for reaching decisions: ask which of the conflicting goods is more important for the achievement of the highest good and then resolve the conflict in favor of the more important one. It may be difficult to answer that question in particular contexts, nevertheless it must be attempted because the alternative is to make arbitrary decisions. But this leaves defenders of ideological politics with problems they can neither resolve nor avoid. First, making reasonable decisions by relying on the ideological approach is not merely difficult but impossible. Second, there is an alternative to the ideological approach, which is non-arbitrary, non-ideological, and reasonable.

The first problem arises because there is no agreement about what the highest good is. Many of the generally recognized political goods have been regarded as the highest by one ideology or another. Reasonable people in contemporary Western democracies will agree that equality, justice, liberty, and rights are indeed good, but why should any of them be regarded as the highest? Why suppose that when a good selected as the highest conflicts with some other good, then the conflict should always be resolved in favor of the supposed highest good? Assume that the highest good is equality and it conflicts with justice or liberty. Why suppose that a great increase in justice or liberty is not worth some decrease in equality? Why is it always more important for a society to have more equality than to have more justice or liberty?

Egalitarian ideologues would reply that the reason why equality is more important than justice or liberty is that the latter presuppose the former. They would say: justice is to treat equals equally, and liberty presupposes that everyone should be equally free. Suppose this is true. It is, however, also true that equality presupposes justice and liberty. For equality is not a good if everyone is treated equally unjustly, or if everyone is equally enslaved. Equality presupposes that the respects in which it should hold are good to have. In the course of specifying these respects equality takes for granted the goods of justice and liberty, for they are some of the good respects in which equality should hold. This is not a unique feature of equality. All political goods presuppose other political goods. Each political good is complex, partially constituted of other political goods. Political goods are interdependent, overlapping, and reciprocally reinforcing. Arguing about which is more important is like arguing about whether the roof, or the walls, or the foundation of a house is more important. There is no habitable house that lacks any one of them. All generally recognized political goods in contemporary Western democracies are important and none is always more important than the others. The mistake of egalitarian ideologues is not that they elevate the wrong good to the highest status. All ideologues are mistaken for the same reason as egalitarians: for regarding a political good—any political good—as the highest.

Suppose, however, that ideologues manage in some way to avoid this problem. Suppose there is a highest political good that is presupposed by the other political goods, but it presupposes none of them. Another problem for ideological politics becomes evident if we ask how anyone could know that this supposedly highest good is in fact good and the highest good? There are after all supposed political goods that have been mistakenly regarded either as good or as the highest. The Nazis made this mistake about racial purity and the Communists about the dictatorship of the proletariat. How do we know that any supposed political good is really good or really the highest?

There is only one way this can be known: through experience. It is reasonable to regard a supposed political good as the highest only if it meets three conditions: there is or was a society whose political arrangements are or were based on according the highest status to that good; people living in that society were generally satisfied with the resulting political arrangements; and they had no reason to want to change them. But ideologues never assign the highest status to a supposed political good on the basis of these conditions. They could not because there has never been any good that met these conditions.

Instead of subjecting their favored good to the test of experience, ideologues deem it highest on the basis of a theory expounded in a book. But this is a deeply flawed way of proceeding because it has no answer to the obvious question of how the theory in the book can be known to be correct if it has not passed the test of experience? No theory of the highest good propounded in any book has ever passed the three conditions of the test of experience. Anyone who doubts this should consider whether a society ever existed whose political conditions were actually, not rhetorically, based on equality, justice, liberty, or rights as the highest good. And in the very unlikely event that a historical example could be found, would it be true of it that the people living in that society were so satisfied with the political conditions as to wish no changes in them? Think of the fate of France following the revolution of 1789, or of Nazi Germany, or of Communist Russia, societies that came closest to basing their political conditions on a supposed highest good.

The Balanced View

Think of what would happen if an ideology took hold of the political conditions of contemporary America. Would a tremendous increase in equality improve the wretched educational system or cope with the threat of terrorism? Would the elimination of injustice make the environment healthier or find a cure for AIDS or cancer? Would much greater liberty reduce the crime rate, drug addiction, or teenage pregnancy? All societies have to cope with a wide variety of conflicts and problems. There can be no blueprint for how to do it. Something rightly valued is always shortchanged. Sometimes one endangered political good must be protected, at other times another. Costs must be weighed against benefits. Useful policies may be unfeasible because public opinion would not accept them. Resources are always limited. Pivotal people die or fall ill. Charismatic politicians persuade voters to favor stupid measures. Unexpected events in distant countries impinge on internal affairs. Long-term interests must be balanced against short-term ones. These and like contingencies are the realities of politics.

Ideologues, however, ignore them. They are hell-bent on making politics fit their theories, rather than the reverse. They are the terrible simplifiers moved by passionately held but untested ideals and they want to transform people's lives whether they like it or not. They claim to know what is good for everyone, and they are quite prepared to force people to live according to it. Their justification is always that they are acting for the common good, that if people only knew what they know, they would willingly follow the ideologues. But the ideologues do not know what they claim to know. They only believe it passionately on the flimsy basis of a theory that is untested by experience.

On that flimsy basis, however, ideologues aim to politicize society by continually expanding the sphere of politics to make more and more activities conform to their unfounded ideal. And as politics expands, so liberty shrinks. Consider for a moment how intrusive has become the moralistic bullying of ideologues in contemporary America. It has become a political matter whether and how children are taught about sex; whether or not they join a labor union; how they should invest their money; what jokes they are allowed or forbidden to tell; what kind of car they should buy; whether they refer to God as "he"; whether they belong to a private club that restricts membership to reflect the preferences of its members; whether they use words like statesman, fireman, Indian, or Negro; whether they think of homosexuality as a sin; whether they own a gun; or whether they eat meat, care about whales, favor or oppose voluntary euthanasia, abortion, contraception, cross-dressing, or sex-change operation. On all of these and similar issues ideologues hold passionate views, condemn those who do not share them, and thereby polarize society, intrude into private lives, and create enmity. They are a menace.

Politics, however, can be free of the pathology of ideology. It can respect privacy and liberty, avoid polarization, and resist moralistic bullying. The key to these highly desirable goals is to keep ideology out of politics. Politics should not aim at the pursuit of some passionately held Utopian ideal, but at the amelioration of the unavoidable dissatisfactions with some of the prevailing political conditions. What follows is an attempt to show how this may be done.

1.5 THE BALANCED VIEW

The easiest way to explain non-ideological politics is to specify how it differs from ideological politics. The primary difference, from which other differences follow, concerns the system of goods. Defenders of the balanced view deny that political goods form a permanent hierarchy, that there is a highest good, and that conflicts among political goods can be resolved by appealing to a highest good. Ideologues regard their ideal system of political goods as good because, given their conception of human nature, they think that the goods are needed for human well-being. The starting point of the balanced view is the system of actual political conditions of a particular society, which in our case are those of contemporary Western democracies. The political goods the balanced view is concerned with derive from this context, as do the disagreements about the interpretation and the respective importance of the political goods these conditions aim to secure.

People living in such societies are satisfied with some of the prevailing political conditions, and dissatisfied with others. It is a characteristic feature of their dissatisfactions, however, that they result from the failure of political conditions to reflect one or more of the recognized political goods. It is felt, for instance, that there is not enough equality, or justice, or liberty, or rights. Such dissatisfactions are not deep because they appeal to agreed upon political goods. A deep dissatisfaction would be with the supposed political goods the conditions were meant to reflect. In contemporary Western democracies, however, such deep disagreements are rare. There is widespread agreement about what the political goods are, even if their interpretations are disputed. Consequently people have something to lose, namely the way of life in which the political goods are enjoyed because the prevailing conditions generally reflect them.

This is a happy state of affairs, but of course it does not remove particular dissatisfactions with faulty conditions. According to the balanced view, the aim of politics is to remove them if possible, or, if not, ameliorate them as much as circumstances allow. Dissatisfactions have various causes. One is that a particular condition fails to reflect an agreed upon political good. Equality, justice, liberty, and rights may generally prevail, but one or more of them may not be extended to people belonging to some unpopular ethnic, religious, political, or racial minority. The remedy then is to make the condition more inclusive. Another source of dissatisfaction is scarcity. Health and education are political goods but there may not be enough competent physicians or teachers and then the underlying need remains unsatisfied. Whether scarcity can be remedied depends on the available resources and the priorities assigned in their distribution.

Contemporary Western democracies, however, are affluent and make an effort not to discriminate against minorities. In such societies, perhaps the most frequent cause of dissatisfactions is that the agreed upon political goods conflict. That is one main reason why the prevailing conditions do not reflect them adequately. They do not because they cannot. There is not enough equality, justice, liberty, or rights because having more of one would result in having less of another. In such cases, the resulting dissatisfactions cannot be removed, but they may be ameliorated by finding a better balance between the conflicting goods.

How might this be done and what would a better balance be? Ideologues answer by appealing to the standard set by whatever happens to be their highest good. But since the balanced view rightly denies that there is a highest good that could be a standard, its defenders must find some other standard to which they could reasonably appeal. Part of the rhetorical force of ideologies is that they deny that an alternative standard could be found. Ideologues thus confront their opponents with a stark choice between accepting their highest good as the standard or having no reasonable standard. They insist that the choice is between the authority of their ideology and the unacceptable consequences of nihilism. But this is a false dilemma. There is a standard to which defenders of the balanced view can appeal, and it is an obvious one.

The standard is the generally agreed upon system of political goods. When two goods of the system conflict, the reasonable approach to ameliorating their conflict is to choose the balance between them that is best for protecting the whole system. The system is always more important than any of the individual goods that are parts of it. Individual goods are valued, of course, but the system of individual goods is rightly valued more. The reason for this is that people living in a society have come to regard the protection of the system as protecting the political condition of their well-being. Its protection is the aim of politics. If the best way of protecting them is to have more of one of the conflicting goods and less of the other, then that is what politics should aim at. If a policy serves this purpose, dissatisfaction with it is unreasonable, for the policy is the best under the circumstances. If dissatisfaction persists, it ought to be directed at the contingencies of life that made it best to accept less of a needed good. Politics can only cope with the contingencies of life, not change them. The approach to politics that aims at the balance of generally agreed upon political goods is what I am calling the balanced view. My aim throughout the book is to defend it.

Ideologues may say that this allegedly non-ideological balanced view is in fact ideological because it appeals to a standard set by a highest good, just as other ideologies do. The highest good in question is the system of political goods. But this would be a bad misunderstanding of the balanced view. It is committed to no such universally applicable principle, no permanent ranking of political goods, no once-and-for-all resolution of conflicts as the ideological approach promises, requires, and fails to deliver.

In the first place, the standard appealed to is not one good deemed highest, but all the generally recognized political goods in a particular society. Secondly, the standard set by the system of goods varies from context to context because the generally recognized political goods in one society differ from those of another. And the standard also varies historically within a particular society because what goods are generally recognized changes as public opinion changes. Equality, liberty, and rights, for instance, have become generally recognized goods only during the past 200–300 years, and the understanding of justice has also undergone basic changes. Thirdly, when the system of political goods is appealed to in order to ameliorate a particular conflict, then the suggested amelioration differs as the contingent circumstances and priorities change. If the conflict is between liberty and security, it makes a great difference whether the society is at war or whether the crime rate is high. If the conflict is between equality and prosperity, it matters whether the living standard is high or low or whether some have less because of misfortune or imprudence. When the standard is appealed to, therefore, the same conflict may be ameliorated differently in different contexts.

Lastly, the ideological standard of the highest good can be and routinely is used to criticize and revise the generally accepted political goods. The criticism and revision are based on the claim that some particular generally recognized good actually hinders the realization of the highest good. The balanced view, by contrast, presupposes the generally accepted goods, so it cannot be used to criticize or to revise them. The standard of the balanced view is the system formed of generally recognized goods. It cannot, therefore, fail to accept them.

Could it not be, however, that the general recognition of particular goods is mistaken? The answer depends on what the general recognition is based on. If it is based on indoctrination, manipulation, fear, ignorance, or stolid refusal to adapt to changing conditions, then of course the general recognition is mistaken. But if it is based on people's satisfaction with the political conditions of their way of life, if the prevailing conditions generally and faithfully reflect the political goods, then the general recognition is as correct as it could be. For the aim of politics conditions is to secure the well-being of individuals living together in a society, and their satisfaction indicates that they have been, in that context, at that time, secured. No matter how desirable this is, it has never been achieved and it is most unlikely that it will be. Contingency, scarcity, and conflicts will always lead to dissatisfactions. That is why the balanced view aims to minimize dissatisfactions as much as possible.

Defenders of the balanced view think that when politics is going as it should, it is like keeping up the old house in which we live. It suits our needs, we have made it comfortable over the long years we have lived in it, but it takes work and effort to keep it up. Things constantly go wrong and they need to be repaired. The house also has to be protected from burglars, unwanted visitors, meddlesome inspectors, and ambitious contractors proposing radical and costly alterations. Its upkeep costs money and takes energy. Both are limited and we have need of them for other purposes as well. Moreover, keeping up the house is not our main interest in life. It has to be done but not for its own sake. We need it as a place where we can be private, enjoy personal relationships, and pursue interests. We may think from time to time that the money and effort we have put into its upkeep over the years is not worth it. But if we stop and reflect, we realize that we need a house to live in, and if we give up the one we have and move to another, it too will have inconveniences, although they will be unfamiliar and we will have to learn all over again how to cope with them. So we should keep up this old house of ours, rely on our experience to handle its problems, and do so as well as we can, knowing that no house is without imperfections.

CHAPTER TWO

✦   ✦   ✦

REASON AS PRUDENCE

A belief about the nature and scope of rational understanding, which, on the one hand, confines it to the promulgation of abstract general propositions and, on the other hand, extends its relevance to the whole of human life . . . may be called 'rationalism'. And there is as much difference between rational enquiry and 'rationalism' as there is between scientific enquiry and 'scientism', and it is a difference of the same kind. Moreover, it is important that a writer who wishes to contest the excessive claims of 'rationalism' should observe the difference, because if he fails to do so he will . . . make himself appear the advocate of irrationality, which is going further than he either needs or intends to go.

MICHAEL OAKESHOTT
Religion, Politics and the Moral Life

IN CHAPTER ONE I introduced themes, made claims, and drew distinctions I will develop, deepen, and defend in the rest of the book. Both the criticism of ideological politics and the defense of the balanced view involved claims about reasonable ways of coping with conflicts among political goods. This chapter is about the conception of reason I have relied on. I begin with an illustration of how reason led to success in coping with a very difficult political conflict.

✦   ✦   ✦

Reason as Prudence

2.1 A Case in Point

One of the encouraging developments during the past quarter century or so has been the transition of many countries from right or left-wing dictatorship to a less barbaric regime. This process of transition is fraught with dangers in all contexts, but I will discuss it in the context of Argentina, as it was leaving behind the brutal military dictatorship that lasted from 1976 to 1983. Low estimates put the number of people murdered between eleven and fifteen thousand, but many thousands more were kidnapped and survived terrible torture and brutal imprisonment. The junta's justification for taking power was the genuine threat to stability presented by Marxist guerrillas, who themselves murdered about a thousand civilian, police, and military supporters of the not too savory Peronist regime that preceded the military coup. I will not dwell on the horrors inflicted by military officers on their largely innocent victims. Those wishing to know the gory details can find them in the works listed in the Notes to this chapter. It is a particular conflict involved in the transition that I want to discuss.

The names of the generals who ordered the terror and of the officers who worked out the details, diligently executed the orders, and did the ghastly deeds were well-known. It was undoubtedly an elementary requirement of justice that these people be tried and punished. This, however, was not possible. The new democratically elected regime was in a precarious position, partly because the military had the arms and the will to defend their own and because the police, the only other arms-bearing force, largely sympathized with the military. To have done what justice required was not practically possible, and if it had been possible, it would have risked civil war, great bloodshed, and the further destabilization of the already unstable society. The new government, in my opinion rightly, took the view that their primary responsibility was to lay the ground for a better future, not to punish the evildoers of the past. But the many thousands of survivors and the much more

23

numerous family members of the murdered victims understandably demanded justice. They argued convincingly that a better future cannot be built without coming to terms with the past. It was a moral outrage that the perpetrators of the terror lived in comfort, continued to be paid high salaries, and enjoyed other advantages that traditionally came to military officers in Argentina. And many members of the new government, several of them former victims themselves, shared this sense of moral outrage. The result was a deep conflict between justice and stability at this time in Argentina. The more there was of one, the less there could be of the other. Since there was urgent need for both, their conflict could not be ignored.

The reason for doing justice was not merely that the evildoers deserved to be held responsible, but also the more intangible needs of re-establishing the moral order that the dictatorship systematically violated, communicating to the citizens that this was being done, and thereby assuaging the justified moral outrage felt by so many people. But the reason against doing justice was the no less strong consideration of the threat of civil war and bloodshed that would have involved the continuation of the moral anarchy that the new government was committed to putting behind the country.

There were equally weighty reasons for and against maintaining stability. Perhaps the strongest reason against preferring stability to justice was that the vile dictatorship offered precisely that justification for its crimes. The responsibility of the new government was to break with the past, not to continue it. If they had ignored what justice required, they would have been guilty of the same wrongdoing, although not to the same extent, as the generals and officers who unleashed the terror. But if they had opted for justice over stability, then they would have risked in another way the continuation of the past through the strong likelihood of another military coup with the all too predictable consequences. All the alternatives the new government had, therefore, appeared to be unacceptable. But, then, they thought of a further alternative, and it saved the day.

This alternative was setting up a truth commission. The people appointed to it were among the most respected citizens of Argentina who were uncompromised by collaboration with the dictatorship. The commission's task was to hold widely publicized hearings in which anyone who wished could testify to the kidnapping, imprisonment, and torture he or she had to endure during the dictatorship. Their testimonies were recorded, deposited in archives open to the public, and selections from them were subsequently published by the commission in a volume called *Nunca Mas*, the Spanish for never again. In the testimonies the perpetrators of the crimes were named, and their names were publicized.

The commission had no legal powers. It could not prosecute or sentence the guilty, nor hear lawyers' arguments condemning or defending the named perpetrators. It heard only the victims, searched the prison and court archives for corroboration of the testimonies, visited the places of detention where the victims were kept, but its brief did not include investigative powers to determine the truth of the victims' testimonies. Their testimonies, however, were corroborated by widespread agreement among them of precise and very detailed descriptions of the physical properties of various detention centers, procedures followed in the kidnappings, tortures, and the exceptionally brutal circumstances of imprisonment. Their testimonies were further corroborated by the very few military officers who actually confessed to the crimes and came to repent what they had done. There could be no reasonable doubt that the horrors reported actually occurred and that they caused great suffering to tens of thousands of innocent victims.

The work of the truth commission defused the crisis. It resulted in a national catharsis in the course of which people faced and acknowledged the horrors of the dictatorship and the sufferings of their fellow citizens. The perpetrators were named but not prosecuted. The catharsis was the first step toward a moral regeneration. Not the least among the effects of the hearings was that it allowed the surviving victims and the families of the murdered ones to express their moral outrage, to have the victims' innocence and suffering publicly acknowledged, and to make it psychologically possible to try to rebuild a normal life. Justice was not quite done because the guilty were not punished, but they were tried in the court of public opinion. Another coup and civil war had been avoided, and it became possible to get on with the task of re-establishing stability. The work of the commission coped with this conflict and was an admirable illustration of the role of reason in politics.

I turn now to the conception of reason that is appropriate and another that is inappropriate in politics. I will proceed by distinguishing between different types of reason and then identifying the ones appropriate in politics. I will argue that the balanced view is committed to reason in politics, but its commitment is to a conception of reason that leads only to limited and fallible conclusions. The balanced view, therefore, excludes the excessive claims ideologues make on behalf of reason.

2.2 THEORETICAL AND PRACTICAL REASON

Theoretical reason aims at true beliefs; practical reason aims at successful actions. They overlap in some ways, diverge in others. They overlap because successful actions often depend on true beliefs and true beliefs often lead to successful actions. But they also diverge because successful actions may involve no beliefs (e.g. waking up in the morning at the usual time) and true beliefs may lead to no action (e.g. that WWI started in 1914). Reason in politics is primarily practical because its aim is to propose a policy for coping with a conflict among political goods. This usually involves true beliefs, and thus theoretical reason, but it is secondary to the practical aim of formulating successful policies. True beliefs in politics are means to successful policies. In other contexts, as in science or history, true beliefs are primary and successful policies only secondary.

Beliefs are true if the facts believed are what they are believed to be. The truth of a belief is thus independent of what goes on in the minds of believers. Everyone may hold a belief that is in fact false and a belief may be true even if no one accepts it. Whether there is intelligent life elsewhere in the universe does not depend on what anyone believes about it. If a belief is true, it is true universally: anyone who holds it holds a true belief and anyone who denies its truth is mistaken. Of course people may reject true beliefs and accept false ones but that has no effect on the truth or falsity of the beliefs themselves. And of course people may accept or reject beliefs on the basis of insufficient evidence or because they willfully or involuntarily ignore evidence, but that too has no effect on whether the facts are as they are believed to be.

The success of policies, however, is a quite different matter. Their success depends on whether they are acceptable means to particular ends and whether the ends are acceptable. The legalization of drugs may or may not be an acceptable means to greater liberty and greater liberty may or may not be an acceptable end to aim at. The appropriateness of both means and ends depends on what alternatives to them are available, and their availability varies with contexts. Whether the legalization of drugs is an appropriate means to greater liberty in a particular society at a particular time depends on whether the addiction rate is high or low, whether it is likely to increase or decrease the crime rate, whether attractive alternatives to drug use are available, and so forth. And whether aiming at greater liberty is appropriate depends on how much liberty there is already, how greater liberty would affect other aims, such a maintaining order, protecting public health, winning a war, and so on. There is, therefore, no such thing as a universally successful policy, as there are universally true beliefs. Whether a particular policy is successful depends on the context, and it may be successful in one context and unsuccessful in another.

This points to a basic difference between true beliefs and successful policies. The truth of beliefs is independent of their context, whereas the success of policies is context-dependent. The source of this difference is that the truth of beliefs depends on facts, but the success of policies depends not just on facts but also on judging their relative importance. True beliefs reached by theoretical reason provide the facts that successful policies formulated by practical reason must both take into account and go beyond to judge their relative importance. The task of practical reason, therefore, cannot merely be to implement true beliefs reached by theoretical reason.

Ideologues fail to recognize the context-dependence of practical reason and the central role of judgment in it. That failure is the source of their mistaken central assumption that once an ideology is constructed out of true beliefs, context-independent policies will follow from it. They falsely suppose that an ideology could determine once and for all the relative importance of political goods and thus provide a blueprint for resolving conflicts between political goods independently of the context in which the conflicts occur. But the ideological approach is bound to fail even if it is constructed out of true beliefs because coping with conflicts depends on judgments that go beyond the facts reached by true beliefs. If those judgments are reasonable, they must take into account particularities that vary with contexts. These particularities concern the appropriateness of means and ends, and they vary because their appropriateness depends on what alternative means and ends are available.

Defenders of the balanced view, however, recognize that coping with conflicts depends both on true beliefs and reasonable judgments about context-dependent means and ends. And that is one reason why they reject the doomed aspiration of ideologues to formulate policies that would successfully resolve conflicts between political goods in all contexts. It is, for instance, folly to suppose that the truth commission that coped admirably with the conflict between justice and stability in Argentina in the 1980s would have been successful in achieving the same end in the transition in Russia following the collapse of Communism, in Iran following the fall of the Shah, or in the Congo following the death of Mobutu.

There is another line of argument that leads to the same conclusion about the failure of ideological politics and the need for a non-ideological balanced approach. The true beliefs that theoretical reason yields are expressible as true propositions. True propositions are consistent with one another. One true propositions cannot contradict another because if it did one or the other must be false, which true propositions cannot be. But it is otherwise with practical reason in a political context. There may be strong practical reasons for pursuing a policy that aims at justice and for pursuing a policy that aims at stability. But unlike true propositions, the two policies may be inconsistent because justice and stability may conflict in a particular context, as they did in Argentina in the 1980s. Politics is riddled with such conflicts of political goods and policies.

The ideological approach to coping with such conflicts is always wrong-headed and sometimes disastrous, as it would have been in Argentina. Regardless of whether ideologues had acted on the assumption that the claims of justice always took precedence over the claims of stability, or vice versa, their attempted conflict-resolution would have seriously jeopardized the political conditions on which the well-being of Argentineans depended. For giving precedence to justice would have, in all likelihood, led to a coup and the re-establishment of the vile dictatorship. And giving precedence to stability would have alienated precisely those citizens on whose support the new government depended and who supported it because they passionately wanted it to do justice. Any reasonable policy would have had to balance in some manner the conflicting claims of justice and stability, rather than simply choose one or the other. But finding the optimal balance crucially depended on judging how likely it was that the military would stage another coup, that those clamoring for justice would understand how dangerous it would be to try the evildoers, whether the military would be deterred by the likely international condemnation of another coup, whether the Church would use its considerable influence to encourage or discourage the military, whether the police would side with the military, whether the courts could be counted on to render just verdicts, and so on and on. There could be no blueprint for making such judgments. Making them well required experience, local knowledge, and intimate familiarity with the Argentinean political context. That is why finding a reasonable balance required the non-ideological approach that led to the admirable policy of setting up the truth commission.

I conclude that in politics practical reason is primary, and theoretical reason is secondary. But practical reason in politics is unavoidably context-dependent and particular because political goods routinely conflict, their conflicts can be coped with only by balancing them, and that requires taking into account particular circumstances that differ from context to context. This depends on the balanced view and excludes all ideological approaches regardless of which political good they rank highest. Defenders of the balanced view are right to want to protect the whole system of political goods that citizens agree in valuing and they are also right to reject all ideological attempts to impose a blueprint that ignores the particularities of the context.

2.3 WHAT REASON REQUIRES AND ALLOWS

I postpone (until 2.4) the question of why it is desirable to be reasonable in politics and assume that it is desirable. Given that assumption, we can say that reason requires policies to meet certain conditions. If a policy fails to meet any of them, it is unreasonable and should be rejected. These conditions are elementary requirements that set only minimum standards: a policy must be logically consistent, take into account the generally available relevant facts, and propose a possible way of achieving its aim. In a typical conflict of political goods, many policies of coping with the conflict are likely to meet these conditions. All the policies that do meet them are allowed by reason as possible policies but they may or may not be adopted. Whether a policy allowed by reason should be adopted depends on whether there are reasons for preferring it to alternative policies that are also allowed by reason.

What reason requires and what it allows, therefore, are different. Reason requires that policies should meet minimum standards to be considered as candidates for adoption. To adopt a policy that fails to meet the minimum standards is unreasonable, but all policies that meet them are allowed by reason. The question, then, becomes which of the policies allowed by reason is justified to adopt. This is a complicated question because typically there are reasons for preferring more than one of the policies allowed by reason. If these reason were all the same kind, then justifying the adoption of one would be a simple matter of weighing the strength of the same kind of reasons. If two policies differ only in how safe they are, then obviously the safer one should be adopted. But the reasons for adopting policies are usually of different kinds. Reasons may have to do not just with safety, but also with cost, popularity, legality, morality, past success or failure, and so forth. It is often unclear what comparative weight should be assigned to these different reasons. It makes the justification of the adoption of a policy even more complicated that it often depends also on decisions that have been made about quite different policies. If the justified policy in another context was very unpopular, then the comparative popularity of policies in this context may become important even if it does not affect the policies themselves. The consequence of these complications is that there may be reasonable disagreements about which of the policies allowed by reason is reasonable to adopt.

Politics is full of such disagreements, but they are reasonable disagreements. The parties to them can agree about the relevant facts, the appropriateness of the available means and of the ends aimed at, and still disagree because they attribute different importance to the agreed upon considerations. One cares more about future generations, another about the well-being of the present generation; one stresses the importance of reducing inequality, another of growth in prosperity; one is more concerned with liberty, the other with order. They can acknowledge and respect the other's concerns, but they may have reasoned preference for their own.

These disagreements can go on and on, but the contingencies of life sooner or later require that a decision be made. In America the decision is made by putting the question to vote. The vote will not determine what the most reasonable decision is, but it will result in a decision, and that is better than having none. These are the realities of political life as we know it. Having no better choice, we live with its inconveniences.

Ideologues, however, are unwilling to accept this. They are moved by an impassioned certainty to claim that all political conflicts have a simple resolution required by reason, and that they know what that resolution is. The failure to accept this resolution is a failure to follow the dictates of reason. Ideologues, therefore, regard their opponents as unreasonable because they fail to see what is there to be seen, if only they would look. The ideologues, however, do see it. And what they see is the highest good or the supreme principle that is the ultimate standard with reference to which reason requires that all political conflicts be resolved. For Plato, the standard was the metaphysical form of the Good; for Stoics, tranquility; for Hobbes, safety; for Rousseau, the general will; for the Jacobins, the rights of man; for Kant, the categorical imperative; for Bentham, pleasure and the avoidance of pain; for Fichte, the German State; for Mill, utility in one work and liberty in another; for Marx, the classless society; and for contemporary ideologues in Western democracies, it is equality, or freedom, or justice, or rights.

The passionate conviction of ideologues that there is a highest good or a supreme principle is not weakened by the enormous gap between the realities of actual politics and what, according to their ideal, politics ought to be. For they attribute the gap to the unreasonableness of those engaged in actual politics. It causes no doubt to ideologues that other ideologues also imbued with passionate conviction regard other goods as the highest and other principles as supreme. For these other ideologues are also said to be unreasonable. The well-known reciprocal criticisms of all ideologues of other ideologies merely strengthen the efforts of ideologues to come up with a more sophisticated formulation of their own ideology. For they are certain that a refined enough formulation will meet all criticisms. Nor are ideologues troubled by the dismal historical record of societies that have attempted to model their political arrangements on an ideology. For, ideologues say, if their attempts had been guided by the right ideology and if they had been reasonable enough, they would not have ended dismally.

Nothing is allowed to affect the unquestioned assumption that what ideologues seek is there to be found. They attribute all failures to not having been reasonable enough, and they continue undeterred to search for the highest good or the supreme principle that would resolve all political conflicts once and for all. They are like the alchemists who searched for the philosopher's stone that would transform everything into gold. And as the alchemists were not deterred by centuries of failure, so the ideologues remain undeterred by the cumulative weight of reasons against continuing with their doomed enterprise. Ideologues remain undeterred partly because they believe that there is no reasonable alternative to their approach. They suppose that to abandon it is to abandon reason in politics. But they are mistaken because they mistakenly suppose that reason in politics must be theoretical and must yield conflict-resolutions required by reason.

In the Argentinean context what reason required was to find a way of coping with the conflict between the demand for justice and the need for stability, but reason did not require any particular way of doing that. Setting up the truth commission was one way, but reason allowed other ways as well. The truth commission merely made the truth public without holding the evildoers legally accountable. It might have been possible to go further toward justice and hold public hearings at which the victims were permitted not merely to tell of the horrors they have suffered but to confront their torturers, and demand to know from them how they squared their ghastly deeds with their conscience. Or they might have gone even further and risked the actual trial of one or two of the most egregious offenders. How best to balance the justified claims of justice and stability called for judgment, and, in retrospect, it seems that the judgment that led to the setting up of the truth commission was the right one. This, however, means only that the judgment was the best among those reason allowed, not that reason required making it.

The upshot of the argument so far is that reason in politics should be primarily practical, not theoretical; that political conflicts can only be coped with, not resolved; and that reason routinely allows different ways of coping with them. But this account is still incomplete.

2.4 REASON AS DELIBERATION AND AS JUSTIFICATION

We can now return to the assumption I have made (in 2.3) that it is desirable to be reasonable in politics. Why is it desirable? Because politics is about coping with conflicts among political goods, and reason is the most reliable means to it. Ignoring such conflicts is politically unacceptable because people living together in a society want to secure the political conditions of their well-being, and the political goods they recognize specify what they take those conditions to be. But if the goods conflict, then the conditions are endangered. So coping with the conflicts is politically necessary. The task of reason in politics is to minimize this danger and to secure the political conditions of well-being. Since both goods in a particular conflict are regarded as such conditions, simply opting for one and neglecting the other is no more acceptable than is ignoring the conflict. For neglecting either good would be a willful failure to secure the conditions that the aim and justification of politics is to secure. The only acceptable alternative is to balance the conflicting goods to ensure that there is as much of both as possible, given the contingencies and the scarcity of resources in the context in which the conflict occurs.

Coping with a political conflict thus involves finding this optimal balance, and that is what reason in politics is meant to do. The question, therefore, is not whether it should be done, whether reason should guide politics, but how it should guide it. I have argued that the ideological approach is unacceptable because it consists in preferring one of the conflicting goods and neglecting the other, and because, unacceptable as that is, the preference for one of the goods is based on an appeal to a good or to a principle that is arbitrarily held to be the highest or supreme. This leads to the balanced view that is based primarily on practical, not theoretical, reason, and seeks a way of coping with conflicts that reason allows, but does not require. Reason usually allows several ways of coping, and the task of the balanced view is to find a reasonable way of choosing one of them. The distinction broached earlier between reason as deliberation and reason as justification points to how that may be done.

Deliberation in politics involves forming policies by means of certain cognitive processes, such as thinking, analyzing, estimating likelihoods, and so forth. These processes may be called collectively reasoning. Reasoning, however, is only one way of forming policies. Some other ways rely on emotion, intuition, inspiration, faith, or imagination. Justification in politics is indifferent to the processes by means of which policies are formed. It is concerned with determining the reliability of policies. And that is done by asking and answering critical questions: Does a policy pass the minimum tests of being logically consistent, taking account of all the relevant facts, and offering a possible way of coping with a conflict? If it passes, then further questions are asked about how the policy compares with other possible policies in respect to efficiency, cost, risk, public acceptability, consequences, morality, and so forth. Deliberation is concerned with forming policies; justification with testing them.

Deliberation and justification may or may not lead to the same conclusion. A policy formed on the basis of reasoning is much more likely to be justified than one formed by relying on non-cognitive processes. But the two may also lead to different conclusions because policies formed by reasoning may succumb to subsequent criticism and non-cognitive processes may lead to policies that are later justified. The Japanese decision to bomb Pearl Harbor was based on much reasoning, but it led to the unjustified policy of provoking an unwinnable war. The policy of moderate Jacobins to execute Robespierre was based on their visceral fear of what Robespierre may do to them, but it nevertheless turned out to be justified because it put an end to the great evil of the Terror. In politics, the important question about a policy is whether it will cope with a conflict. Examining the deliberative processes by means of which a policy has been formed is much less likely to yield a reliable answer than accepting the policy only after it has been rigorously justified. Good reasoning may lead to bad policies, but a rigorously justified policy is less likely to fail. The reason for this difference is deep, and it further strengthens the case for the balanced view and weakens the case for ideological politics.

Consider how ideologues proceed. They behold the messiness of actual politics. They see the contingencies, the scarcity of resources, and the conflicts, and they are appalled by the compromises and negotiations involved in policy-making. They want clarity and principles in policy-making rather than the opportunistic, often self-serving, and always partisan wrangling that characterizes American politics. They think that the imposition of order on this chaotic clash of competing interests depends on formulating an ideal of a highest good that policies ought to aim at. Once the ideal is clear, a principle can be derived from it that prescribes how the ideal is to be achieved. Policy-making, conflict-resolution, and justification, then, will have an objective, reliable basis, and the prevailing chaos will be replaced by order. To achieve this end, ideologues formulate an ideology that provides the ideal to be aimed at. And they arrive at the ideology by deliberation.

In this manner, socialists and left-of-center liberals claim that the ideal is equality; centrist liberals that it is justice; libertarians and right-of-center liberals that it is liberty; fundamentalist Protestant conservatives that it is the will of God as found in the Bible; and Catholic conservatives that it is conformity to natural law. Defenders of the balanced view reject the ideological approach on which these political views rest. They argue that none of them has an acceptable answer to the question of justification: what reason is there for accepting the ideology on which these ideals of the highest good and the resulting principles rest?

To answer it by pointing at the careful reasoning that has led to the formulation of the ideology is no answer at all. For equally careful reasoning has led to different and incompatible ideologies, and, in any case, defenders of the balanced view question the reliability of the reasoning in all of them. They say that the reliability of reasoning arrived at by deliberation can be ascertained only by the justification of the ideology. Deliberation without justification yields only dogmatically held ideologies. And such ideologies are dangerous because, if they are mistaken, they destroy the political conditions of well-being, as Communist and Nazi ideologies have done. How, then, can ideologies be justified?

No justification based on any consideration internal to an ideology can be adequate, for it merely appeals to what is in question. Few ideologies fail to be logically consistent, account for the relevant facts, and yield a possible policy. But these are only minimum requirements. They are met by all the currently held ideologies I mention above, yet they are incompatible with one another. If an ideology is to be justified, therefore, it has to be on the basis of something external to it. That something, however, can only be the actual politics of a society whose political conditions were based on the ideology and in which the political conditions of human well-being were better served than they would have been by another ideology. There are two reasons, however, why such a justification cannot be found.

First, the justification would have to compare two societies that differed only in respect to their political conditions. This cannot be done because political conditions are responses to a society's historical, religious, economic, social, and cultural conditions, and these non-political conditions vary from society to society and from time to time within the same society. Whatever conclusion the comparison of two societies might yield can always be attributed to differences in these non-political conditions rather than to differences in political conditions.

Second, in American politics there is general agreement about what the political goods are. There are, of course, persistent disagreements but they are about the respective importance of the agreed-upon goods. The comparison, therefore, would have to be based on two societies that differed, not about the political goods valued in them, but about the political good that should be ranked highest. And ranking a good highest would have to be shown by consistently forming policies for conflict-resolution that appealed to the supposed highest good. But American politics has never proceeded that way. It has always been in precisely in that messy state that ideologies want to replace with what they regard as a preferable order.

There is, therefore, no way to justify the ideological claim that a political good should be elevated to the highest status and serve as the ideal that ought to guide policy-making and conflict-resolution. Without such a justification ideologies are just blueprints of magic castles to be built on air. Although the ingenuity of the architects may be aesthetically pleasing to some, American society never has or should have replaced the political goods it is enjoying with the untried and untestable blueprints of rightist, leftist, or centrist ideologues.

Is there no way, then, in which policies can be justified? Is there is no reasonable approach to coping with conflicts among political goods? Of course there is. The alternative to the ideological approach is not to abandon efforts at justification but to keep them within reasonable limits. What are these limits?

To begin with, the limits are set by the context of American politics. There are other contexts of course, and the role of reason in them may or may not be the same as they are in ours. In any case, it is in our context that the balanced view is meant to hold. One feature of that context is consensus about the political goods. There is general agreement that policies ought to be guided by these goods. People may be dissatisfied with particular policies, and they may be justified. The policies, then, ought to be changed and the politicians who formed the defective policies ought to be held accountable. But if the dissatisfactions are justified, they are so by appealing to the system of political goods in the background. One of the limits of the balanced view, then, is that it presupposes a general consensus about the system of political goods. People living in the context agree that this system ought to be preserved, even as they disagree about the relative importance of the constitutive goods and about the best means of preserving them. This is a significant agreement because it follows from it that the long-term aim of policies is to preserve the system of political goods.

Policies also have a short-term aim, which is to minimize the dissatisfaction with the extent to which particular political goods are available. If their availability is limited because two political goods conflict, then the dissatisfaction will persist. That, however, is not the fault of policy-makers who could be replaced with less fallible ones, but a consequence of unavoidable contingencies or of the scarcity of resources. From this follows a further limit on the balanced view, namely, that the short-term aim of policies is to cope with dissatisfactions by balancing the conflicting goods that cause the dissatisfactions. The best balance is one that allows having as much of both goods as possible, given the particular circumstances of the context in which the conflict occurs.

The long-term aim of the balanced view is thus to preserve the agreed-upon system of political goods. Its intermediate aim is to cope with conflicts between particular political goods in particular contexts. Justification involves finding the most reasonable policies for pursuing these aims. And those will be ones that compare most favorably with other reasonable policies. But this makes justification unavoidably context-dependent and particular. The policies to which it leads may be the best in one context, but this implies nothing about what policy would be the best in another context. Nor does justification rule out reasonable disagreements about which of several policies allowed by reason is the best. The choice of the best is a matter of judgment about the relative importance of agreed-upon considerations. Such judgments are fallible and reasonable people can disagree about them. It is often practically necessary to make a decision even when such disagreements persist. In American politics this is done by elections. Since the disagreements are about choosing the best among reasonable policies, not even the worst outcome of the vote would be disastrous, since the policy favored will be reasonable, even if it might not be the most reasonable.

It may be thought that this account is naively optimistic. It would be that if it were meant to be a description of how American politics actually works. It is, however, meant to be something else: a description of how American politics might work if it were guided by the balanced view. Of course actual politics is not as it might be. Ideologues misdirect it by chimerical schemes and politicians are often shortsighted, unreasonable, and, I am afraid, corrupt. There is some reason for expecting improvement because we know why and how politics could be made more reasonable. And there is some reason for expecting that politics will continue to stumble along in its customary flawed manner because of human imperfections.

As Argentina was recovering from the military dictatorship, politics stumbled in the right direction. The government found a policy that managed to cope with the conflict between justice and stability. The policy was justified by its success at preserving as much of justice and stability as was possible under the wretched conditions left behind by the previous regime. And that was the primary consideration. How the policy-makers deliberated, what had gone on in their minds, whether they relied on cool calculation, political experience, optimism or pessimism, insight into the attitudes of their fellow citizens, or precedent imported from other contexts was secondary. What mattered was that the policy was justified, not how it was arrived at.

2.5 REASON AS PRUDENCE

Reason in politics is primarily practical, allowing, and justifying. I say primarily because it would be a bad mistake to deny that reason in politics also involves true beliefs, provided by theoretical reason; that reason requires minimum standards that policies must meet; and deliberation based on reasoning is most likely to lead to justified policies. But true beliefs, minimum standards, and reasoning are all instrumental to the primary aim of politics, which is to formulate policies for coping with conflicts between political goods. Pursuing this aim is politically necessary because it protects what are regarded as the political conditions of the well-being of individuals in a society. For ease of reference, I will refer to this view of reason as prudence. Prudence yields good judgment. And good judgment in politics consists in formulating policies that actually succeed in coping with these conflicts.

One main difference between the ideological and the balanced views of politics turns on this conception of prudence and good judgment. Ideologues think that good judgment is not good enough; defenders of the balanced view think that good judgment is the best we can have in politics. Ideologues are dissatisfied with good judgment because they think that reason in politics should be theoretical and provide policies that are required by reason. They regard policies that are merely allowed by reason and reached by practical reason as inferior precisely because they are matters of judgment rather than of certainty. Ideologues seek universally applicable policies that can be relied on to resolve all conflicts between political goods in the same way in all contexts. They seek certainty, not fallible, context-dependent judgments. They seek it through a metaphysical theory; or a theory about human nature; or a theory about the laws of history, or sociology, or biology, or economics, or psychology; or faith in God, the revelation contained in a sacred book, the inspiration of a charismatic prophet; or the altruism of human motivation.

What they seek cannot be found because successful policies must take into account the contingent circumstances, the scarcity of resources, and the historical, cultural, moral, religious, and aesthetic differences that unavoidably make the contexts of policies vary with societies, times, and places. Taking these matters into account is not just to recognize relevant facts, but also to form a view of their comparative importance in coping with a particular conflict. Forming that view, however, is also affected by these varied influences. That is why successful policies must remain a matter of judgment, and why there may be reasonable and incompatible policies reached by as good judgments as are possible in a particular context. Dissatisfaction with this is dissatisfaction with the human condition. This is an understandable but wasted sentiment. The energy expanded on it would be better spent trying to make small and local improvements within the limits set by our condition.

The balanced view, then, excludes all ideological attempts to go beyond these limits by metaphysical speculation, religious faith, or scientific research. This is emphatically not an objection to metaphysics, religion, or science. The objection is to the attempt to deny the unavoidable context-dependence and particularity of political judgments and replace them with propositions derived from very different contexts. Defenders of the balanced view are committed to reason in politics, provided it is understood as prudence, but they eschew inflated expectations of what prudence can achieve in politics. The upshot of this chapter is, then, to have identified and provided an interpretation of a political good that the balanced view is committed to defending. The chapters that follow aim to do the same for other political goods.

CHAPTER THREE

THE PLURALITY OF GOODS

Pluralism ... seems to me a truer and more humane ideal than the goals of those who seek [it] in ... authoritarian structures. ... It is truer, because it does, at least, recognise the fact that human goals are many, not all of them commensurable, and in perpetual rivalry with one another. To assume that all values can be graded on a scale, so that it is a mere matter of inspection to determine the highest, seems to me to falsify our knowledge that men are free agents, to represent moral decisions as an operation which a slide-rule could, in principle, perform. ... It is more humane because it does not (as the system-builders do) deprive men, in the name of some remote, or incoherent ideal, of much that they have found to be indispensable to their life as unpredictably self-transforming human beings.

ISAIAH BERLIN
"Two Concepts of Liberty"

IN THE PREVIOUS CHAPTER I argued that the balanced view is committed to defending reason as prudence as a political good. I will argue in this chapter that pluralism is another such political good. I begin with the conception of human nature that underlies pluralism.

+ + +

The Plurality of Goods

The biblical story of Adam and Eve is a profoundly suggestive allegory of human nature. There they were in perfect, childlike innocence, in idyllic conditions, their needs easily met, and they ate the forbidden fruit from the tree of knowledge. They learned about good and evil, lost their innocence, and were sentenced to what we know as an ordinary human life of contingency, scarcity, and conflict. They had to fend for themselves, to contend with evil, and to seek the goods on which they depended. Part of the suggestiveness of this allegory comes from the questions it prompts one to ask. The question I ask is why they ate the fruit. The snake has tempted Eve, and Eve has tempted Adam, but why did they succumb to the temptation? They were not hungry; and they did not suffer from any of the frustrations, adversities, and social ills that are all too familiar to us.

I came to think that they succumbed because they were bored. After they quelled their hunger, made love, rested, and played with the animals to their hearts' content, they had nothing else to do. All their days were alike, and equally monotonous. As the English advertising catchphrase has it: for them the waiting was taken out of wanting. They had only to feel a need, and they could satisfy it. In this manner, their lives predictably and repetitiously had gone on. Who would not be bored after concluding that this is all there is to life?

They ate the fruit to relieve their boredom; learned about good and evil; and their lives became interesting. All of a sudden possibilities occurred to them, they had to choose between them, and the choices were not easy because some of their possibilities were good and others bad, although they could not have been always clear about which was which. They could not rely on the Bible to tell them because they were making the story the Bible told. They had to think for themselves and ask whether they wanted to realize one possibility or another. They were forced to make decisions about how they wanted to live. Their future was open, and it was up to them to make it good or bad. When they realized this, they became one of us, who are their progeny.

Reflection on this allegory brings us to understand that our nature imposes on us necessities and opens up possibilities. We are alike in respect to the necessities, but unalike because we choose different possibilities. We have the needs we have, and some of them we must satisfy or die. But we also have options, and we make very different choices about them. How we think about human nature and politics depends in part on how we answer the question of whether what matters most are the ways in which we are alike or the ways in which we are different. Does human well-being depend on meeting the necessities of our nature, and thus the same for all of us, or on the possibilities we may explore in various ways, depending on our characters and circumstances?

Consider two impassioned answers, both by fine stylists. David Hume says that "it is universally acknowledged that there is a great uniformity among the actions of men, in all nations and ages, and that human nature remains still the same, in its principles and operations. The same motives always produce the same actions. . . . Ambition, avarice, self-love, vanity, friendship, generosity, public spirit: these passions, mixed in various degrees, and distributed through society, have been from the beginning of the world, and still are, the source of all the actions and enterprises, which have been observed among mankind. . . . Mankind are much the same, in all times and places, that history informs us of nothing new or strange in this particular. Its chief use is only to discover the constant and universal principles of human nature, by showing men in all varieties of circumstances and situations, and furnishing us with materials from which we may . . . become acquainted with the regular springs of human action." Let us call this the *universal view* of human nature, since it claims that human nature is the same always, everywhere.

The second answer is Isaiah Berlin's: "The conviction common to Aristotelians and a good many Christian scholastics and atheistical materialists alike, that there exists a basic knowable human nature, one and the same, at all times, in all places, in all men—a static, unchanging substance underneath the altering appearances, with permanent needs, dictated by a single, discoverable goal, or pattern of goals, the same for all mankind—is mistaken; and so, too, is the notion that is bound up with it, of a single true doctrine carrying salvation to all men everywhere, contained in natural law, or the revelation of a sacred book, or the insight of a man of genius, or the natural wisdom of ordinary men, or the calculations made by an elite of utilitarian scientists set up to govern mankind." This is the *relative view* of human nature because it claims that human nature is relative to times and places.

At first glance these two views seem to be incompatible, but they are not, and, although both seem to be patently mistaken, they are not that either, or so I will argue. What is at issue between the universal and relative views is not merely whether there are characteristics shared by all human beings. For there could be such characteristics without any effect on human well-being. It is hard to see why it would matter to our well-being if it were true, for instance, that only human nails grow at a specific rate. The question is not simply whether there are universal human characteristics, but whether there are such characteristics that are important for human well-being. Let us call them *important universal characteristics*. The universal view, then, is that there are important universal characteristics, and they follow from human nature. The relative view, by contrast, denies that there are any important universal characteristics because human nature is plastic, malleable, formed by variable social, cultural, historical, environmental, and other influences.

The reason why both views appear to be obviously mistaken is that they seem to deny incontestable facts. The universal view seems to be contradicted by the enormous diversity among people in different historical periods and cultures. But universalists recognize this diversity and attribute it to variable but unimportant characteristics human beings have in addition to the universal and important ones. According to universalists, variability is superficial, universality is deep. The relative view seems to be refuted by the plain fact that we readily identify as human the subjects whose characteristics are supposed to vary with contexts. How could we do this if human beings did not share some universal characteristics? The relative view explains this by saying that the characteristics on which the identification is based are indeed universal, but they are not important because it is not on them that human well-being depends. According to relativists, universality is superficial, variability is deep.

If we reflect on this disagreement, we can see that it is not about the facts but about the interpretation of agreed upon facts. Universalists can readily accept anthropological and sociological reports about human diversity, and relativists need not be disconcerted by ethological or sociobiological evidence tracing facts of social life to our biological make-up. Both attribute anomalous facts to superficial aspects of human nature and continue to hold fast to what they regard as important. Their disagreement is about which of these facts are important. The first think that it is the respects in which we are the same, the second that it is the respects in which we differ.

I have said above that this disagreement is only apparent, and we can now see that the two views can be reconciled if we recognize that some of both universal and variable characteristics are important for our well-being. These characteristics create needs for goods whose enjoyment is necessary for our well-being, but they are different kinds of goods. What, then, are these different kinds of goods?

3.2 Goods and Conventions

There are of three kinds of such goods: universal, social, and personal. Goods are good because having them is beneficial and not having them is harmful. Universal goods are the satisfaction of basic needs. They are the same for all human beings at all times and places and under all conditions. The most obvious are physiological needs for nutrition, oxygen, protection from the elements, rest and motion, consumption and elimination, and so forth. To these may be added basic psychological needs for companionship, appreciation, the absence of terror and self-loathing, and the like. These are the goods Adam and Eve had in the Garden of Eden. Having them is necessary but hardly sufficient for well-being, and that is why they wanted more. Unlike them, however, we live in a society and we also have basic needs for order, security, division of labor, protection against crime and illness, and for a life beyond mere subsistence.

The satisfaction of these basic needs is a condition of human well-being. For their prolonged frustration damages and incapacitates everyone in normal circumstances, and their satisfactions are *universal goods*. According to defenders of the balanced view, one of the political conditions of the well-being of people in a society depends on their enjoyment of universal goods. They are, therefore, committed to conventions that govern the distribution and possession of these goods and provide protection against being deprived of them. We may refer to them as *required conventions* because human well-being is impossible without them. One aim of the balanced view is thus to secure universal goods. Required conventions are the means by which this is done.

By way of illustration, consider the universal good of life and the required convention prohibiting murder. Disagreements about whether an act constitutes murder are likely to occur. People may agree that a homicide has occurred, but disagree whether suicide, abortion, euthanasia, capital punishment, or killing in self-defense or in war constitutes murder, and, if it does, whether it is justifiable or excusable. These disagreements are not intractable because the opposing sides are committed to the universal good of life and to the required convention that protects it, so the burden of proof can be assigned. Those who accept the convention prohibiting murder, but deny that a particular homicide is a violation of it, owe an explanation of why it is an exception. Good explanations excuse the act on the ground that it was accidental or done in ignorance, or, if it was deliberate and informed, justify it on the ground that the alternatives were worse. Bad explanations lack a convincing excuse or justification. There are also explanations that are not clearly good or bad because it is difficult to weigh the reasons adduced in support of them. But unclear cases do not cast doubt on the need to distinguish between clear cases in which the required convention is unambiguously violated and unclear cases that stand in need of interpretation. Murder for fun, pleasure, or profit are clear violations of the required convention.

All universal goods and required conventions must leave room for unclear cases that make interpretation and judgment necessary. But unclear cases do not change the fact that human well-being depends on the enjoyment of universal goods and the enforcement of required conventions. In this respect, the universal view of human nature is undoubtedly correct.

Defenders of the balanced view recognize that there are also many *social goods* in any society, and different societies have many different social goods. In all societies, however, there are rules aimed to secure social goods and prohibit their violation. These rules may be called *variable conventions* because they vary with societies and changes within the same society. But when they do hold, they apply to everyone in that society, so they are general. Social goods and variable conventions form an essential part of the evaluative frameworks of societies. The upbringing and socialization of people living together partly consists in acquainting them with this evaluative framework. They derive from it both their *moral identity* and the standard by which they justify or criticize actions and variable conventions in that society.

There are two types social goods. One is formed of the particular ways in which the universal goods are interpreted in a society.

The Plurality of Goods

Consider for instance the basic need for food. It must be met or we die. But there are great differences in how it is met. In all societies people reject some perfectly nutritious food, such as beef, pork, human flesh, or insects, regard some as delicacies, and often what is rejected in one society is treasured as a delicacy in another. In all societies there are customs about mealtimes, about what is eaten, when, with whom, what should be raw and what cooked, who prepares the food, what is served to guests, and so forth. In all societies there are shared ways of interpreting universal goods and shared conventions aiming to secure the goods thus interpreted, but the interpretations and conventions vary with societies. This is why the goods are social and the conventions variable.

The second type of social goods includes aspects of life whose connection with universal goods is more remote, such as ethnicity, religion, work, education, patriotism, sports, music, literature, crafts, hobbies, and so forth. It includes also the countless customs, rituals, and ceremonies of common life that mark significant occasions, like birth, marriage, and death; conventions about flirtation, competition, clothing, and housing; and the appropriate ways of expressing gratitude, regret, contempt, resentment, admiration, and the like. It includes as well what counts as politeness, tact, generosity, insult, making a promise, being superficial, and so on.

People in a society are familiar with both types of social goods. Their familiarity creates expectations and forms the character of people who have lived there for a sufficiently long time. The social goods are the building blocks of the evaluative framework from which individuals derive the personal goods which they try to realize in their own lives. Their expectations, characters, and styles of life jointly constitute a significant part of their social identity.

As the satisfaction of basic needs is a condition of well-being, so also is the maintenance of social identity. And as the required conventions may be justifiably violated because the protection of universal goods collectively may require the violation of a required convention in a particular case, so variable conventions may be justifiably violated because the protection of social goods collectively may require the violation of variable conventions in a particular case. There is, however, a difference. The violations of required conventions must be exceptional if well-being is to be possible, but the violations of variable conventions are likely to be frequent. For universal goods depend on unchanging basic needs, whereas social goods depend on the prevailing evaluative framework that continually changes in response to changing technological, demographic, cultural, social, and other conditions.

Changes in social identity do not make it a dispensable condition of well-being. Social identity is as important for well-being as the satisfaction of basic needs because without it people would be doomed to a barely human life that lacks an evaluative dimension. Through social identity societies coordinate the satisfaction of basic needs, establish customary ways in which people can relate to each other, provide a range of alternative styles of life, and help people to make the choices that are open to them. The importance of social identity, however, is as consistent with changes in it as the importance of one's language is with changes in usage. And just as speaking a language is to know what and how to communicate, so having a social identity is to know what to do and how to do it.

The balanced view, therefore, is committed also to the protection of social goods and variable conventions. The protection, however, is of the *system* of social goods and variable conventions, not of changing constituents of it. It is the *having* of a social identity that is a condition of well-being, not the particular social goods and variable conventions that temporarily constitute it. Recognition of the importance of protecting social identity must be combined with a great deal of flexibility in allowing changes in its constituents. The conditions of well-being in different societies, having to do with the satisfaction of unchanging basic needs, will therefore be largely the same, but the social conditions of well-being will be the same only as far as the protection of social identity is concerned. They will differ in respect to the changing social goods and variable conventions that constitute social identity in different societies or in different periods within the same society.

Thus there are both similarities and differences between universal and social goods. The similarities are that they are both necessary conditions of well-being and they are protected by conventions. The differences are that universal goods are unchanging, whereas social goods are always changing; the conventions protecting universal goods are required and universal, whereas the conventions protecting social goods are variable, hold generally in a particular society, not universally in all societies; and universal goods are independent of social context, while social goods are context-dependent. In respect to social goods and variable conventions, therefore, the relative view of human nature is correct. Having a social identity is a universal requirement of human well-being, but what particular social identities amount to vary with time and place.

This brings us to personal goods, having to do with individual styles of life. These goods are ones that individuals make their own from the social goods that are available in their context. They have to do with their personal relationships; their attitudes to illness, death, sex, work, and leisure; whether they seek pleasure, power, wealth, love, salvation, knowledge, or beauty; whether they prefer solitude or a busy social life, having or not having children, depth or breadth, intellect or passion, comfort or adventure, and so forth. Adam and Eve were bored and wanted more because they lacked most social and personal goods. But the key to having more is to have choices among possibilities, and with that comes knowledge that choices can be good or bad.

That is the knowledge the forbidden fruit gave them with the able assistance of the snake. It is perhaps worth mentioning that there is a minority tradition in Christian theology according to which the expulsion from the Garden of Eden was a necessary step toward the fuller realization of human capacities, and thus a good thing.

I discuss personal goods last not because they are least important but because they depend on universal and social goods. For, without universal goods we die or are seriously damaged, and without social goods we can make only severely restricted choices about how we want to live. The fact remains, however, that universal and social goods are good only because they contribute to the well-being of individual human beings. The central concern of the balanced view is with the well-being of individuals. The required and variable conventions that protect universal and social goods should be enforced only because and only to the extent to which they are necessary for individual well-being. It is certainly true that we are physical and social beings, but our well-being depends on what we make of ourselves after our physical and social requirements have been satisfied.

Politics can make these satisfactions more likely, but, according to the balanced view, politics is an activity secondary to the primary activity of individuals making what they can of their lives. One main reason why the balanced view is opposed to ideological politics is that ideologues intrude into the lives of individuals and prescribe—always for their supposed good—what they should make of their lives. Politics is important but it should be kept in its place. And its place is to enable individuals to seek their own well-being, rather than bully them into conceiving of their well-being in an ideologically correct way.

Our well-being, then, depends on a system of universal, social and personal goods, and on the required and variable conventions and styles of life that enable individuals to realize these goods. This system is the evaluative framework of a society. It contains many particular traditions, which may be legal, moral, religious, educational, economic, aesthetic, and so forth. Participants in these traditions favor a particular selection of goods and conventions from all those that constitute the evaluative framework. This framework is at once enduring and changing: it is enduring because it is changing. The goods, conventions, and traditions that make up the framework must be continually revised to adjust them to changing economic, demographic, technological, cultural, and other circumstances; they must accommodate the influences of the traditions of other societies; they must respond to internal dissatisfactions and to each others' reciprocal influences. But there is also continuity throughout these changes because the reasons for or against changing in specific ways are evaluated in terms of the temporarily unchanging parts of the evaluative framework.

One aim of the balanced view, then, is to protect the evaluative framework of a particular society because it enables individuals to satisfy their basic needs, maintain their social identity, and follow their styles of life. The protection is successful if the frustration of a basic need, the breakdown of a social identity, or the failure of a style of life is the result of individual misfortune, imprudence, criminality, or immorality, and not of defects in the evaluative framework.

It is an obvious implication of this account that human well-being depends on the plurality of goods that holds not only because there are many different universal, social, and personal goods, but also because there are religious, aesthetic, psychological, economic, and medical goods, as well as many different goods within each of these and other types of good. Human well-being depends on the enjoyment of goods, but the identity and respective importance of these goods vary with contexts and individuals. As a result of this extensive plurality, there can be no universal account of human well-being that applies to all contexts and individuals. In each case, the identity and respective importance of the goods needed for the well-being of specific individuals can be reasonably judged, but such a judgment does not—cannot—carry over to other contexts and individuals.

One of the reasons why defenders of the balanced view reject ideological politics is that all ideologues, regardless of their specific views, assume that there is a hierarchy of goods that holds universally for all contexts and individuals. They assume that equality, or justice, or liberty, or rights, or something else is the highest good always, everywhere, for everyone, and that the respective importance of other goods depends on how much they contribute to the realization of the highest good. Ideologues, then, feel morally obligated to coerce people to follow the universally applicable hierarchy. And they can self-righteously say to themselves and to others that the coercion is justified because it serves the well-being of those coerced. It gives ideologues no pause that other ideologues favor other universal hierarchies as passionately as they favor their own.

The ideological approach to human well-being is like the approach to health that supposes that one of our organs—the brain, or the heart, or the digestive tract, or the immune system—is the most important. All such approaches are mistaken, not because what they regard as important is unimportant, but because they stress the importance of one condition of human well-being at the expense of other conditions that are also necessary. By neglecting these other necessary conditions, they actually endanger what they are most concerned with achieving.

3.3 HUMAN NATURE AS MIXED

What, then, is the political significance of the just completed account of human nature and the plurality of goods that follows from it? Its significance is that human nature determines some of the goods on which our well-being depends. It is because we are the kind beings we are that these goods are good for us. There are goods for fish, birds, non-human mammals, plants, and angels and ghosts if there are any, but their goods are different from ours because their natures are different. If we now return to the claim I have made earlier that the universal and the relative views of human nature are both true and not incompatible, it is easy to see why this is so.

The universal view is right: human nature is the same always, everywhere in respect to basic needs, the necessity of satisfying them, and their satisfactions being universal goods. The universal view is also right: human nature requires that there be a system of social goods and variable conventions and that individuals should construct a style of life for themselves that suits their characters and circumstances. These requirements hold because human nature dictates some of the conditions on which our well-being depends. But the universal view is also wrong in supposing that human nature determines all or most conditions of our well-being. Human nature allows a great plurality of different systems of social goods and variable conventions, and a like plurality of individual styles of life. Human nature includes only some of the important universal characteristics on which our well-being depends, but those characteristics are not sufficient to specify all that our well-being requires.

The respects in which the universal view is wrong are the respects in which the relative view is right. There are great differences among societies and individuals in respect to social goods, variable conventions, and styles of life. These differences are the result of differences in their contexts—contexts shaped by climatic, economic, religious, historical, cultural, technological, demographic, and countless other influences. The relative view is right in emphasizing the great plurality of forms human well-being may take. But the relative view is wrong in supposing that all the conditions of our well-being vary with contexts. Universal goods and a system of social goods and variable conventions are some important universal, context-independent conditions of our well-being.

The universal and relative views of human nature make the same mistake. They pass from the justified insistence on the importance of some facts of human nature to the unjustified dismissal of the importance of some other facts of human nature. The way they go wrong suggests that the right view of human nature avoids the unjustified dismissal of any of the important facts of human nature. Human nature is invariable in some respects and variable in others. Consequently human well-being has some universal and context-independent requirements, as well as some requirements that are relative and context-dependent. A reasonable view of human well-being must recognize both types of requirements. The mixed view of human nature combines the respects in which the universal and the relative views are right and avoids the respects in which they are wrong. And this is just what the balanced view does.

According to the mixed view of human nature, it is an important universal condition of our well-being that our basic needs be satisfied. But this is only a minimum condition and our well-being also depends on what happens after the minimum condition is met. It is of great importance that societies and individuals can develop plural forms of human well-being. In fortunate circumstances, when contingencies, scarcity, and conflicts do not prevent it, our nature leaves us free to choose among these forms. Unlike other beings with other natures, we are not driven solely by genetic inheritance and environmental conditions. We have evolved in a way that enables us to control to some extent what inherited dispositions we cultivate, what we do in response to environmental conditions, and occasionally we can even alter our environmental conditions. The importance of this is that we have some control over our well-being, we can shape how we live, and we are, therefore, responsible for some of the ways in which we live and act. This is at once the boon and the burden of the human condition.

The mixed view of human nature has significant consequences for politics. Any acceptable approach to politics must aim to protect the political conditions of the well-being of people in a particular society. It must recognize, therefore, the important universal characteristics that follow from human nature. All such approaches must be committed to satisfying basic needs, maintaining the prevailing social identity, and enabling individuals to develop styles of life. One reason in favor of the balanced view and against numerous alternatives to it is that it recognizes these conditions, whereas many competing approaches fail to do so. Their failure is the result of exaggerating the importance of one of these conditions at the expense of the importance of the others.

3.4 MISTAKEN ALTERNATIVES

The most widely held conservative alternatives to the balanced view are natural law theories. The Thomistic attempt to combine an interpretation of Aristotle's ethics and politics with Christian beliefs is perhaps the most prominent version of such theories. What I have been saying about the universal conditions of human well-being is congenial to natural law theorists, but they go far beyond what I take to be the extent of these conditions. Natural law theorists assume that there is a moral order permeating the scheme of things. It is a law of nature that human well-being depends on living in conformity to this moral order. Doing so is a universal requirement of the well-being of all societies and individuals. Natural law theorists are in effect saying that the important universal characteristics extend well beyond the satisfaction of basic needs and determine also what social goods and styles of life human well-being requires. Thus they reject the mixed view of human nature. They think that required conventions should regulate also the education of children, abortion, euthanasia, contraception, divorce, the relation between church and state, homosexuality, the status of women, and so on.

The balanced view excludes this version of conservatism because there is no good reason to believe that there is a moral order in the scheme of things. And even if there were one, it is very doubtful that anyone could have reliable beliefs about what it is. Defenders of the balanced view find the plain facts testifying to the plurality of social goods and styles of life that are conducive to human well-being far more plausible than the metaphysical speculations on which natural law theorists base their denials of these facts. Defenders of the balanced view rely on the evidence supplied by history, anthropology, and personal experience that there are many more forms of human well-being than natural law theorists allow. The mistake of natural law theories is to inflate the importance of the universal condition, deflate the importance of the plurality of social and individual conditions, and thus fail to recognize that human nature is mixed.

A strikingly similar mistake is made by liberals who regard the individual condition of human well-being as paramount and recognize the relevance of social and universal conditions only insofar as they are instrumental to meeting the individual conditions. The main inspiration of such theories is the Kantian view that individual autonomy is the key to human well-being. Autonomy is generally understood as the capacity to make unforced choices among adequately understood alternatives. Kantian liberals think that individuals are in control of their lives to the extent to which they make such choices, rather than live in conformity to the prevailing conventions. They think of autonomy as freeing oneself from the constraints of conventions. And they think that the aim of politics is to create the conditions in which individuals can do this. Now this is an undoubtedly attractive possibility, but a little reflection shows that Kantian liberals actually presuppose what they deny, namely the importance of the required and variable conventions for human well-being. Reflection also shows that Kantian liberalism leads to absurdity. The emphasis on the individual condition of human well-being and the demotion of its universal and social conditions to a merely contingent, instrumental status is thus a mistake.

First, autonomous choices can have a significant effect on well-being only if they concern important matters, such as the choice of styles of life, rather than trivial ones, like what to have for lunch. Where do alternative styles of life come from so that individuals could choose one among them? Very few people construct original styles of life. Most of us choose among styles of life that reflect some of the social goods that are recognized as such in our society. But then the autonomous choices among styles of life depend on the prevailing system of social goods that provides the alternatives among which we can make autonomous choices. Autonomous choices, therefore, presuppose and are enabled by the social conditions whose importance for such choices Kantian liberals neglect.

Second, individual choices must be restricted because they cannot be allowed to violate the required conventions on which human well-being depends. If individuals can make autonomous choices, it is only because the required conventions are well enough protected to provide the universal goods necessary for choice-making, such as nutrition and security. We find, then, once again that autonomous choices presuppose that the universal conditions of human well-being have been met. The universal condition of human well-being on which autonomy depends cannot be less important than the individual condition that presupposes it.

Third, making autonomous choices requires adequate intelligence, education, leisure, reflection, prosperity, peace, and security. There have been few people in human history who met these requirements. If autonomous choices were necessary for human well-being, then people who are uneducated, or unintelligent, or poor, or unreflective, or live in tumultuous times are unavoidably deprived of well-being. Since this has been the condition of the vast majority of people who ever lived, it is an unintended consequence of Kantian liberalism that they could not have lived well. General well-being, therefore, must be restricted to contemporary Western democracies where these conditions are usually met. This is an absurdity that no reasonable approach to politics could accept. But it follows from Kantian liberalism and tells against it.

Fourth, since individuals often make autonomous choices that are detrimental to human well-being, autonomous choice cannot be sufficient for well-being. But whether an autonomous choice is conducive to human well-being depends on whether it recognizes the universal and social conditions of well-being, and this shows, once again, that it depends on those conditions.

Kantian liberalism and natural law theories go wrong in the same way. They stress one condition of human well-being and forget about the others. The trouble is not that they stress an unimportant condition of human well-being. The trouble is that natural law theorists and Kantian liberals alike fail to recognize that there are other important conditions as well, and the three conditions—universal, social, and individual—are mixed and reciprocally presupposed by one another. And this is what the mixed view of human nature claims.

Relativists also reject the mixed view of human nature. Their mistake is similar in an important respect to the mistake of natural law conservatives and Kantian liberals: relativists recognize the importance of only one condition of human well-being—the social—and fail to acknowledge the importance of its universal and individual conditions. But there is also an important way in which relativists differ from these conservatives and liberals. Natural law theorists and Kantians stress the universality and context-independence of reasons, relativists deny them. The relativists' view is that social goods and variable conventions determine what is politically acceptable in the context of a particular society. They deny that there is any fact, principle, or standard external to a society's evaluative framework. Their view is that human well-being is what people in a society regard as human well-being. Thus they think that the dominant condition of human well-being is social. What the mixed view claims are universal and individual conditions are recognized by relativists as conditions of well-being only if they have been incorporated in the prevailing evaluative framework of a society. But then the reason for recognizing them is not that they hold universally for everyone or individually for a particular person, but that they are recognized as one of the social goods.

Natural law and Kantian theories accept that human well-being partly depends on conformity to standards external to one's society. Relativistic theories, however, deny that there are any external standards, consequently they deny that their own view can be rightly criticized for the failure to conform to them. According to relativists, what is politically acceptable depends solely on considerations internal to the evaluative framework of a society. This view, however, has patently mistaken implications for human well-being.

First, if a policy, action, or belief conforms to the evaluative framework of a society, then, according to relativists, it could not be misguided. If slavery, child prostitution, or magic are generally approved in a society, that is sufficient to make them right and reasonable. For there is no consideration external to the society's evaluative framework that could show otherwise. Second, if relativism were correct, it would be impossible to compare two societies and say that one is better than the other in some particular respect, for that would involve appealing to a standard that those living in the worse society do not recognize. It could not be reasonable, for instance, to say that a society that burns witches, kills dissenters, or requires the genital mutilation of women is in that respect worse than another society that rejects these barbaric practices. Third, if individuals feel dissatisfied with their lives even though they meet the prevailing social conditions of human well-being, or if they feel satisfied even though their lives do not conform to the social conditions, then relativists would have to say that the individuals are mistaken in feeling that way. For relativists claim that individual judgments about well-being are acceptable only if they reflect the social conditions. Fourth, if a society did not accept that security, peace, or adequate nutrition, for instance, were among universal goods, then that would show that they were not universal goods, since what is good or bad depends on what are thought to be the social conditions of well-being. For, according to relativists, there is nothing external to the prevailing social conditions that could be appealed to in order to show that the social conditions are mistaken. Relativism leads to these absurdities, so it has much less going for it than natural law conservatism or Kantian liberalism. Yet relativism is virtually the official view of sociologists, anthropologists, and of those literary critics who have drunk deeply of the strange brew concocted in France.

I conclude that the alternatives to the balanced view represented by natural law conservatism, Kantian liberalism, and relativism are mistaken. Moreover, they are mistaken for the same reason, namely, for failing to take into account incontestable facts of human nature.

These facts are that human nature makes it a condition of human well-being that basic needs are satisfied, social identity is protected, and a style of life is developed. Meeting these conditions provides the universal, social, and personal goods that jointly constitute an essential component of human well-being. The shared mistake of these three theories is not they ignore these facts, but that they attribute the wrong importance to them. Each theory privileges one type of fact and regards the other types as important only so far as they contribute to the favored type.

In criticizing these views, I have endeavored to point out the unacceptable consequence of each that beliefs that virtually everyone rightly holds in our context are actually false. Natural law theorists exaggerate the importance of universal goods they derive from a supposed cosmic moral order and on this basis deny that human well-being also depends on social and personal goods that vary with societies and individuals. Kantian liberals exaggerate the importance of autonomously chosen personal goods and this leads them to deny that autonomous choices presuppose universal and social goods. And relativists exaggerate the importance of social goods derived from the evaluative framework of a society and this leads them to deny that a society's evaluative framework may be mistaken about universal and personal goods and thus be detrimental to human well-being.

3.5 PLURALITY OF GOODS

Each of the alternatives to the balanced view begins with a view of human nature, derives from it a system of goods, attributes our dissatisfactions to a failure to live in conformity with the system of goods, and proposes policies for closing the gap between how life in our context is and how it ought to be. This, of course, is the ideological approach to politics. We can now conclude that the ideological approach is mistaken not only because it is based on a mistaken conception of reason (as I have argued in Chapter Two), but also because it is based on a mistaken conception of human nature (as I have argued in the present chapter).

Showing that the ideological approach to politics is mistaken does not show that the balanced view is right. Showing that requires improved conceptions of reason, human nature, and the political goods required for human well-being. I hope to have provided such a conception of reason by arguing that it should be prudential, that is, practical, allowing, and justifying, rather than theoretical, requiring, and deliberating. And I hope to have done the same for the plurality of goods that follows from a conception of human nature as a mixture of a universal component, making us need a plurality of different universal goods, and of a variable component, making us need a plurality of social and personal goods.

I have, then, identified and interpreted reason as prudence and the plurality of goods as two of the political goods to which the balanced view is committed. But the account I have given of the mixed view of human nature and the plurality of goods is incomplete. For when we think of human nature, we must think not only of our needs but also of our characteristic dispositions. Are our dispositions basically good, bad, mixed, or are we perhaps without any basic good or bad dispositions? The answers we give have obvious political implications. The questions, the answers, and the political implications are the topics of the next chapter.

CHAPTER FOUR

✦　　✦　　✦

NECESSARY LIMITS

I feel at times identified with the good, as though all my self were in it; there are certain good habits and pursuits . . . which are natural to me, and in which I feel at home. And then again there are certain bad habits and pursuits . . . in which perhaps I feel no less at home, in which I also feel myself to be myself . . . whichever way I go, I satisfy myself and yet fail to do so. . . . I am driven to believe that two opposing principles are at war in me, and make me at war with myself; each of which loves what the other hates, and hates what the other loves.

F. H. BRADLEY
Ethical Studies

THE DISCUSSION OF HUMAN NATURE in the preceding chapter led to the conclusion that human nature is mixed. This is true as far as it goes, but it does not go far enough because human nature is doubly mixed. It is a mixture of universal and variable components, as we have seen, and also of good and bad components, as we will see in this chapter. If we think that the good contributes to human well-being and the bad detracts from it, then it follows that the balanced view must be committed to political conditions that promote the good and limit the bad.

We have also seen that there is a great plurality of universally, socially, and personally good and bad things. A full account of

66

human well-being would require a consideration of all of them. My present purpose, however, is not to give such an account, but only a much more limited one that considers what is good and bad from the American political point of view. And even within that narrower aim, I will concentrate only on basic political goods whose importance is generally recognized. What is politically bad, then, can be specified with reference to these political goods. There are, of course, deep political disagreements, but they are not about the identity of the most important political goods, but about their interpretation and respective importance. The reason why these political goods are good and their violations bad is that the goods are conditions of human well-being and the violations are contrary to it.

It is a lamentable fact of life that such violations are frequent. Crime, discrimination, drugs, ignorance, ill-health, injustice, persecution, poverty, terrorism, violence, and so on abound. These violations are caused by human actions. Why do people act in ways that threaten the political conditions of human well-being in general and of their own well-being in particular? The aim of this chapter is to provide an explanation in terms of human nature. This will strengthen the case for the balanced view and weaken the case for some ideological alternatives to it.

4.1 AN ANCIENT MYTH

The myth is about Heracles, Deianira, and Nessus. Heracles is the greatest hero in the heroic age of ancient Greece; the son of Zeus, who by a ruse impregnated Alcmene, a mortal woman. Heracles is the embodiment of what in archaic Greece was thought to be the best in human beings. Deianira is Heracles' innocent and simple wife. She waits patiently at home while Heracles is away meeting challenges. Nessus is a centaur, half human, half beast. He is a wicked, cunning creature who falls short of ordinary humanity, just as Heracles rises above it. As Heracles is almost divine, so Nessus is almost brutish. Nessus has a special reason to hate Heracles because he killed all the centaurs, with the exception of Nessus, who is now a ferryman.

As it happens, Deianira is being ferried by Nessus across the river. He realizes who she is and tries to rape her. Heracles, however, prevents it by shooting Nessus with a poisoned arrow that causes Nessus excruciating pain and a slow death. As Nessus is dying, he feigns repentance, and by way of pretended expiation gives Deianira a vial, which he says contains a powerful love potion, but is in fact Nessus' poisoned blood. Time passes, Heracles is away again demonstrating that he is the best, and Deianira is afraid that Heracles no longer wants her. Her fears are reinforced when Heracles returns with a lovely woman he has enslaved. Deianira, wanting to regain Heracles' affection, then, soaks his shirt with what she believes is the love potion. Heracles puts on the shirt. He is poisoned, suffers the same excruciating pain Nessus had suffered, and, like Nessus did, dies slowly and terribly. Heracles is thus killed by the very poison with which he killed Nessus. And Deianira, in her innocent simplicity, killed the best of all humans whom she truly loved.

The myth has many versions. Perhaps the best known is Sophocles' treatment of it in *The Women of Trachis*. I take the myth to represent three aspects of human nature: brutish cunning, innocent simplicity, and the pursuit of the good. Brutish cunning and innocent simplicity cause the pursuit of the good to fail. As Sophocles sees it, brutish cunning is the dark side of human nature. There hangs over it "a murderous cloud"; it is "treacherous," "sets traps," and is "soaked with venom" (831–833). Innocent simplicity, by its very nature, is helpless against it, for it is shocked by what appears to it "unspeakable, incomprehensible to human reason" (693–694). This incomprehension, however, has the terrible consequence of leading the innocent to do "unwittingly the will of the beast" (935), to do wrong while intending the good (1136), and ending up "killing the best . . . [in] man" (811). It is no use for the innocent to lament after the destruction that "I could not bear to live and hear

myself called evil when my only wish is to be truly good"
(721–722). Good intentions are not enough because they easily
lead to doing "the will of the beast".

Sophocles represents the destruction of the best in man as the
outcome of the conflicting dispositions of three distinct characters.
I think, however, that the deep significance of this myth appears
only when we see that the conflict is not between the dispositions
of different characters, but between conflicting desires each of
us has: desires of the dark side of our nature, desires for a life of
innocent simplicity, and desires for the good. The desires for innocent simplicity are untrustworthy and ought to be suspected
because they are easily led astray by the dark side of our nature. We
must realize that our desires for the good can be satisfied only if
we recognize and struggle against the desires of our dark side for the
bad, only if we acknowledge bad desires and do not regard them
as "incomprehensible to human reason." We must also realize that
our desires for a life of innocent simplicity are unattainable because
coping with the complexities of life depends on reflection, and
innocent simplicity is incapable of it.

These conflicting desires affect all the conditions of our well-
being, but my present concern is only with the political ones. The
first lesson this understanding of the myth teaches is that it is
innocent simplicity to trust our good intentions. Being imbued with
a vision of the good is not enough, for it may in fact have been led
astray by the bad side of our nature, just as Deianira's was by Nessus.
All political visions, therefore, ought to be treated with great suspi-
cion. Since, at the core of ideologies there is always a simple vision
of the good, we have another reason against being guided by them.

The simplicity of the vision of the good, however, is not the only
reason against ideologies. Another reason is that they fail to recognize the political significance of the bad. Each ideology rests on two
assumptions: one is that it has identified the political conditions of
human well-being, and the other is that if people can be brought
to realize this, they would join the ideologues in establishing and

protecting these conditions. In the preceding three chapters I have argued against the first assumption. In this chapter I will argue against the second that even if the first assumption were true, the second would remain false. For knowing what the political conditions of human well-being are is not enough to motivate people to adhere to them. The dark side of human nature may lead us to pursue the bad even if we know what the good is.

Ideologues miss this because they do not take into account the complexities of human motivation. They fail to see the significance of there being psychological tendencies that motivate us in a direction contrary to human well-being. The second lesson we should learn from the ancient myth is that our bad desires are enemies of the good ones; we have contrary and conflicting desires; their conflict is permanent; and no ideology, no matter how successfully it may identify the political conditions of human well-being, can eliminate the bad desires and their conflicts with the good ones. The myth teaches us that our psychology is deeper than our politics because the politics we tend to favor is a reflection of our psychological dispositions.

I begin to explore the implications of the myth and its lessons with the fact acknowledged by everyone that, although there is a consensus about the most important political goods, practices contrary to them are ubiquitous in contemporary Western democracies. Why is there so much crime, discrimination, drug addiction, ignorance, ill-health, injustice, persecution, poverty, terrorism, and violence, if people know that they are contrary to the political goods on which depend their own and other people's well-being in a society?

4.2 Moral Monsters and Uncharacteristic Bad Actions

I will consider three inadequate explanations: two in this section and a third in the next one. They are inadequate because, although each explains some violations of political goods, each fails to explain many other violations. Their failure, however, is instructive because it provides the clue to what an adequate explanation would be. The first inadequate explanation is that the violations of political goods are caused by bad people, whom I will call moral monsters. They knowingly, intentionally, and habitually cause serious harm to others in their society. They are multiple murderers; those who deliberately infect others with AIDS; terrorists motivated by ethnic, racial, or religious hatred; greedy embezzlers who defraud the elderly of their life-savings; wholesale drug dealers who entice children into addiction; sadists who take pleasure in inflicting grievous injury on innocent victims; and so on. These moral monsters make it a policy for themselves to destroy the conditions of others' well-being. They may be motivated by virulent prejudice, thirst for power, self-loathing projected outward, cynicism, destructiveness, or passionate resentment of supposed injustice.

Moral monsters, however, are surely rare, probably even rarer than moral saints. For monsters not only have to have as clear vision, great strength of character, and exceptionally strong sense of purpose as saints have, but they must also do what saints do not, namely, hide from others their true nature, since public opinion generally favors the good. Being a moral monster, therefore, is very difficult, and it takes capacities that most people lack. There certainly are people like Stalin, Hitler, Mao, and others of their ilk, but there can be only a few like them who cultivate monstrosity and make it a lifelong policy to act on it.

Since moral monsters are few, the prevalence of the bad cannot be attributed to them. Crime, the drug trade, injustice, and so forth depend on the active engagement of a substantial number of people, not just a handful of moral monsters. The murder, torture, and enslavement of millions of people in Communist Russia and China, and in Nazi Germany, for instance, could not have been caused by the dictators alone. It required thousands of henchmen to commit the atrocities. There certainly are moral monsters, and they certainly cause much harm to innocent people, but the violations of political goods are considerably more widespread than what could be attributed to the deliberate acts of rare moral monsters.

The second inadequate explanation is that many violations of political goods are caused by the uncharacteristic acts of normally decent people. They cause serious harm to innocent victims, but they do not realize what they are doing because they are ignorant of relevant facts, or they act uncharacteristically because they are under great stress, have been provoked, or are incapacitated by drugs or alcohol. Such acts do account for some violations. Sometimes they may be excused, or the blame assigned for them may be reduced. But crime, the drug trade, injustice, and so forth are only rarely the exceptional acts of otherwise blameless people. The violations of political goods are usually part of the violators' customary pattern of actions, rather than uncharacteristic episodes. Of course, people sometimes do act in uncharacteristic ways, but most people most of the time act characteristically.

What people usually do is what they would predictably and routinely do: sleep at night, go to work, eat at mealtimes, make love, pay bills, and so on. Emergencies, great provocations, or disorienting stress are rare in civilized circumstances. A large part of everyone's life is routine. Actions normally flow from the agent's character. When the need arises, liars will lie; thieves will steal; kind, just, honest people will act kindly, justly, honestly. Actions are prompted by motives; motives reflect settled dispositions, habits, and aims; and they partly constitute the characters of agents. Because uncharacteristic actions are rare and the violations of political goods frequent, many violations cannot be explained in terms of uncharacteristic actions.

4.3 UNINTENTIONAL BAD ACTIONS

If the prevalence of the violations of the political conditions of human well-being cannot be attributed to moral monsters or to the uncharacteristic actions of normally well-intentioned people, then the obvious possibility is to attribute it to the characteristic acts of bad people, who are not bad enough to be called moral monsters. This is in fact the third inadequate explanation I will consider. The explanation is that such people habitually violate the political conditions of human well-being, but they do not see the serious harm they cause as bad. Their actions are bad, but they are convinced that they are not. They do what they do, but they do it unknowingly and unintentionally because they misinterpret the moral significance of what they are doing. They see that their actions seriously harm people, but they do not see their victims as innocent. They see their persecution of innocent people as deserved punishment; dealing in drugs as a transaction in the free enterprise system; murdering their opponents as justified defense of their country, religion, ethnic group, or race; infecting others with AIDS as righteous revenge for having been infected themselves; embezzling the life-savings of elderly people as well-earned compensation for business acumen; and burglary as the fair redistribution of wealth from the rich to the poor.

These people genuinely fail to understand the true nature of their actions; they may see the serious harm they cause, but they do not see it as unjustified. They are not moral monsters who know and intend their bad actions, but moral idiots who fail to see what is obvious. Their idiocy is not a cognitive deficiency, for they are often quite intelligent, but a kind of moral blindness. Defenders of this third explanation, therefore, must explain what blinds these benighted agents to the absurdity of their misdescriptions of what they are doing.

The explanation they offer is that the agents of unintentional bad actions are blinded by their understandable reactions to the prevailing bad political conditions. They are enraged by injustice that was done to them; brutalized by the poverty in which they grew up; desensitized by the terrible education they have received; deprived of enjoyment by the soul-destroying work they have to do; filled with resentment by inequalities of the wealth; and dominated by the desire to avenge the harm that was done to them. Their blindness to the true nature of their actions is thus not self-imposed but inflicted on them by their society. They are not acting badly because they are bad but because they were corrupted by bad political conditions.

We may put this explanation in terms of the ancient myth by saying that the innocent simplicity of Deianira aiming at the good is our basic motivation. If it is corrupted, it is because bad political conditions darken our nature, teach us the treacherous cunning of Nessus, blind us to the good, and destroy the best in us, as it had destroyed Heracles.

The attractions of this explanation are numerous. It has a certain psychological plausibility; makes understandable how unexceptional, ordinary people, like countless Nazi and Communist functionaries, can come to cause horrendous harm to many innocent people; acknowledges that bad actions are widespread; and it is free of the implausible attribution of the majority of bad actions to moral monsters or to the uncharacteristic acts of normally decent people. The explanation recognizes that the agents who habitually cause harm to innocent people are motivated by ill-will, but denies that being so motivated is their fault. The fault is ascribed to the society in which they live and whose political conditions have corrupted them. Many ideologues enthusiastically embrace this explanation because it reinforces their view that there is urgent need for the radical reform of the corrupting political conditions.

There are nevertheless several reasons why this explanation is inadequate. First, it does not account for the fact that there are significant differences in how people react to the same corrupting political conditions. True, injustice may enrage some and provoke them to act unjustly, but it may lead others to become reformers, scrupulous defenders of justice, seek consolation in religion, become resigned and turn inward, or leave the unjust society. Poverty may

74

brutalize some, but it may spur others to excel, to organize the poor in order to improve their lot, or to disdain the goods of which they are deprived. Bad education may desensitize some, but it may inspire others to become autodidacts, self-made artists, fanatical devotees of the first creed to which they happen to be exposed, or compensate by becoming athletes, body-builders, or disciples of some crank.

The point is not that these alternatives to being corrupted are easy to choose and cultivate. The point is that there are alternatives, and their mere existence shows that corruption by bad political conditions cannot be the full explanation of bad actions. A full explanation must take into account individual differences in willingness to explore alternatives and in receptivity and resistance to corruption. An adequate explanation of bad actions, therefore, must be at least partly psychological, and cannot be merely political.

Second, if bad actions were the result of bad political conditions, it would follow that the worse political conditions are, the more bad actions there will be. This may in fact be true in disintegrating societies whose conditions approximate anarchy. But the cause in such cases is the breakdown of political conditions, not their badness. If we consider firmly established dictatorships whose political conditions are very bad indeed, we find that violent crimes committed by individuals, as opposed to the dictators and their henchmen, are infrequent. Repressive societies repress their citizens, consequently they repress both their criminal and non-criminal actions. The rates of murder, mayhem, and other violent crimes were much lower in Nazi Germany and Communist Russia than they are, say, in contemporary America.

The bad political conditions of dictatorships have some good consequences, and the good political conditions of democratic societies have some bad consequences. This is so because in democratic societies people are much freer to act on their psychological dispositions than in dictatorships. From which it follows that the explanation of bad actions merely in terms of bad political conditions is inadequate. An adequate explanation must take into account the psychological dispositions of the agents who act badly.

Third, historical, anthropological, and literary examinations of human conduct show that bad actions are motivated by the same depressing psychological dispositions under very different political conditions. Aggression, cruelty, envy, fear, greed, hatred, jealousy, prejudice, self-deception, and selfishness are familiar and recognizable motives for bad actions in the context of all societies, no matter how different are the political conditions that prevail in them. The actions that follow from these motives, of course, are directed toward different objects in different contexts, but the motives are the same. Greed may lead to seeking more money, land, honors, paintings, or slaves; prejudice may be directed against tribes, races, women, religions, homosexuals, foreigners, heretics, dissenters, the rich, the poor, the bourgeois, and so forth. Fear may be of strangers, ghosts, novelties, God, social disapproval, poverty, pain, shame, death, or illness. What varies, however, are the objects of the motives, not the motives themselves. If this were not the case, we could not do what we do all the time, namely, understand and explain the bad actions of people in contexts very different from our own. Bad political conditions, therefore, may explain why motives lead to desiring or avoiding specific objects, but they do not explain the motives that remain the same even though political conditions vary.

Fourth, let us grant for the moment that what blinds us to the badness of our actions are bad political conditions. This would explain why we do not see our bad actions as bad, but it would not by itself explain why the actions are bad. The explanation requires the further assumption that bad political conditions do not merely blind us to the true nature of our actions but also cause us to act badly. Deianira was not merely deceived by Nessus, she inflicted excruciating pain on Heracles and killed him. The deception was clearly caused by Nessus, but were Heracles' pain and death also caused by him? Heracles, after all, would not have been destroyed if it had not been for Deianira's actions. Expressed differently, the explanation assumes that if people were not blinded to the badness of their actions, then they would not act badly. Only if this further assumption were true could bad actions be explained by the corrupting effects of bad political conditions. But the assumption is false.

Take people whose actions violate political conditions of human well-being, but who do not see that their actions are bad. They see them under a different description. They persecute innocent victims, but they see it as deservedly punishing them; they deal in drugs and entice children into addiction, but they see it as a free market transaction; they murder their opponents, but they see it as justified defense of a righteous cause; and so forth. Unknown to these agents, the underlying motives for their actions are very different from what they take them to be. The truth to which they are blind is that they persecute because they are driven by hatred; they deal in drugs because they are greedy; they murder because they are fanatics.

Suppose, then, that they come to see that they have been blinded to the truth, perhaps because it is convincingly explained to them, or they have emigrated to a better society. They now recognize that hatred, greed, fanaticism, and the like motivated them. Why should we think that their reaction would be to stop acting on these motives? What reason is there for thinking that the change from blindness to seeing aright would change the motives? Why would their reaction not be to shrug, say to themselves: yes, I am driven by hate, greed, or fanaticism, and continue to act precisely as before, except they would know what they are doing? They may conclude that harming those they hate, satisfying their greed, or defending the cause to which they are fanatically committed is more important than the well-being of their victims. Their newly acquired knowledge may merely change them from being unknowingly and unintentionally bad to being bad knowingly and intentionally.

The belief that bad actions are the effects of bad political conditions rests on the assumption that people would not act badly if they knew that that is what they are doing. But we all know that this assumption is false from our own case: we often know that we are venting our frustration on people who have not caused it; that we are lying because we are afraid to tell the truth; that we are breaking a promise because we have found something better to do; or that we are blaming others for our failure although it is caused by our lack of effort. Such self-knowledge is quite common and having it rarely has anything to do with what political conditions happen to prevail.

There can be no serious doubt that our nature has a dark side and we are sometimes motivated by it. It may be, but it need not be a snake, or a Nessus, or poverty, injustice, or bad education that causes us to act badly. The reason why innocent simplicity is not enough is not just that we are at risk of being corrupted by external influences, but also that we are at risk of acting on the dark side of our nature. The cause of bad actions can be both internal and external. The fourth reason why the explanation of bad actions in terms of bad political conditions is inadequate is that it ignores the internal causes of bad actions. And the significance of the ancient myth is that it reminds us of this basic truth about human nature.

The last reason I will adduce against the explanation of bad actions in terms of bad political conditions emerges if we ask the obvious question of why political conditions are bad. Their badness consists in violating conditions of well-being in a particular society. Why do they do this? The first thing that must be said is that strictly speaking political conditions do not violate anything because they are not the sorts of things that are capable of action. The violations are done by people who act in conformity to political conditions. If there is avoidable poverty, it is because some people impoverish others; if there is injustice, it is because some people treat others unjustly; if education is bad, it is because teachers are incompetent, schools are badly run, and taxes are insufficient or ill-spent. The question is, then, why do people act in conformity to bad political conditions?

To answer that people do this because they have also been corrupted by bad political conditions merely postpones facing the implausibility of the explanation. For the question remains of why people have acted in conformity to this second kind of political conditions. Sooner or later it has to be acknowledged that people come first and political conditions can only follow. There could be no political conditions unless there are people who create them. In the order of explanation, people must precede the political conditions they create. If political conditions are bad, it must be the fault of the people who made them. The fault may be intellectual or moral. But it is far more likely to be moral because those who make bad political conditions could hardly fail to realize that they will violate conditions of human well-being. Who could fail to know that poverty deprives people of resources they need; that injustice results in some people not getting what they deserve and others getting what they do not deserve; or that bad education fails to provide knowledge and skills that children need to make their way in life? The unavoidable conclusion is that most bad political conditions are created by people who cannot be ignorant of the harm the conditions cause to innocent victims. It is, therefore, the badness of people that explains the badness of political conditions, not the other way around as this explanation mistakenly assumes.

We must conclude that the explanation of bad actions by attributing them to moral monsters, or to decent people acting uncharacteristically, or to people who are blinded by bad political conditions are all inadequate. Each accounts for some bad actions, but all of them fail to account for many others. In one way or another all of them refuse to face the fact that many bad actions must be explained by the badness of the agents who perpetrated them. But why do the defenders of these inadequate explanations go to such lengths to refuse to face the rather obvious reasons I have given against their accounts? The answer, I think, is that they wish to think well of human beings. It is comforting to believe that, with the exception of rare moral monsters, we are all basically good and we act badly only uncharacteristically or because external influences have interfered with our benign native dispositions and spontaneous good will. This comforting belief is a sentimental and dangerous falsification of the facts of life because it stands in the way of a realistic approach to making bad actions less prevalent.

4.4 THE AMBIVALENCE OF HUMAN MOTIVATION

To conclude that the causes of many bad actions are internal to agents is not, of course, to conclude that human nature is basically bad. That conclusion is as implausible as the opposite one that human nature is basically good. The conclusion that should be drawn is that human nature is basically ambivalent. We have both good and bad desires, and sometimes we act on one, sometimes on the other. External circumstances, including political conditions, influence which desires we aim to satisfy and what forms their satisfaction may take, but we have desires prompted by aggression, cruelty, envy, fear, greed, hatred, jealousy, prejudice, self-deception, selfishness, and so forth, regardless of what external circumstances prevail. This is why psychological explanations are indispensable to understanding why human beings act badly.

Recognizing the necessity of psychological explanations is one thing, providing them is quite another. But providing them is particularly important because it is far from obvious why we act on our bad desires, when we could act on the good ones. To put this in terms of the ancient myth: even if we grant that our nature has a dark side, we must recognize that it also has another side, and the question remains why we often act as Nessus did rather than trying to approximate an ideal of human excellence, even if we do not think that it takes the heroic form as represented by Heracles and loved with an all too innocent simplicity by Deianira.

The explanation I will now propose is that people act badly because they are committed to some other aim they regard as more important than their own or other people's well-being. Their bad actions are contrary to well-being but they are instrumental to their pursuit of another aim. Their bad actions, therefore, are not done in ignorance or by inadvertence. They recognize the significance of what they are doing. They need not share the ill-will that motivates the misanthropy of moral monsters. They are uncorrupted by bad political conditions. And yet they act in ways that cause serious harm to others. They know that morality normally prohibits such actions, but they think that there is some consideration that overrides the dictates of morality when they come into conflict. What might be such a consideration?

It might be faith that leads them to subordinate their will to God's. They say: "Thy will be done," as Abraham said as he was preparing to sacrifice his beloved son Isaac when he felt that God commanded him to do so. It might be commitment to a life dedicated to the creation of works of art, even if the life involves the systematic violation of moral obligations. It might be an overpowering desire for wealth, power, glory, or fame that leads them to do whatever is necessary to achieve it. It might be passionate love of another person, a people, or a cause that is so strong as to silence contrary considerations and compel individuals to act as their love dictates no matter what the cost is to themselves or others.

When people act in these ways, they think that they are justified. Their justifications, of course, are not moral, if by moral we understand commitment to human well-being in general. But it is, nevertheless, an evaluative justification that rests on some ideal they regard as higher than any other. Such people can be charged with immorality, although not with irrationality. For they can be logically consistent, take account of relevant facts, be efficient in pursuing an ideal, and have accepted the ideal only after due consideration. Such people are guided by an overriding commitment to religion, art, personal ambition, or love.

This explanation, however, does not attribute the prevalence of the bad only to people with overriding commitments. It would be implausible to do so because such single-minded people are as rare as moral monsters. The significance of single-mindedness is to call attention to sources of motivation that may conflict with the moral one. The non-moral motives of most people are not single-minded. Most people are ambivalent. They are sometimes moved by moral considerations that override non-moral ones; and sometimes they are moved in the opposite direction. The explanation I am proposing is that the prevalence of the bad should be attributed to perfectly ordinary people who act on their non-moral motives, rather than on the moral motives they also have. Because their non-moral motives are stronger, or their circumstances are conducive to it, they violate the political conditions of well-being in the context of their society. That is why crime, the drug trade, injustice, and so forth are widespread. This explanation accounts for the prevalence of the bad in a way that moral monsters, uncharacteristic acts, and bad political conditions by themselves cannot do.

If this explanation is right, then many bad actions are the consequences of bad desires. But it is crucial to see that the motivating desires are bad only from the moral point of view. From the point of view of those who are motivated by religious, aesthetic, or personal commitments to ambition or love, the desires are not bad, even if they are acknowledged to be morally bad. Just as a moral commitment may override a religious, aesthetic, or personal commitment on account of being morally bad, so a religious, aesthetic, or personal commitment may override a moral commitment on account of being religiously, aesthetically, or personally bad. It is not a requirement of reason that desires be evaluated primarily from the moral point of view. And the reasonable moral evaluation of a desire may conflict with its reasonable non-moral evaluation.

This point is strengthened by the recognition that commitments motivated by religious faith, art, ambition, or love are very common indeed. When people are so motivated, they may well say that the commitment that motivates them is more important than the moral commitment to human well-being, which they can acknowledge to have but judge to be less important. The fact remains, however, that by being so motivated these people may violate political conditions of human well-being. What reason can be given against such violations?

The reason is that the political conditions in America enable people to live in accordance with their religious, aesthetic, or personal commitments. The political goods the prevailing conditions protect are preconditions of the pursuit of all the various commitments that people may have. If people violate these preconditions, they violate conditions that enable them to live as they want, and that is a strong enough reason against violating them. The violators, of course, may not acknowledge that this is so because they have not thought it through, or because they are fanatical about their non-moral commitments, or because their faith, sense of beauty, ambition, or love is so strong as to silence the voice of reason. If this happens, the prevailing political conditions should still be enforced, even against the will of the violators. The reason for doing so is available for all to see. That some people fail to acknowledge this reason does not affect its force. It only shows what is hardly news, namely, that some people are unreasonable.

4.5 NECESSARY LIMITS

The view I have been defending in this chapter is a secular version of the Christian belief in original sin. Sin is a religious notion but, the bad can be discussed without having to choose between religious and secular beliefs, and that is how I have discussed it. The basic idea is that good and bad desires are both parts of human nature. We all start out in life with dispositions to promote and to act contrary to human well-being, including our own. The realistic view of human nature regards this ambivalence as a basic truth about us. In most lives the ambivalence persists because we seldom succeed in the total suppression of either good or bad desires. Moral monsters and saints may succeed, but they are rare.

Having these desires does not, of course, mean that we will act on them. We may or we may not depending on their respective strength, the nature of our upbringing, the contingencies of our experiences and our interpretation of them, and the goodness or badness of our society and of our position in it. The extent to which we act on our good or bad desires, therefore, depends on these external and internal influences, but not on them alone. For we can reflect on these influences and we can often, although not always, shape how we interpret and respond to them. But our interpretations, responses, and reflections are also subject to external and internal influences and are motivated by our good and bad desires. We are, therefore, never in full control of our motives and actions, but nor are we without some control over them. Reason and responsibility dictate that we should increase the control we have. For the greater is our control the more likely it is that we will promote rather than jeopardize our well-being.

The ancient myth with which I began this chapter illustrates the need for reflection and control. Deianira in her innocent simplicity did not reflect at all. She happened to be dominated by good desires, but they were easily corrupted because she was naïve and unreflective. Nessus reflected but he was ruled by bad desires. They corrupted his reflection and turned it into cunning. He cunningly destroyed Deianira and Heracles, but not before he was himself destroyed. Heracles was the best of humans because he was half divine. He did not have to reflect to overcome his bad desires because he spontaneously and heroically acted on his good desires, as they were conceived in archaic Greece. His good desires and actions, however, did not exempt him from the contingency of life and he fell afoul of it through Deianira's well-intentioned but much too innocent and simple-minded actions. We learn from the myth that not even the best of us are free of contingency because not even the best of us are in full control of our well-being, Being unreflective, Heracles was shocked by what happened. The facts would not have been different if he had been reflective, although reflection would have made it easier for him to bear his misfortune.

Our immediate concern, however, is not with the tragic view of life that permeates the ancient myth, but with the political implications of the realistic view of human nature. Realism about human nature cannot but create doubts about the possibility of a steady improvement of the human condition. It would be foolish to doubt that great improvements have been made in life expectancy; infant mortality; living standards; responses to crime, insanity, and dissent; the reduction of ethnic, racial, and religious discrimination; and in numerous other areas of life. But with undeniable improvements have come equally undeniable scourges. Drug addiction and AIDS are epidemic; the rates of murder and other forms of violent crime are very high; the disgraceful educational system is deteriorating; the environment is threatened; a large proportion of the population lacks skills necessary to cope with the complexities of life; vast bureaucracies create alternatives among which we are forced to choose and remove alternatives we would prefer to have; great advances in medicine come with great increases in cost that few people can afford to pay; longer lives brought with them nursing homes in which an ever-growing number of old people are kept alive in a virtually vegetative and certainly undignified state; terrorism and the interdependence of national economies threaten our physical and financial security; and so on. The ways in which our lives have become worse are as many as the ways in which they have become better.

This is precisely what realism about human nature leads one to expect. For the great changes in the conditions of life have not changed the ambivalence of human motivation to which these changes are ultimately traceable. We continue to have good and bad desires, and the great changes have affected only the ways in which these desires are expressed. The undoubted political goods secured in America have given greater scope to the expression of both good

85

and bad desires. And it is these desires that the improvements and deteriorations we witness reflect. The underlying problem for us is psychological, not political. It has been rightly said that out of the crooked timber of humanity nothing straight has ever come.

The ideological approach to politics is driven by optimistic illusions that pretend that these facts of human nature do not exist. Ideologues put forward ideals and derive from them policies that supposedly will bring us from the unsatisfactory present circumstances to a more perfect future state. They fail to see that the ideals and the policies are just as much at the mercy of our ambivalent motivation as are our present circumstances. Ideologues are blind to the fact that the remedy they propose is infected by the disease they hope to cure by it. And, of course, the attempt to cure the cure suffers from the same liability. Does it follow then that there is no hope, that policies are unavoidably corrupt; that we should not try to correct our present ills?

No, it does not follow. It is a false alternative that we have to choose between hope derived from some ideology and hopelessness that follows from abandoning the ideological approach. The balanced view is another option. But it favors keen awareness of our fallibility, ambivalent motivation, and of unrealistic illusions and enthusiasm. It is the politics of caution, trial and error, and of small, piecemeal attempts to ameliorate our existing dissatisfactions. It does not aim at future perfection; it aims at making the present less imperfect. It cannot change the ambivalence of human motivation, but it can encourage the realization of good desires and discourage acting on bad desires.

A society must discourage actions motivated by bad desires. This requires setting and enforcing limits to what people can do to each other. These limits are set by law and their aim is to protect the political goods on which everyone's well-being depends. Such laws do not make people good but they do make it more difficult for them to act on bad desires. Pluralism and liberty are political goods but it is a consequence of the ambivalence of human motivation that they conflict with other political goods, such as order and security. The aim of the balanced view is cope with this and other conflicts among political goods. Coping in this case requires the imposition of limits on pluralism and liberty that are neither more nor less restrictive than what is needed for the protection of the other political goods. Finding optimal limits takes prudence, good judgment, realism about human motivation, and intimate knowledge of the prevailing circumstances in a particular society at a particular time. There is no blueprint for how this should be done. We know only that it has to be done differently in circumstances that are always different.

The conclusion, then, that follows from this chapter is that necessary limits must be added to reason as prudence and the plurality of goods as a basic political good that the balanced view is committed to defending.

CHAPTER FIVE

✦   ✦   ✦

LIMITED LIBERTY

*I should ... suspend my congratulations on ... liberty ...
until I was informed how it had been combined with government; with public force; with the discipline and obedience of
armies; with the collection of an effective well-distributed
revenue; with morality and religion; with the solidity of
property; with peace and order.... All these (in their way)
are good things too, and without them, liberty is not a benefit
whilst it lasts, and is not likely to continue long. The effect of
liberty to individuals is, that they may do what they please: we
ought to see what it will please them to do, before we risque
congratulations, which may be soon turned into complaints.*

EDMUND BURKE
Reflections on the Revolution in France

THIS CHAPTER IS ABOUT liberty, another generally accepted
political good in American society. I will discuss three conceptions
of liberty, explain why the shortcomings of the first lead to the
second, and why the second needs to be improved by the third.
Each successive conception rejects parts and accepts other parts of
the preceding one. The discussion is thus cumulative, leading to a
conception of liberty that defenders of the balanced view have
reason to accept. I will not discuss liberty in areas other than the
political, nor the difficult questions connected with freewill and
determinism.

✦   ✦   ✦

Limited Liberty

5.1 THE LIBERTARIAN CONCEPTION

Sisyphus was the legendary King of Corinth, reputed to be the cleverest of all humans. He presumed to deceive even Zeus, who punished Sisyphus for it by sentencing him to an eternal life of futility. He had to roll a rock uphill, and when he reached the summit, the rock rolled down. Then he had to roll it up again, and again, and again forever. We may think that his punishment was too harsh, but the ancient Greeks knew that the gods were to be feared and that opposing them was bound to end very badly. Sisyphus too should have known that, but he was carried away by his own cleverness. The myth thus served to caution the ancient Greeks against opposing formidable powers.

We do not believe in Zeus, but we also need to be aware of the danger of falling afoul of formidable powers that are no less real now than they were then. The powers we have to fear are political. The transactions between political rulers and their subjects, however, are not nearly as straightforward as they were between Sisyphus and Zeus. Zeus made no bones about compelling Sisyphus to endure the miseries of rock rolling, but the rulers now are less forthright. They strive to convince their subjects by indoctrination and manipulation that the rock rolling they force on them serves a higher ideal. If their subjects were convinced of this, they would realize that what seems like a burden is really a benefit because their well-being consists in working for the higher ideal that their rulers have discerned and of which they themselves are ignorant. Their ignorance prevents them from knowing where their own interests lie, but rulers who see more clearly know, and work selflessly to protect the ignorant. Those who do not like to roll rocks do not know what is good for them.

This sophistical perversion of the truth has been a standard ideological tool much used, among others, by Communists. The millions of laborers building Stalin's roads that led to nowhere, canals that irrigated nothing, factories that produced shoddy goods no one wanted were told that they were working for the ideal society. And the millions starving during Mao's insane Great Leap Forward and the physicians, scientists, intellectuals, engineers, and artists whom the Mao-inspired Red Guards humiliated and sent to the countryside for useless drudgery when their expertise was desperately needed elsewhere were told that their hardships served the same ideal as was mouthed by Stalin. These victims of a noxious ideology were not only compelled to roll their rocks, they were subjected to ceaseless propaganda proclaiming that it was for their own good. One horrifying consequence was that many of them came to believe the lies and turned into enthusiastic rock rollers.

Not all ideologies are as bad as Communism, and not all who have political power are ideologues. But with the possession of power comes the temptation to believe that the rulers know better than their subject what is good for them. And since the rulers feel responsible for the well-being of their subjects, they regard themselves obligated to compel their subjects to live and act as they would if they understood as well as their rulers wherein their well-being lies. The temptation for the rulers is thus to override the preferences of their subjects and to justify doing so by misrepresenting the dictates of reason and morality. In this way, the use of political power tends to become self-righteous and coercive, and coercion is presented as a benefit to the coerced. Individual well-being depends on resisting this sort of abuse.

The *Oxford English Dictionary* (1961) gives as the first meaning of coerce: "To constrain or restrain (a voluntary or moral agent) by the application of superior force, or by authority resting on force; to constrain compliance or obedience by forcible means." And coercion is: "Constraint, restraint, compulsion; the application of force to control the action of a voluntary agent." I will use these definitions with the slight amendment that force need not be applied; the threat of it is often sufficient for coercion. Coercion, then, involves both constraining voluntary agents to act and restraining them from acting in particular ways. Coercion compels if resistance to it is credibly indicated to have far worse consequence than compliance.

There are many different kinds of coercion but I will discuss only the political kind, which is typically legislative, judicial, or executive. It operates through laws, judicial rulings, and police or military forces. Political coercion (from now on simply "coercion") may or may not be justified. It is always dangerous, however, because it involves forcing people to do or not to do what they would not or would do if they were not forced. It constrains and restrain how people act and thus compels them to go against their own preferences. Their preferences, of course, may be shallow, hasty, uninformed, perverse, stupid, destructive, and so forth, but, for better or worse, they are their own. Coercion substitutes the no less fallible preferences of rulers for the preferences of their subjects.

Liberty is generally recognized as a political good in American society because its aim is to keep political interference with individual preferences as minimal as possible. One way of thinking about liberty, then, is that it is the absence of coercion. This is negative liberty, liberty from unwanted political interference. A great attractions of liberty understood in this way is that it protects individuals from the abuse of political power by rulers who coerce them for their own supposed good to follow preferences that are not their own.

Liberty defines an area within which people should be free to pursue whatever they regard as their well-being. This area is their private life, the sphere of their individuality, and a good society protects their rights to do or not to do within it as they please. No reasonable person supposes, of course, that people have or should have unlimited liberty. There must be constraints and restraints, and with them comes coercion. The constraints compel doing what is necessary to support the political conditions that make liberty possible. The restraints prohibit interference with other people's liberty.

Liberty does not require the total absence of coercion; it requires only that the coercion necessary for protecting everyone's liberty be kept at the minimum.

In democratic societies there are two general strategies for providing that protection. One is to enact a legally binding a Bill of Rights that specifies the respects in which individuals should be free of coercion. The other is to forgo the legal specification of rights and to require instead that violations of traditionally recognized rights be justified. Both strategies have advantages and disadvantages. The advantage of a Bill of Rights is clarity about when coercion is illegitimate; its disadvantage is that it does not rule out coercion in respects that are not explicitly specified. The advantage of having no Bill of Rights is the implicit demand that coercive interference with any traditional right requires justification; its disadvantage is that it allows that any coercion may be justified if circumstances seem to warrant it. The first strategy—roughly the American—aims to protect narrow but inviolable rights; the second —roughly the English—aims to protect wider but defeasible rights. Both agree, however, that liberty requires that everyone be subject to as little coercion as is consistent with the protection of the liberty of all in a particular society.

There is general agreement across the American political spectrum in that liberty is a political good and its protection is important. Defenders of the balanced view agree. But the agreement comes to an end because many political thinkers hold that liberty is the most important political good. This view is commonly identified as classical liberal or libertarian (I ignore differences between them). It is a political ideology because it holds that there is a hierarchy of political goods; that liberty as the absence of coercion is the highest good in the hierarchy; that conflicts among political goods should be resolved by evaluating their respective importance on the basis of their contribution to liberty; that human well-being is best served by guaranteeing maximum feasible liberty for individuals; that this should be the ultimate aim and sole justification of actual policies; and that the prevailing political conditions should be radically changed to eliminate unnecessary coercion and guarantee the most extensive feasible liberty. The conjunction of these views is the core of what I will call libertarian ideology.

5.2 Objections to the Libertarian Conception

The balanced view is incompatible with libertarian ideology partly because it has the general defect of all ideologies, namely, privileging one political good at the expense of others and holding that it should always override any other political good that may conflict with it. Another reason for rejecting it is that it has defects peculiar to itself. No doubt, an ideology that champions liberty, privacy, and individuality is much better than the alternatives, but it is still an ideology and remains committed to the mistaken supposition that since liberty is good, more liberty is better. I will discuss two main objections to libertarian ideology: one now, the other in 5.4. The first objection, then, is that understanding liberty as the absence of coercion does not explain why liberty is a political good. Many people misuse their liberty, others are incapable of making use of it, and yet others live satisfying lives without it. Libertarians, therefore, must give convincing reasons for supposing that liberty is the most important political condition of satisfying lives. These reasons, however, have not been given.

The most obvious reason that might be given is that it enables people to make uncoerced choices about how they want to live and, unless they make them, their lives cannot be satisfying. But this is patently false. Many Americans live very satisfying lives even though they have made no uncoerced choices about how they want to live. Think of all those who were born, raised, matured, and died in a closely knit family, community, or religious group, and unquestioningly followed its traditional way of life. It is absurd to deny that such people could have been satisfied with their lives. It is no less absurd to deny that people whom unchosen circumstances led

93

to spend their lives and fit happily into a tightly controlled organization, such as the army, a religious order, a corporation, or a ballet group could not have been satisfied with their lives.

It is true, of course, that for many people making uncoerced choices about how they want to live is very important, but that is not enough to establish that liberty is necessary for all satisfying lives. Furthermore, even if liberty is necessary for some lives, it does not show that having it is good because people often use their liberty to make bad choices that make their own and other people's lives worse than they would be if they were deprived of liberty.

The classic, eloquent, and mistaken libertarian answer to this objection is given by John Stuart Mill in *On Liberty*. He says: "The only freedom which deserves the name is that of pursuing our own good in our own way, so long as we do not attempt to deprive others of theirs or impede their efforts to obtain it. Each is a proper guardian of his own health, whether bodily or spiritual. Mankind are greater gainers by suffering each other to live as seems good to themselves than by compelling each to live as seems good to the rest." He adds that for each individual "his own mode of laying out his existence is the best, not because it is the best itself, but because it is his own mode." And he claims that "All errors which he is likely to commit . . . are far outweighed by the evil of allowing others to constrain him to what they deem his good."

The rhetoric is fine but the facts spoil it. *The Diagnostic and Statistical Manual of Mental Disorders*, (Washington, D.C.: American Psychiatric Association, 2000) says that mental disorder "causes clinically significant distress or impairment in social, occupational, or other important areas of functioning." It estimates that 14.8 percent of the population of America suffers from "mental disorder due to a general medical condition." A further 5–9 percent of women and 2–3 percent of men, or 7–12 percent of the population, suffers from "major depressive disorder." Putting these figures together, taking the low number in the estimated range, 21 percent of a population of 300 million, that is, approximately 63 million people, suffer from serious mental disorder. The International Adult Literacy Survey reported by the Plain Language Network puts the number of absolute illiterates in the U.S. at 14,680,000. A report of the Suicide Prevention Resource Center estimates that in 2003 there were 787,000 suicide attempts in America. And according to the Alzheimer Association's web site, there are presently 4,500,000 people suffering from Alzheimer's disease. The actual numbers are far higher than these figures indicate because much mental illness is undiagnosed or unreported, absolute illiteracy does not include the functionally illiterate who cannot read the simplest instruction or write a short letter, many suicide attempts are unreported, and many lonely old people suffer from undiagnosed Alzheimer's disease. If we add up these figures, we find that close to one-third of the population in America is significantly impaired in social or occupational functioning.

In light of these facts, it is utterly implausible to claim, as Mill and his libertarian followers do, that "each [of these people] is a proper guardian of his own health, whether bodily or spiritual," or that "mankind are greater gainers by suffering [them] . . . to live as seems good to themselves than by compelling each to live as seems good to the rest," or that "all errors which [such people] . . . are likely to commit . . . are far outweighed by the evil of allowing others to constrain him to what they deem his good."

It makes the libertarian claim for liberty being the highest political good even more implausible if we bear in mind that, according to the Bureau of Census, there are about 60 million children below the age fourteen in America. Children, the mentally ill, the suicidal, the illiterate, and Alzheimer patients cannot be proper guardians of their well-being; their judgments are severely impaired or undeveloped so they cannot be relied on to know what is good for them; and it is not an evil but a political and moral necessity to constrain or restrain these people's actions, who, it should be remembered, form half of the population. The political goods a society needs for the well-being of these people are education, health care, protection of their security, and sufficient prosperity to provide for them what they cannot provide for themselves. Coercing them for their own good is not an abuse of political power, but a responsible exercise of it.

Nor should we forget that in American society murder, robbery, rape, theft, and fraud are rampant. The illegal drug trade flourishes. Gangs control parts of large cities. The protection of security requires curtailing people's liberty. Millions are imprisoned and millions who should be escape because of technicalities, or because law enforcement is overburdened, or because the shortage of prison space and guards makes plea bargaining and early release attractive.

Libertarians may respond to these facts by saying that liberty being the highest political good does not mean that it allows no exceptions. They do not suppose, they may say, that everyone can benefit from liberty or that no one abuses it. Nevertheless there is an initial presumption in favor of it, but it may be justifiably overruled to prevent violations of other people's liberty or to help those who cannot help themselves. The facts I have pointed to warrant making exceptions. But for at least minimally educated adults, who have committed no crime, and who are not mentally disordered, liberty remains the highest political good because without it they cannot pursue their well-being.

Suppose that this is true. It would still not make it reasonable to regard liberty as the highest political good since the facts show that more than half the population either abuses it or is incapable of benefiting from it. Perhaps there is an initial presumption in favor of liberty for those who do not put it to criminal uses and who are capable of making reasonable choices about how they want to live, but such people constitute a minority of the population. Surely, if there is a highest political good in a democratic society, it must be one that is good for a large majority of the population.

The cumulative force of these objections defeats the libertarian claim that liberty is the highest political good. Some live satisfying lives without making use of liberty; others abuse it; and others still are incapable of using it reasonably. These objections, however, show only that if liberty is understood as the absence of coercion, then it cannot be reasonably regarded as the highest political good. I turn now to another way of understanding liberty and another reason that may be given for regarding it as the highest political good. This other way is to think of liberty in positive, not negative, terms as involving the active pursuit of well-being, rather than merely a passive absence of coercion.

5.3 The Eudaimonist Conception

One of the difficulties of the libertarian conception is that it says nothing about the use that people may make of their liberty. Since, as we have seen, many people misuse it or cannot use it, the question naturally arises why liberty should be thought of as the highest political good in a democratic society if so many people use it badly or not at all. The conception of liberty I will now consider avoids this difficulty by insisting that liberty is the highest political good only if it is used to contribute to one's well-being. A convenient synonym for well-being is eudaimonia. It is a rare English word derived from the Greek, but, unlike well-being, it has various convenient cognates, so I will call the present conception of liberty eudaimonist.

According to libertarians, then, liberty is good because it makes the pursuit of well-being possible; whereas according to eudaimonists liberty is good because it actually contributes to one's well-being. The first sees the good of liberty in enabling people to attempt to pursue well-being; the second sees it in enabling a successful attempt. The first thinks of well-being as something people must make for themselves and repudiates coercion because it interferes with people's efforts to make it. The second thinks of well-being as something people find, and it allows that coercion may lead people to find it. Both libertarians and eudaimonists acknowledge that liberty may be misused. Libertarians, however, do not think that misuse diminishes the political good of liberty, whereas eudaimonists think that liberty is a political good only if it is rightly used.

Eudaimonists, of course, have to explain what the right use of liberty is, how it can be distinguished from wrong uses, and how disagreements about the rightness or wrongness of uses can be settled. Libertarians owe no such explanations because their understanding of liberty has no content beyond the repudiation of coercion. But eudaimonists must provide the explanations because they hold that liberty is good only if it is rightly used, so they must specify what its right use is. This creates a basic division among eudaimonists. Some eudaimonists are monists because they think that ultimately human well-being has only one form and the right use of liberty is to try to realize it. Other eudaimonists are pluralists because they think that human well-being has many forms and the right uses of liberty are correspondingly many.

Monist eudaimonism is the view of many ideologues who suppose themselves to have discovered the highest good whose pursuit is the one and only way to human well-being. Orthodox Jews think that it is revealed in the *Old Testament*, devout Muslims find it in the *Koran*, Thomists suppose that it is conformity to natural law, Calvin located it in his interpretation of the *Gospels*, Rousseau thought that it is to be guided by the general will, Marx believed that the key to it is a classless society, Nazis held that it was the rule of the master race, and Utilitarians claim that it consists in identifying one's own well-being with the common good. Not all of these ideologies are equally noxious, but they all have disastrous political consequences, as history so amply shows. Pluralist eudaimonists reject the monist view. According to them there are many right uses of liberty. Liberty, then, need not be used wrongly if it is not aimed at the realization of one form of well-being, since it may be aimed at the realization of another form. Liberty is used wrongly only if its use is detrimental to the realization of any form of well-being.

Relying on the argument I have given earlier (in 3.2 and 3.3) I assume that monist eudaimonism is untenable because there is a wide plurality of goods out of which many different forms of well-being may be constructed. Many goods are universal because they are required for all forms of human well-being (such as nutrition, health, and security); many others are social because they are constituents of the shared social identity of people living together in a society (such as civility, division of labor, and education); and many further ones are personal because they are essential constituents of one's style of life (such as creativity, friendships, and interesting work). Forms of well-being are alike because they must have the universal goods and some of each of the social and personal goods, but they are also unalike because the particular social and personal goods that constitute them vary greatly. Monist eudaimonism is untenable because it ignores this variety. From now on I will mean by eudaimonism its pluralist version.

Eudaimonists can specify what the right uses of liberty are because they can specify the goods that constitute various forms of well-being. The right uses aim to secure the goods required by the forms of well-being individuals have constructed for themselves, and the wrong uses are those that either violate or are indifferent to these goods. Liberty is the highest good, according to eudaimonists, because it enables people to pursue their well-being. And it is a political good because a good society must protect the political conditions in which people can do this.

The means by which these political conditions are protected are conventions. Some conventions are required because they protect universal goods that all forms of well-being require. Some other conventions are variable because they protect social goods that change in response to changing circumstances and vary with forms of well-being. But all forms of well-being require that there be an evaluative framework that contains the goods and the conventions, and the protection of that framework is required by all forms of well-being, although particular variable conventions that constitute the framework often change. The constituents of particular forms of well-being, then, are universal goods protected by required conventions and some sub-set of social and personal goods protected by variable conventions.

The protection of the political conditions of well-being consists in the protection of the required and variable conventions, and of the opportunity of individuals to construct their preferred form of well-being. But their protection is not sufficient for well-being because what individuals take to be goods may not be, or they may be goods but unsuitable for the characters and circumstances of particular individuals, or the various goods individuals pursue may be incompatible with one another. People can be mistaken about what they regard as their well-being. They may think that they are using liberty rightly, but in fact be using it wrongly. How, according eudaimonists, can such mistakes be identified? This is a crucial question for them because unless they can distinguish between right and wrong uses of liberty they cannot tell what its right uses are, and consequently cannot tell what constitutes a misuse of liberty. I think the best approach to answering this question is to identify central cases in which the use of liberty is obviously right.

Suppose that individuals conform to both the required and variable conventions of their society; they successfully pursue a form of well-being they have constructed for themselves; and they are satisfied with the resulting lives. They want their lives to continue by and large in the same way, they do not regret major choices they have made, and they like their lives. They can honestly say that if they could live their lives all over again, they would want to live it in the same way as they have done. Such people have clearly used their liberty rightly.

What are we to say, however, about individuals whose lives do not meet one or another of these conditions? Are we to say that they have used their liberty wrongly? What we should say depends on why the conditions are not met. There may be good reasons for not meeting them: the prevailing required conventions may fail to protect universal goods, the variable conventions may protect only a much too narrow range of social goods, or individuals may be dissatisfied with their lives because they have met with misfortune beyond their or their society's control. If the reasons for not meeting the conditions are good, liberty has not been misused. If the reasons are bad, then it has been misused.

It must be recognized, of course, that whether the reasons are good or bad is often controversial. But the controversies, at least in principle, can be reasonably resolved by focusing on the concrete details or particular cases. There is a reasonable answer to the question whether making divorce illegal is a good way of protecting family life; whether teenage sex is harmful and should be forbidden; or whether wagering in Russian roulette one's life against a great deal of money is an acceptable way of pursuing one's well-being. Although practical exigencies often preclude the detailed evaluation of individual decisions in such cases, the difficulty is practical, not theoretical.

The reasonable policy to follow in controversial cases depends on the society in whose context the decisions are made. If the society is by and large good because it protects the political conditions of human well-being, then it is reasonable to be guided by the prevailing conventions. If the society is bad or tends toward being bad, then it is better to err on the side of liberty and refrain from coercion that appeals to the prevailing conventions. Many societies, of course, are good in some ways and bad in others. It is unclear in such societies what the reasonable policy is in controversial cases. This, however, only shows that finding the reasonable policy is often difficult and calls for good judgment, not that there is no reasonable policy. Making the right political decision may be hard, but that is not exactly news.

We may conclude, then, that eudaimonists can identify the right uses of liberty, distinguish them from the wrong uses, justify the use of coercion to protect people from the consequences of wrong uses, and explain why liberty is a political good. The eudaimonist conception of liberty thus constitutes an improvement over the libertarian conception. But we are not entitled to conclude that the eudaimonist conception is correct. For, although it follows from it that liberty is a political good, it does not follow that it is the highest political good that should override any other political good that may conflict with it. Two considerations show that no acceptable conception of liberty can regard it as the highest good. These considerations count against the libertarian conception as much as against the eudaimonist one.

5.4 OBJECTIONS TO THE EUDAIMONIST CONCEPTION

The first is a consequence of the plurality of political goods. Liberty is certainly a political good but there are also many others. It is a commonplace of political life that these goods often conflict and the more there is of one, the less there can be of the other. This is as true of liberty as it is of the other goods. One central task of politics is to resolve such conflicts as they occur in particular circumstances. And the circumstances make it reasonable to resolve the conflicts sometimes in favor of one of the goods, sometimes in favor of the other.

The ideological approach to conflict-resolution denies this. Its defenders hold that the conflicts should always be resolved in favor of the highest good, or, if the highest good is not involved in the conflict, then it should be resolved in favor of the good that contributes more to the highest good. According to libertarians and eudaimonists, since the highest good is liberty, when it conflicts with other goods, liberty should prevail. If the threat of terrorism forces us to choose between liberty and security, if the AIDS epidemic makes it necessary to decide between liberty and health, if an uneducated work force compels the choice between liberty and prosperity, then the importance of liberty overrides the importance of security, health, or prosperity. It is crucial to realize that the libertarian and eudaimonist claim is not that liberty happens to be more important in these circumstances, but that liberty, with one exception, is always more important regardless of circumstances.

The exception is when liberty in a particular case may be justifiably violated because the protection of liberty in general requires it. It is, for instance, justified to deprive criminals of liberty, but only because they have violated other people's liberty. That a great increase in security, health, or prosperity may depend on a small decrease in overall liberty is not, according to libertarians and eudaimonists, an acceptable justification for curtailing liberty. What reason could be given in support of this radical claim?

The reason is that liberty is thought to be a necessary condition of the realization of the other political goods. Curtailing liberty curtails the goods that depend on it. Security, health, and prosperity, for instance, require people to make the right choices, and they can make them only if the liberty of making them is guaranteed. This is true but it does not show that liberty is the most important political good. For the same is true of many of the other political goods. The liberty of making the right choices depends on being secure enough to know that one will not be murdered or maimed while making them; on being in sufficiently good health to be able to think clearly; on being adequately prosperous not to have to struggle for the necessities of life and have the possibility of choosing among alternatives. The fact is that political goods are interdependent. They are needed for the realization of the others. They make possible and reinforce one another. The ideological approach that singles out one of them and assigns to it overriding importance misses the fact of their interdependence. Its mistake is like saying that exercise is the most important thing for health, while forgetting that oxygen, nutrition, the immune system, rest, and having the use of limbs and senses are also important.

The second consideration that counts against both the libertarian and the eudaimonist conception of liberty as the highest political good follows from realism about human motivation. If the pursuit of well-being were the dominant human motivation, then perhaps it would be reasonable to assume that people are likely to use liberty rightly. They would, then, use it wrongly only if they were incapacitated, made some understandable mistake, or were greatly provoked. This is what libertarians and eudaimonists tend to think. They do not deny, of course, that human conduct can be bad, but they do think that if human beings are not beset by physical or mental illness, by oppression, poverty, or injustice, if they know the relevant facts and are well enough educated, then they will make right rather than wrong choices.

According to the balanced view, this is an illusion. Human motivation is mixed. We are not very choosy about the cost others have to pay for our pursuit of well-being and we are often motivated to act against the well-being of others because we wish them ill, we are envious or jealous of them, we suspect or fear them, or we recognize that their motives are mixed. We are moved both by virtues and vices. Our psychological constitution is a mixture of love and hate, generosity and selfishness, kindness and cruelty, courage and cowardice, prudence and foolishness, trust and distrust, self-knowledge and self-deception. Whether at any time we are motivated by our good or bad desires depends on our genetic inheritance, upbringing, adult experiences, on how well or badly our personal relationships and work are going; on the state of our health, finances, and comfort; on our capacity to tolerate stress, uncertainty, failure, and disappointment; and so on and on. It is hopelessly simpleminded to assume that if we are not beset by adversity, then our good desires will be dominant and bad ones recessive. History, literature, ethnography, religion, and personal experience all testify that human motivation is mixed in the most varied circumstances. Those living in luxury and comfort often act on their bad desires and people in wretched conditions often act kindly, generously, and courageously.

If we are realistic about human nature and recognize the ambivalence of human motivation, then we will not assume that people will tend to use liberty rightly unless something goes wrong. Nor will we assume, of course, that they will misuse liberty. We will live with the ambivalence and be very careful both about liberty and coercion. And the way to be careful in politics is to rely on conventions that have stood the test of time. Changing circumstances may make it reasonable to revise or abandon conventions that have long commanded the allegiance of most people in a society. This may lead us to increase liberty and decrease coercion, or it may lead us to do the opposite. But it will not lead reasonable people to privilege liberty over all the other goods on which human well-being depends.

5.5 LIMITED LIBERTY

Relying on the conclusions we have reached, it is a relatively simple matter to formulate the third—balanced—conception of liberty. It incorporates the defensible elements of the libertarian and eudaimonist conceptions and avoids the indefensible ones. Libertarians are right: liberty is a political good because it keeps to a minimum coercive interference with individuals. But this is an inadequate explanation of why liberty is a political good because many people misuse their liberty and many others live satisfying lives in which liberty has only negligible importance. Eudaimonists provide a fuller explanation: liberty is a political good only if it is used to pursue well-being, which is its right use. Coercion is justified if liberty is used wrongly to interfere with the pursuit of well-being. So far, this accords with the balanced view.

Libertarians and eudaimonists, however, claim that liberty is not only one political good among others, but that it is the highest, most important political good. Defenders of the balanced view disagree. There is a plurality of political goods and liberty is only one of them, no better or worse than the others. Political goods routinely conflict with one another and there is no way of determining independently of the particular circumstances of the conflicts which of the conflicting goods is more important. The relative importance of conflicting goods varies as circumstances do. Coercive interference with liberty is justified if a conflicting political good is reasonably regarded as more important for the pursuit of well-being. And coercion is also justified when bad desires lead people, as they often do, to misuse their liberty.

Defenders of the balanced view, then, agree with libertarians and eudaimonists that liberty is a political good and coercion should be as little as possible. However, frequent conflicts between liberty and other political goods and realism about human motivation lead the balanced view to recognize that human well-being depends on more extensive coercive interference with liberty than libertarians and eudaimonists tend to suppose. Such interference must be justified of course. The justification depends on explaining why some other political good is more important than liberty for the pursuit of human well-being.

There are, for example, serious disagreements about abortion, voluntary euthanasia, the decriminalization of drugs, the redistribution of wealth, the protection of traditional family life, obligations beyond borders, and so forth. Whether such disagreements should be resolved by appealing to liberty or to some other political good are difficult and divisive questions. The balanced view of limited liberty should have implications about how to think about such issues. And it does. It requires stepping back from these controversies and refraining from joining one side or the other in shouting slogans across the moral divide. People on both sides have something that unites them on a more basic level than the moral stance that divides them. What they share is their allegiance to the evaluative framework of their society, their social identity. Conflicts occur within that framework. The controversies are about the details of a shared social identity, and what the two sides appeal to in their arguments are standards they derive from their shared evaluative framework. They are arguing about the respective importance of political and moral goods that they both recognize as goods.

According to the balanced view, the first step toward resolving such conflicts is to remind the participants in them of what they tend to forget in the heat of the argument: the large area of their agreement about other matters. This will already blunt a little the mutual animosities, but, of course, it will not resolve the conflicts. The second step is to point out that both sides are committed to the evaluative framework about whose details they are disagreeing. If they calm down, reason and reflect, they will realize that the protection of that framework as a whole is far more important than the outcome of their argument about the respective importance of the contested goods. And the third step is to attempt to persuade both sides that they will get nowhere by an increasingly shrill repetition of already familiar considerations. They should welcome changing the question to which they give incompatible answers. They should not ask which of the two conflicting goods is more important; they should ask which of the two conflicting goods is more important for the protection of the evaluative framework to which both sides are committed. This will change the question from being about ends to being about means to an agreed-upon end.

The balanced view, therefore, does not to attempt to resolve controversial questions by proposing yet another answer to them, but by showing how a reasonable resolution may be found and why it is in everyone's interest to seek it in that way. None of this, of course, amounts to the actual resolution of any particular conflict. To show how a resolution may be found is not yet to find it. The balanced view, therefore, must be made concrete. This will be done in the next chapter by considering the difficult question of what should and what should not be tolerated.

The immediate implication of the balanced view for liberty is that it shows how the limits of liberty may be reasonably set in particular cases and what the justification of coercion may be in controversial cases. The more far-reaching implication of it, however, is for conflicts about political goods in general. Recurrent conflicts between liberty and order, justice and equality, security and peace, autonomy and responsibility, and so on can be made tractable by the balanced view. This is more than what can be said for various ideological alternatives to it whose approach to conflict-resolution is to condemn their opponents as irrational, immoral, or both.

Limited liberty, then, is another political good that may be added to reason as prudence, the plurality of goods, and necessary limits that the balanced view is committed to defending.

CHAPTER SIX

✦   ✦   ✦

TOLERATION WITHIN REASON

The delicate and difficult art of life is to find, in each new turn of experience, the via media between two extremes: to be catholic without being characterless; to have and apply standards, and yet to be on guard against their desensitizing and stupefying influence, their tendency to blind us to the diversities of concrete situations and to previously unrecognized values; to know when to tolerate, when to embrace, and when to fight. And in that art, since no fixed and comprehensive rule can be laid down for it, we shall doubtless never acquire perfection.

ARTHUR O. LOVEJOY
The Great Chain of Being

THE CONCLUSION OF THE preceding chapter was that liberty must be limited but I left it open just how and when. I will argue in this chapter that the limits of liberty are the limits of toleration. Liberty and toleration are both political goods but they should not be confused with one another. Although the same activities may be at once free and tolerated, as well as unfree and prohibited, liberty and toleration are nevertheless different. Free activities may be approved, disapproved, or be indifferent, but it makes sense to speak of tolerating only disapproved activities. Another difference is that tolerating an activity implies that we could interfere with it but refrain from doing so, whereas an activity may be free even if no one could interfere with it. It follows from these differences that defenders of toleration must answer the obvious question of why it should be thought good to tolerate an activity of which we disapprove. The aim of this chapter is to discuss and answer this question.

6.1 PROHIBITION

In 1954, at the height of the Cold War, the U.S. Congress passed Public Law 637, known as the Communist Control Act. The Act in effect outlawed the Communist Party in the U.S. and made membership in it a criminal offense. The Act was based on "Findings of Fact", which state that "the Communist Party is ... dedicat[ed] to the proposition that the present constitutional Government of the United States ultimately must be brought to ruin by any available means, including resort to force and violence." The Party is "the agency of a hostile foreign power" and this "renders its existence a clear and present danger to the security of the United States."

The Act was controversial from the beginning but the Courts upheld it in the 1950s against various challenges. The controversies centered on the Findings of Fact. Opponents of the Act denied that the Communist Party presented a clear and present danger. I will not enter into this controversy and discuss the Act on the assumption that the Findings of Fact were accurate. Given that, the Act was a clear instance of the justified prohibition of a subversive activity. The protection of security is a basic obligation of any government. If the Communist Party was a serious threat to American security, its prohibition was justified. The freely and democratically elected government, functioning within the Constitution and using powers explicitly granted to it, would have been irresponsible if it had failed to defend the Constitution and the rule of law it was sworn to uphold. Toleration has limits, and one of them is the prohibition of activities that seriously threaten the very social identity that makes toleration possible.

This point can be expressed in a number of ways: liberty is justifiably limited in order to prohibit activities that make liberty impossible; a society is justified in prohibiting activities that would endanger its evaluative framework, composed of the goods, conventions, and traditions, on which the well-being of its members depends; prohibiting the violation of conditions of well-being is not a sign of intolerance but a necessary condition of toleration; quite generally, defenders of any beneficial activity are surely justified in prohibiting any particular use of the activity that undermines the very possibility of the activity in general; and finally and crudely, it is stupid not to prevent the destruction of the house in which one comfortably lives.

These different expressions of the same point make clear that there is a very good reason for setting limits to toleration: to prohibit activities that violate a condition on which the very possibility of the well-being of people in a society depends. The prohibition is not based on the moral disapproval or dislike of the activities in question, nor on finding them distasteful or disgusting. They are prohibited for the completely impersonal reason that has nothing to do with psychological attitudes, or with moral, religious, or aesthetic commitments: they subvert their own possibility. There may also be moral, religious, or aesthetic objections to the prohibited activities but their prohibition is not justified by these objections. The justification is that the failure to prohibit them would be unreasonable.

There are, of course, many other contexts in which the question arises of whether or not a particular activity is within the limits of toleration. And of course toleration in general is much preferable to lack of it. Fanaticism, dogmatism, narrow-mindedness, prejudice against the unfamiliar, and the distrust of ways other than one's own are deplorable at worst and silly at best. But none of this changes the fact that some limits of toleration, some prohibitions are reasonable. The question, therefore, is not whether there are some activities that ought not to be tolerated but what should and what should not be tolerated. I now turn to this question.

THE ART OF POLITICS

6.2 THE PROBLEM

How could toleration be good if it involves acting contrary to one's belief that the tolerated activity is in some sense wrong? If one's disapproval is genuine and one could interfere with the disapproved activity, why should one refrain from it? And if one refrains, does that not indicate that its disapproval is hypocritical?

The simple answer is that it is not hypocritical to tolerate a disapproved activity if the reasons against interfering with it are stronger than the reasons for it. But this requires explaining what these reasons are and why the reasons against interference are stronger than the reasons for it. The required explanation, however, faces the problem of double-mindedness. The *Oxford English Dictionary* defines double-minded as "having two 'minds'; undecided or wavering in mind." Toleration seems to involve double-mindedness, and that is not a good state to be in.

To be double-minded is to have two sets of strong reasons for action that exist in a state of tension because acting on one excludes acting on the other. People in this state feel the force of both sets of reasons but neither is obviously stronger than the other. This leads them to waver, to become ambivalent, to be of two minds about what they should do. Double-mindedness may be a temporary state or a lasting disposition. As a temporary state it is a common experience that most of us have when we try to decide, as we must, between immediate and distant satisfactions, between the demands of morality and self-interest, between institutional and personal loyalties, between duty and pleasure, and so forth. Such a state is virtually unavoidable on occasions but if it is temporary and infrequent, it causes no great harm. Reasonable people can put up with occasional uncertainty and indecision and still have a sense of overall well-being. If, however, double-mindedness is a lasting disposition, if it is an essential element in one's psychological condition, then it is a serious threat to well-being because it habitually and predictably dooms one to frustration.

To see why this is so consider the psychological condition of those who are committed to living according to a particular tradition, such as Catholicism, humanism, or romanticism. This shapes their beliefs and feelings, which may or may not be conscious or articulate, about race, religion, sex, violence, beauty, risks, authority, family, work, death, and so forth. Clusters of these beliefs and feelings may be called formative attitudes. Part of people's social identity consists of their formative attitudes. The beliefs and feelings embedded in these attitudes constitute perhaps the strongest personal reasons people have for living and acting as they do.

Alongside personal reasons, people also have impersonal reasons that derive from legal prohibitions, customary political institutions and economic practices, conventions of justice, rights to property, limits of liberty, and from the expectations they have of each others' conduct. These reasons are impersonal in the sense that they hold for every member of a society but they need be no more conscious or articulate than personal reasons are. They also form part of the social identity of people living together in a society.

Personal reasons vary with individuals and traditions. Impersonal reasons, however, are largely shared by individuals because they derive from the shared evaluative framework of their society that includes, enables, and protects the goods, conventions, and traditions on which their well-being depends. Double-mindedness is a serious problem for individuals if their personal and impersonal reasons are strong and prompt them to act in incompatible ways. The strength of both kinds of reasons derives from people's social identity, and acting contrary to either is to act contrary to their deepest beliefs and feelings. It involves a split in their social identity and, whichever set of reasons becomes dominant, it leads them to violate their own social identity.

Personal reasons lead people to disapprove of some activity that is contrary to the formative attitude they derive from a particular tradition, while impersonal reasons lead them not to interfere with the very same activity because they realize that the toleration of activities that follow from formative attitudes is a condition of everyone's well-being. If they tolerate it, they violate their own formative attitude; and if they do not tolerate it, they violate a condition on which everyone's well-being, including their own, depends. So of course they are double-minded, waver, are ambivalent, and cannot decide what to do. The problem of toleration, therefore, is a problem indeed. As a preliminary to proposing a resolution of it, I will consider how the problem arises in our context between two limits in the first of which the problem does not arise and in the second it has an obvious resolution.

The first limit is when an activity conforms to the goods, conventions, and traditions of the evaluative framework of our society. Toleration, then, is not an issue because the activity accords with our social identity and it is not disapproved. There is, for instance, no question of whether we should tolerate a legal activity that follows a pattern of established practices, such as an author and a publisher signing a contract for the publication of a work. Both are acting within their rights so whether signing the contract should be tolerated simply does not come up.

The other limit is when an activity seriously threatens our social identity and thus the evaluative framework of our society. It is obvious, then, that the activity should be prohibited. If the Findings of Fact were correct, then the subversive activities of the Communist Party obviously should not have been tolerated. Equally obvious is that activities like suspending the Constitution, selling military secrets to foreign powers, or causing anarchy by obliterating public and financial records ought to be prohibited.

The problem of toleration arises between these limits; between obviously rightful and obviously wrongful activities; between activities for which there are clear, non-conflicting impersonal and personal reasons and activities that seriously threaten our social identity from which both impersonal and personal reasons are derived. In the intermediate context between these two limits, impersonal and personal reasons may yield incompatible answers to the question of whether an activity should be tolerated. There may be strong impersonal reasons for disapproving an activity and there may also be strong personal reasons for approving it. Or vice versa.

Consider a person who has a strong, consistent, lifelong commitment to a particular tradition according to which the protection of human lives is more important than any other good that may conflict with it. He is a pacifist; he opposes capital punishment, abortion, suicide, and euthanasia; he wants to lower the highway speed limit and outlaw dangerous occupations; and he refuses to pay a portion of his income tax that would support military expenditure. He feels so strongly about these matters that he does not merely advocate changing the relevant laws but as a conscientious act of protest he openly breaks the laws he opposes. He clearly has strong personal reasons for this. Equally clearly, there are strong impersonal reasons for discouraging his law-breaking: although human life is obviously good, there are also other goods, such as liberty, security, the rule of law, prosperity, and so forth, and human life would not be good if these other goods were not protected, even at the cost of risking some human lives. The consequences of adopting his policies would be disastrous. And the example he sets might encourage others to violate laws they happen to dislike. Should, then, the activities of this person be tolerated?

There is much to be said on both sides. We want independent people who have the courage of their convictions; the pacifist may actually encourage others to stand up for their beliefs; and in actual fact his symbolic law-breaking does not directly threaten our social identity and evaluative framework. But we also want law-abiding citizens; we do not want to leave it optional whether people conform to properly enacted laws; the reasons the pacifist has for his conscientious activities are quite weak if viewed impersonally; and the laws apply to citizens equally, regardless of what their conscience tells them.

The simple resolution of the problem of toleration says that we should weigh these reasons for and against toleration and follow the weightier ones. We can now see that while this is obviously true, it is no less obviously unhelpful because our problem is precisely that we do not know what weight we should attach to the conflicting reasons. In order to resolve the problem, therefore, we need a standard to which we could appeal in assigning the appropriate weight to incompatible reasons. I will now propose such a standard and then apply it to the pacifist's case (in 6.4).

6.3 THE PROBLEM RESOLVED

The standard we need is the evaluative framework of our society. I described it earlier (in 3.2) but here I need to repeat the main points. Our well-being depends on having universal, social, and personal goods. Universal goods are the satisfaction of basic needs that are the same for everyone, and they are protected by a society's required conventions. Social goods are the particular legal, religious, educational, political, aesthetic, commercial, and other customs, ceremonies, institutions, and practices embedded in the traditions that have evolved in the course of a society's history. They are protected by variable conventions that differ from society to society and from time to time within the same society. The social goods and variable conventions form part of the social identity of those who live in a society. Personal goods are some subset of the social goods that individuals adapt to their characters and circumstances in order to form their conceptions of well-being. An important part of these conceptions is the participation of individuals in some of the traditions of their society. Personal goods are also protected by variable conventions but they vary with individual conceptions of well-being. Personal goods, allegiance to particular traditions, and the variable conventions that protect them form individual styles of life.

The evaluative framework of a society, therefore, makes the well-being of those living in it possible by satisfying their basic needs, protecting their social identity, and enabling them to live according to their own styles of life. My claim is that by appealing to this standard we can make reasonable decisions about what should and should not be tolerated. The weight of reasons for and against the toleration of disapproved activities depends on whether they violate basic needs, social identity, or styles of life.

If the disapproved activities violate required conventions that protect universal goods, they are disapproved because they prevent the satisfaction of basic needs, as do, for instance, murder, torture, and mutilation. Under normal circumstances, the reasons against tolerating these activities are overwhelmingly stronger than the reasons that may be adduced for tolerating them. A society must protect the well-being of its members, and murder, torture, mutilation, and other activities like them violate minimum conditions of the victims' well-being.

Circumstances, however, may not be normal. In rare cases, there may be strong reasons for murdering a tyrant (like Hitler), torturing a terrorist (in order to extract information that would save thousands of innocent lives), or mutilating a person (by cutting off a limb pinned under a huge boulder) rather than allowing him to die. But the reasons for tolerating normally prohibited activities that violate basic needs are strong only if their violation in particular rare cases is the best way of satisfying basic needs in general. Understanding why rare exceptions may be made, therefore, strengthens, rather than weakens, the case for protecting the satisfaction of basic needs and the reasons against tolerating activities contrary to it. The prohibition of such activities is one of the cases in which the problem of toleration has an obvious and uncontroversial resolution.

I consider next activities that are disapproved because they violate some particular social goods, variable conventions, or traditions that form the social identity of people in a society. These are the disapproved activities whose toleration or prohibition is usually the most problematic because it is difficult to judge the relative weight of the reasons for and against toleration. It helps to cope with this difficulty if we bear in mind that social identity is always changing and if we draw a crucial distinction.

The changes in social identity we need to recognize result from tensions internal to social identity and from the need to adapt it to changing external conditions. Consider, for example, how effective contraception, television, computers, terrorism, increase in life expectancy, globalization, drugs, and life-prolonging medical technologies have forced changes in prevailing moral, religious, commercial, legal, medical, political, educational, and sexual goods, conventions, and traditions that define our social identity. As a result of these changes, it is often difficult to know whether an activity that violates one of these components of social identity is a threat to social identity or an attempt to adapt it to changed circumstances.

The distinction we need to draw is between activities that violate particular goods, conventions, and traditions but do not seriously threaten social identity as a whole and activities that do threaten it. Adultery, obscenity, prostitution, pot smoking, drunkenness, and hypocrisy offend against components of our social identity but their threats are slight and do not seriously endanger it. Let us call them weak threats. There are also activities that might become serious threats to social identity as a whole, such as outlawing religions, punishing criminals by mutilation, abolishing the income tax, allowing unrestricted immigration, and banning atheists from holding public office. If there were movements that seriously advocated such measures, they would be serious threats to our social identity, but there is presently virtually no chance that they might attract widespread support. Let us call them strong threats. As things stand, our social identity is not endangered by either weak or strong threats. But as a result of changes caused by internal tension and changing external circumstances, the harmlessness of both weak and strong threats may change. If weak threats became widespread and if movements advocating strong threats were successful, they would endanger our social identity.

Toleration within Reason

The reasonable attitude toward the toleration of weak and strong threats follows from these considerations. Both should be tolerated because they do not cause serious harm. They offend against particular social goods, conventions, and traditions we have good reason to value, so it is reasonable to disapprove of them, but they do not offend seriously enough to endanger our social identity, so we should put up with them even though we rightly disapprove of them. The toleration of them, however, should be passive, by which I mean that they should be allowed but not encouraged. Acting in our private capacity, we may express disapproval of them, encourage public opinion to turn against them, dislike and avoid those who engage in them but there is presently no strong impersonal reason to prohibit them. This may change. The respective weight of reasons may shift from personal to impersonal, and if it does, it may become reasonable to prohibit them because they have become serious threats to our social identity.

Let us lastly consider activities involved in individual styles of life derived from individual conceptions of well-being. These activities may offend against the personal goods that others derive from their own but very different styles of life. In this way, individuals in a society may disapprove each others' sexual preferences, child rearing, marital arrangements, religious or irreligious positions, vulgarity, personal hygiene, patriotism, profligacy, ignorance, political views, or prejudices. In a pluralistic society like ours, where there are many traditions and styles of life, such reciprocal disapprovals are likely to be frequent. The disapproved activities give offense but normally cause no serious harm to those who are offended by them. This makes the reasons for tolerating them in most cases much stronger than the reasons against it.

This is true in most cases, but why not all cases? Because we should leave room for cases in which the weight of reasons may shift and favor prohibition over toleration. Styles of life may prompt activities that violate the basic needs of others: they may be sadistic, obsessed with power or money, fanatical, and so forth. Then the activities that flow from them should not be tolerated. Barring such cases, the reasons for tolerating activities that reflect a particular style of life but are disapproved from the points of view of other styles of life are much stronger than the reasons against tolerating them.

Schopenhauer's lovely parable explains why this is so. "One cold winter's day, a number of porcupines huddled together quite close in order through their mutual warmth to prevent themselves from being frozen. But they soon felt the effect of their quills on one another, which made them again move apart. Now when the need for warmth once more brought them together, the drawback of the quills was repeated so that they were tossed between two evils, until they had discovered the proper distance from which they could best tolerate one another. Thus the need for society which springs from the emptiness and monotony of men's lives, drives them together; but their many unpleasant and repulsive qualities and insufferable drawbacks once more drives them apart. The mean distance which they finally discover, and which enables them to endure being together, is politeness and good manners."

Politeness and good manners are the social graces possessed by those to whom toleration has become a habitual second nature. It leads them to be tactful rather than judgmental, and to respect the privacy of others rather than meddle with their styles of life. Such people have a style of life of their own, and they use their time and energies to concentrate on it rather than on criticizing other styles of life. Active toleration, consisting in the encouragement of a wide variety of styles of life, is the key to the enjoyment of peace and harmony in a society once the basic needs are reliably satisfied, the prevailing social identity is secured, and the most important political goods are protected. Individual members of a society, then, can get on with making what they can of their lives and possibilities.

In summary of this resolution of the problem of toleration, I have argued that the evaluative framework of a society provides a reasonable standard for weighing the reasons for and against the toleration of disapproved activities. Our well-being depends on the protection of that framework, and the respective weight of reasons derives from how seriously an activity threatens a component of the framework. Activities that violate the satisfaction of basic needs should be prohibited, except in rare cases when the violation is the best way of protecting the satisfaction of basic needs in general. Activities that seriously threaten the prevailing social identity should also be prohibited, provided they are not attempts to adapt social identity to changed circumstances. Activities that violate particular social goods, variable conventions, or traditions but do not seriously threaten the social identity itself should be passively tolerated. And, although activities that follow from particular styles of life but do not violate the satisfaction of basic needs or seriously threaten social identity may still be disapproved by those who have other styles of life, they should nevertheless be actively tolerated, since they cause only negligible harm to those who are offended by them. Whether or not a disapproved activity should be tolerated, then, depends on how seriously it threatens the well-being of people in a society.

This is a method for answering the question but not an answer to it. It shows only how a reasonable answer may be found. What the actual answer is in particular cases depends on judging the seriousness of threats to well-being and the respective weights of reasons for and against toleration. These considerations vary with changing goods, conventions, traditions, and external circumstances. Consequently reasonable judgments are context-dependent, and, because they involve the interpretation of complex facts, they are fallible and disputable. What I have offered, therefore, is not a specification of what should and should not be tolerated but a way of identifying the relevant considerations on which reasonable judgments should be based.

+ + +

The Art of Politics

6.4 Impersonal vs. Impersonal Reasons

The method I have proposed proceeds from the point of view a society and calls for weighing the reasons for and against toleration impersonally, rather than from the personal perspective of the individuals who are affected by them. From the personal point of view, individuals may well arrive at a different judgment. This leads us back to the problem double-mindedness in which personal and impersonal reasons conflict, and, by way of concrete illustration, to the pacifist's case to which I promised earlier to return.

The pacifist, it will be remembered, believes that human life is the highest good, more important than any other good. He thinks that it has to be protected even if it involves drastic interference with pluralism, limits, liberty, or any other political or non-political good. He does not merely believe and advocate this view, he sincerely and selflessly acts on it by breaking laws that in his judgment lead to risking or taking human lives. In this way, he expresses his opposition to capital punishment, abortion, euthanasia, suicide, military expenditure, risky occupations and sports, dangerously high speed limits, and so forth. But he often goes beyond the open advocacy of basic changes in the laws and constantly looks for and often finds ways of illegally interfering with and disrupting the activities involved in what he sees as morally abhorrent practices.

What conclusions will the method lead to about tolerating the pacifist's activities? It will lead us to conclude that his illegal activities should not be tolerated and his legal advocacy of fundamental changes in the laws governing the practices he abhors should be passively tolerated. Let us discuss first why the reasons against tolerating the pacifist's illegal activities are overwhelmingly stronger than the reasons for tolerating them.

In the first place, the laws that the pacifist violates have been properly enacted in accordance with democratically mandated constitutional procedures. They are designed to protect the prevailing social identity composed of particular goods, conventions, and traditions, and thereby protect a condition we regard as necessary for our well-being. Each good, convention, and tradition may be challenged and there are procedures for changing the laws so as to reflect agreed-upon changes. But the pacifist is not merely advocating changing the laws, he is breaking them. And by doing so he endangers what we regard as our well-being.

The pacifist does this because he believes that we are mistaken. He thinks we misconceive our well-being because we fail to realize that human life is the highest good. We think otherwise. We think human life is one basic good among others and its claims must be balanced against the claims of pluralism, limits, liberty, justice, property, equality, and democracy. For this we have our reasons and he knows what they are. He has his reasons and they lead him to break the laws that embody our reasons. He also knows that there are penalties for this. If he nevertheless breaks them, he knowingly makes himself liable to the penalties. If we actively or passively tolerate his illegal activities, we collude in endangering the laws on which we believe our well-being depends. This would be unreasonable, so the pacifist should be punished for his breaking the laws. We should recognize, however, that his law-breaking is motivated by good will and conscience, so the punishment should be as mild as possible. But punishment there should be because we should protect the laws on which we believe our well-being depends.

These reasons against tolerating his law-breaking are based on three considerations. One is that the existing laws reflect a long process of public deliberation and a very wide consensus among those who are subject to them. We have no reason to question the legal system as a whole, even if we have reasons for wanting to change parts of it. We want the rule of law to prevail and that means that we cannot leave it optional whether the laws are obeyed. A second consideration is that the pacifist has other ways of expressing his opposition than by breaking the laws. He could follow the appropriate procedures for trying to change them. Or, if he thinks this would be futile, he could leave the society for another. But if he stays, he must obey the laws or accept the penalty for breaking them. The third consideration is that the pacifist's belief that human life is the highest good and that we misconceive our well-being unless we recognize this is untenable.

No matter how consistent, sincere, and selfless the pacifist is, a little reflection shows that it is absurd to believe that taking human lives is the worst thing we can do. It may be perfectly reasonable to do so if it is unavoidable in self-defense, in resisting unprovoked foreign aggression, in preventing terrorist outrages, or in saving innocent lives. Furthermore, acting on his belief has unacceptable consequences, such as having to disarm the military and the police, ban mining, high rise constructions, contact sports, parachute jumping, rock climbing, and downhill skiing; forbidding sunbathing and compelling overweight people to diet. We would have to condemn, rather than admire, people who have lost their lives and inspired others to risk theirs in order to defend justice, liberty, their country, their religion, or their family. The pacifist's belief is contrary to the virtually universal conviction that lives may not be worth living under certain conditions, such as extreme pain without the possibility of relief, continuing debasement and gross humiliation, unrelieved Sisyphean drudgery, and so forth. The pacifist's belief is untenable because what we value is not human life but human life on acceptable terms that include many other goods that we have excellent reason to value, such as liberty; justice; lack of pain, humiliation, and self-loathing; having some pleasure and enjoyment; self-respect; intimate relationships; at least moderate comfort; and so forth. These considerations provide strong reasons against tolerating the pacifist's illegal activities. The only consideration in favor of tolerating them is that he is sincere and selfless, but that is not a strong enough reason because his illegal activities threaten a condition of our well-being, regardless of what motivates them.

The mistake of the pacifist is the mistake all ideologues make:

the exaggeration of the importance of a particular good at the expense of other goods. Their mistake is not to exaggerate the wrong good but to exaggerate any good. Their self-imposed blinkers allow them to see only one good and, because they prevent themselves from seeing the others, they accuse those who do see them of delusion. It has been well said by Hume that ideologues "are always clamorous and dogmatical, even in the nicest questions, of which from want of temper, perhaps still more than of understanding, they are altogether unfit judges." They do not see that "all political questions are . . . complicated, and that there scarcely ever occurs, in any deliberation, a choice, which is either purely good, or purely ill. Consequences, mixed and varied, may be foreseen to flow from every measure: And many consequences, unforeseen, do always, in fact, result from every one." Possessed by a moralistic fervor derived from indefensible personal reasons, they violate the widely accepted impersonal reasons embedded in the long tradition of the rule of law. Falsely believing themselves to be the true champions of our well-being, ideologues actually endanger it. They may be sincere and selfless but that makes them even more dangerous. A society would be suicidal if it failed to enforce its laws against ideological, as well as other, law-breakers.

But, unlike the pacifist, we should not allow ourselves to get carried away. Only some of the pacifist's activities involve breaking the law. His public advocacy of outlawing all practices that involve risking or taking human lives is within legal limits. If we apply the method I proposed to deciding whether his advocacy should be tolerated, we find that the reasons for toleration are stronger than the reasons against it. The reasons against tolerating his advocacy have to do with the great weakness of the case he is making and with the damaging consequences that would follow from accepting it. But these reasons against toleration are outweighed by the reasons for it.

The basic reason for toleration is that it is important to keep the legal system flexible. Particular laws may be obsolete, ill-defined, unable to cover new situations, inconsistent with other laws, or flawed in other ways. Public criticism helps to expose flaws or to compel defenders of the criticized laws to make clear the reasons in favor of the laws. The pacifist's public advocacy is such a criticism, so it should be tolerated. But what he advocates is not a small change in a particular law but a radical transformation that would fundamentally alter the existing legal system. If all the existing laws that protected various liberties, private property, the administration of justice, contracts, security, and so forth were altered so as to eliminate risks to human lives, our society would be radically transformed and this would have incalculable consequences. Reason requires great caution in contemplating such changes and taking the attendant risks. The pacifist's public advocacy of making these changes and accepting the risks involved should be tolerated, therefore, but only passively. He should be allowed to voice them, to try to attract public support for them, but it should not be encouraged.

I have discussed the pacifist's case at length to illustrate how the method I have proposed could be used to resolve the problem of toleration in a particular case. The resolution always depends on weighing the reasons for and against toleration by judging how serious would the likely harm be if we tolerated or interfered with the activity. Such judgments are often difficult and always fallible, for they concern the future consequences of present actions and we can never know what else may happen in the future that would invalidate even the most reasonable present judgments.

The reasonable course, therefore, is to rule in favor of toleration if the judgment is reasonably disputed. Toleration must have limits but we should have very strong reasons for placing an activity beyond them. We should be exceptionally careful not to confuse our moral, religious, political, aesthetic, or other disapproval of some activity with strong reasons for prohibiting it. The reasons against toleration are that the activity endangers the evaluative framework from which the reasons for the activity are derived.

The reasons should not be that our commitment to the goods and conventions of a particular tradition leads us to condemn an activity that is prompted by the goods and conventions of another particular tradition. We should be like the porcupines in the parable and cultivate politeness and good manners toward other people's activities, especially if we disapprove of them.

6.5 TOLERATION WITHIN REASON

The justification of toleration, as well as of the limits of toleration, is prudential. This is contrary to the widely held view that their justification is moral. There is a tangled dispute behind this disagreement. If we are to understand why toleration is a political good, we need to disentangle this dispute. To begin with, morality may be understood in a narrow and a wide sense. Understood narrowly, the domain of morality is restricted to impersonal evaluations of actions on the basis of how they affect others. Understood widely, the domain of morality includes all the conditions of human well-being, both personal and impersonal, self-regarding and other-regarding, and not just actions but also virtues, vices, duties, obligations, characters, traditions, agents, and institutions. When I say that the justification of toleration is prudential, not moral, I mean it in the narrow sense. And so do those who hold that its justification is moral. In the wide sense, the dispute is obviously moral because toleration is among the conditions of human well-being. The dispute, however, is substantive, not merely verbal, because both parties to it understand morality in the narrow sense.

Using morality in the narrow sense, then, we must note that it is an obvious feature of morality that there are many different moral traditions from which many different and often incompatible moral evaluations follow. Moral traditions may be Catholic, Protestant, Jewish, or Moslem; within each religion, they may be traditionalist or reformist; or moral traditions may be secular, and within that conservative, liberal, or socialist; they may be

classically or romantically oriented; realistic or idealistic; abso-
lutist, relativist, pluralist, or skeptical; individualist or communitar-
ian; they may center on duty or on happiness; they may give
priority to choice, or actions, or motives, or character; they may
aspire to universal or merely local validity; and so on and on.

Those who think that the justification of toleration is moral
cannot just leave it at that. They must show what that justification
is. When they do that, they must do it from the point of view of a
particular moral tradition. And this is in fact what they do. They
proceed from the point of view of liberalism. They claim that toleration is an essential and characteristic feature of liberalism and
liberal societies because it is an essential condition of the individual exercise of autonomy, which has a good claim to being the
central liberal good.

It is against this background that I have been insisting that the
justification of toleration is not moral but prudential. My reasons
for doing so are that it is not true that liberal societies are particularly tolerant; that the implied claim that non-liberal societies are
bound to be less tolerant than liberal ones is false; and that it is a
disservice to the undoubted good of toleration to make its justification depend on the fortunes of liberalism, which, it should be
remembered, is only one particular moral tradition among many
others, even though liberals often talk as if no evaluations but
theirs were morally acceptable.

American society, I suppose, is as liberal as any and it is
undoubtedly true that it is tolerant of a wide variety of religions,
sexual practices, and pornography. But I have not noticed a great
deal of toleration of those who oppose affirmative action, homosexuality, or the policies advocated by feminists; or of those who
deny the Holocaust, think that racial profiling by the police is
warranted, belong to private clubs that exclude women, or want to
conduct research to determine whether there are genetic racial differences in intelligence. There is much toleration of the abuse of
fundamentalists, the CIA, President Bush, and corporations, but the

abuse of African Americans, Jews, or homosexuals is criminalized as hate speech. Universities tolerate radical rabble-rousers but there are speech codes forbidding anything that might offend minorities or women. Cocaine and pot use are tolerated but cigarette smoking is not. These examples of intolerance could be multiplied but perhaps I have said enough to show that American liberals are not particularly tolerant.

Nor is it true that liberals tend to be more tolerant than non-liberals. For long periods between the end of WWII and the present, conservative governments were in power in Britain, France, Germany, Sweden, Italy, and America, but the level of toleration during their rule was not discernibly different from its level during the rule of liberal governments that preceded or succeeded them. Liberalism began in Europe as a movement to tolerate religious diversity, but the Ottoman Empire, surely not a liberal regime, practiced wide religious toleration centuries before European liberals began it. Toleration, therefore, is not a characteristic feature of liberal societies.

Moreover, if toleration were an essential characteristic of liberalism, then the endless liberal condemnation of societies and traditions that rejected both liberalism and toleration would simply be an exercise in futility. For if toleration were a liberal good, then non-liberals would have no reason to be tolerant. If liberals are right to claim that all societies and traditions should be tolerant, then they cannot reasonably suppose that toleration is a characteristic only of liberal societies and traditions. Liberals must hold that it does or should transcend particular societies and traditions.

Toleration in America is fairly widespread. It makes no difference to this whether or not the majority party is liberal. The reason why toleration is widespread is that the society is pluralistic. Americans have realized that the cost of being allowed to enjoy the goods, follow the conventions, and maintain their allegiance to their preferred traditions is to allow others to do the same. They let others live as they please, so that they themselves could live as they please. They are led to do so by prudence, not by commitment to a particular moral tradition.

The justification of toleration, therefore, is the prudential attitude that allows people with allegiances to different goods, conventions, and traditions to live side by side without too great a friction. They put up with the minor inconvenience of having to tolerate activities of which they disapprove, provided they are not seriously harmed by them. But if the disapproved activity threatens them with serious harm, then the reasons against toleration outweigh the reasons for it. This is a reasonable attitude, and it is the prudential justification of both toleration and its limits. We can, then, add another component to the balanced view. In addition to reason as prudence, the plurality of goods, the necessity of limits, and limited liberty, we now have toleration within reason.

CHAPTER SEVEN

✦ ✦ ✦

JUSTICE AS HAVING WHAT ONE DESERVES

It is just . . . to render to each his due.

PLATO
The Republic

SUPPOSE YOU HAD THE POWER to impose on a society one of two patterns. In the first, good and bad things are distributed randomly across the population. In the second, there are exactly the same good and bad things, but good people have the good things and bad people the bad ones. Let us call the first pattern random, and the second ordered. Which pattern would you impose? I have asked this question of many people and I have yet to meet one who would not impose the ordered pattern.

This leads to a second question: why is the ordered pattern preferred? My answer is that a society with the ordered pattern (from now on "ordered society") is preferable because it is just: people in it have what they deserve and do not have what they do not deserve. The trouble with the society in which the random pattern holds (from now on "random society") is that it is unjust because people in it have no reason to believe that they will have what they deserve. Hard work, intelligent choice, and self-discipline, for instance, have exactly the same chance of success as sloth, stupidity, and self-indulgence. The view I aim to defend is that the ordered society is just because its political conditions increase the likelihood that good actions will have good consequences and bad actions will have bad consequences. I also aim to show that if reasonable people think through what they believe, they will realize that they are, in fact, committed to this view of justice.

7.1 WHY SHOULD PEOPLE GET WHAT THEY DESERVE?

Consider a simple sequence leading to an action. I am hungry, want to eat, decide to go home for lunch, and I walk there. Implicit in the sequence is that I have a set of obvious beliefs (my house is nearby, there is food in the fridge, there are no obstacles in the way, and so on) and I have the required ordinary capacities (I can walk, rely on my memory, estimate distance, and the like). The sequence that precedes action, then, has the following elements: motive, belief, capacity, goal, and decision. Each may be defective: motives may be irrational, beliefs false, capacities inadequate, goals unattainable, and decisions wrong-headed. Suppose, however, that they are not defective and I perform the action to which the conjunction of these elements leads. I expect, then, that my action will be successful, that it will achieve its goal. In simple sequences of this sort, normal people in normal circumstances have normally good reason to suppose that the elements are free of defect and no reason to doubt it. Their expectation that their actions will be successful is generally reasonable. The well-being of individuals requires that such reasonable expectations be generally met.

It would be comforting if simple sequences were adequate for the business of living, but they are not. Complexities unavoidably arise because it is often difficult to tell whether an element is defective. Motives conflict and we constantly have to make choices about which of them we should act on. We routinely have to evaluate the reliability of our beliefs on the basis of imperfect knowledge and insufficient evidence. Our capacities are always limited and we have to estimate whether they are adequate for the achievement of difficult goals. We usually have several incompatible goals and we must decide about their respective importance. But what seems important at one time may become less so at another. The world changes, we change, and we have to make guesses about how these changes might affect our goals. The choices we make depend on understanding our circumstances and what we want, all things considered, out of life. We are often unclear about them at the time we have to choose, and we are also unclear how we may change in the future. Coping with complexities requires, in addition to getting the facts right, judging the significance of available facts. Good judgment about such matters is difficult.

Suppose I act on the basis of a complex sequence and my judgment is good. Might I, then, reasonably expect that my action will be successful? No, because even if I act as reasonably as anyone in my position could, I may nevertheless fail because others justifiably prevent me from succeeding. Most of the time my success depends on the cooperation of others, and they may have more important concerns; or they may also want what I want and are better at getting it; or what I want may run counter to their interests or to the interests of an institution or cause they wish to protect. More is needed, therefore, before I can reasonably expect to get what I want, and the same, of course, is true of everyone else. We all have to take into account that we live together in a society and depend on the cooperation of others. The terms of cooperation, therefore, have to be more or less clearly articulated and made customary. These terms are the conventions of justice (from now on, just "conventions"; there are, of course, numerous other conventions, political and non-political, affecting matters other than justice). In the vast majority of complex sequences, we can get what we want only by conforming to these conventions.

Can we reasonably expect that our actions will be successful if they are based on good judgment and conform to the prevailing conventions? The answer is still no for two reasons. One is that the conventions may be defective. I will say more about this shortly, but let us assume for the moment that the conventions are adequate.

133

The other reason why the expectation of success may be premature is that not even adequate conventions can eliminate competition. We may fail to achieve our goals, although we have good judgment and conform to adequate conventions because we lose out in a competition with others whose judgment is also good and who also conform to adequate conventions. Only one person can win the race, get the job, be the first to make the discovery, and only a few can get elected, add to the canon, or make a lasting contribution to science. For each of those who succeed, there are many who try and fail. Not all goals are competitive, of course; having a good marriage, enjoying nature, developing a historical perspective, listening to music are not. But many are, and because of them we may have good judgment, conform to adequate conventions, and still fail to achieve our goals.

Putting all this together, the following requirements of successful action emerge: having good judgment; conforming to the adequate conventions of one's society; and, if goals are competitive, prevailing in the competition. The expectation of success is reasonable if these requirements are met. This finally allows me to make clear the point of the preceding discussion. What I mean by saying that people should have what they deserve is that they should succeed if their expectation of success is reasonable. And what I mean by saying that people should not have what they do not deserve is that they should not succeed if their expectation of success is unreasonable. The "should" and the "should not" above express requirements of reason as prudence (discussed in Chapter Two).

The aim of reason as prudence is to make human life better. One way of doing that is to make it more likely that good people have good, rather than bad, things in life and that bad people have bad, rather than good, things in life. This is what happens in an ordered society. The reason for making a society ordered is to increase the likelihood that good judgment, conformity to adequate conventions, and doing well in competition will lead to better lives. Justice prevails if these requirements of reason are met. Meeting them is at once the aim and the justification of justice. And justice understood in this way is one of the political goods that the balanced view aims to secure.

People living together in a society should do, therefore, what they jointly can to make justice prevail. Joint efforts, however, are not enough. Individual effort is also necessary because only individuals can make their own judgments good and they alone can make themselves succeed in a competition if the prevailing conventions are adequate. What can be done by joint efforts is to make adequate conventions prevail, which is our next topic.

7.2 CONVENTIONS OF JUSTICE

There are countless conventions of justice because there are countless forms of cooperation. It would be futile to try to list all of them. I will proceed instead by concentrating on three types of variable conventions that a society can hardly do without. These conventions embody habits, customs, practices, and the more or less clearly formulated rules that have emerged in the course of a particular society's history. The conventions change, but usually slowly. There goes with them a continuum of evaluations ranging between the extremes of good and bad, allowing many intermediate judgments in between. The resulting judgments praise or condemn whatever appropriately falls in the domain of one of these conventions; they assign responsibilities people are expected to discharge, or are condemned for violating, or from which, under specifiable conditions, they are exempted or excused; and they create also reasonable expectations of others that these responsibilities will be met. The judgments, then, serve as the bases on which good and bad things are distributed in a particular society. The conventions regulate what people should or should not have in particular areas of life.

One type of convention concerns relationships. Lovers, competitors, friends, colleagues, parents and children, teachers and students, physicians and patients, merchants and customers are connected by conventional ties. These ties create responsibilities and expectations about how people related in these ways should treat one another. The first four of these relationships are symmetrical: lovers, competitors, friends, and colleagues typically have the same reciprocal responsibilities and expectations. The next four are asymmetrical: one party has authority over the other, or provides a service the other needs, or sells something the other wants to buy.

A second type of convention concerns agreements, such as contracts, promises, loans, memberships in organizations, employment, political or legal representation of others, holding a license to drive a car, sell a product, or build a house. Some of these agreements are formal. The responsibilities and expectations are governed by written rules and are legally binding. Others are informal. What is owed or expected rests on a tacit understanding of the parties. The force behind such informal agreements is a shared sense of trust and mutual good will.

A third type of convention is connected with actions that affect the security of others. A society cannot endure unless it protects the security of those living in it, but different societies have different conventions, prompting different judgments about how far the protection of security should go, what violations are permissible, excusable, or prohibited, how people outside of the society should be treated, what counts as cruelty, negligence, accidental injury, and, of course, how security should be understood. Take, for instance, physical assault. All societies must regulate it. But when assault is criminal, when it is excusable or justifiable vary greatly with the prevailing conventions affecting behavior in sports, dueling, self-defense, revenge, the treatment of enemies, prisoners, children, and so on.

Part of the importance of these conventions, and of many others I have not discussed, is that they establish what people in a particular society deserve. They deserve to have what the prevailing conventions prescribe regarding relationships, agreements, and actions, and they do not deserve to have what would be contrary to these conventions. The conventions, thus, provide reasons for the responsibilities and the expectations that people living together in a society have. In our society, children deserve a decent upbringing from their parents because that is part of how parenthood is understood by us. Incompetent physicians deserve to lose their license because a physician is assumed by us to be able to treat illness well. Murderers deserve to be punished because that is how we protect security. These conventions do not merely happen to hold in our society. Our well-being requires that children be brought up well, illness be treated, and life be protected. Such conventions are socially variable but all societies must have them in one form or another. Otherwise the well-being of those living there would be badly served and the society would disintegrate. When we say, therefore, that people deserve this or that, what we are saying is that this is our particular way of protecting what is necessary for our well-being.

Claims about what people do or do not deserve may be mistaken of course. I will consider two ways in which this may happen. One is that the prevailing conditions are adequate but misapplied; the other is that the conventions are defective. I discuss adequate but misapplied evaluations now and defective ones later (in 7.3).

Any convention regarding what people deserve may be misapplied if those applying it get the relevant facts wrong. People falsely accused of murder do not deserve to be punished. Students passing a course by cheating do not deserve credit for it. False friends do not deserve loyalty. But even if the facts are as assumed, the conventions may be misapplied by getting wrong the proportion of what is deserved. A novel may deserve good reviews, but not the National Book Award. A thief may deserve imprisonment, but not to have his arm cut off. A physician may deserve payment for services rendered, but not the deed to my house. Conventions that involve mistakes of fact and proportion lead to people having good or bad things they do not deserve at all or not having as much or little as they actually get.

A less obviously detectable mistake is to be wrong about the goodness or badness of particular relationships, agreements, or actions. Because what is taken to be good or bad may in fact not be, people are rewarded or punished when they do not deserve it. Those who suppose that telling a lie is always wrong, contracts between employers and employees are always exploitative, or suicide is murder are wrong because they suppose that what may be morally acceptable is bad. Similarly mistaken are the suppositions that frugality is a sign of virtue, flogging children is good for their character, and belief in God makes people virtuous.

The prevailing conventions govern a wide array of relationships, agreements, or actions which are judged by a society to be good or bad. These conventions are not invalidated if they are sometimes misapplied. Recurrent misapplications point to the need to reform part of the conventions from which they follow, but they leave their large remaining part intact. It may happen, of course, that not merely a few but most applications of a prevailing convention are mistaken. Then the convention itself should be regarded as defective in its entirety and should be abandoned. This is just what happened, or should have happened, to conventions about testing the credibility of testimonies by torture, making laws retroactive, or allowing people to be judges in cases where their interests are involved.

Another kind of mistake, much closer to home, is to suppose that there is no special reason needed for the distribution of good and bad things. One way of making this mistake is to suppose that everyone is equally deserving of the good things in life and that the bad things are burdens that we all have to be bear equally. If asked why good and bad things are equally deserved, the usual answer is that everyone has equal moral worth, or everyone is entitled to equal respect. This is one of the passionately held ideologies of our egalitarian age. But those whose critical faculties are not numbed by the ceaseless repetition of egalitarian catchphrases will recognize the absurdity of believing that terrorists and hostages, criminals and their victims, friends and enemies of one's society, evildoers and decent, law-abiding citizens have equal moral worth or are entitled to equal respect, and deserve to have the same good and bad things. The familiar indignant reply of egalitarian ideologues is that they believe no such things. What they believe, they say, is that there ought to be an initial assumption that everyone is equally deserving. The assumption may be falsified, and it is falsified in the case of terrorists, criminals, and other malefactors. But this assumption flies in the face of facts whose denial is absurd. Human beings differ in their relationships, agreements, and the effects of their actions on the security of others. In view of these differences, surely the reasonable assumption is that there is an overwhelming likelihood that different people will deserve different things.

The implausibility of the egalitarian assumption is compounded if it is realized that a society betrays its most elementary responsibility to those living in it if it proceeds on the assumption that citizens and foreigners, law abiding and criminal citizens, defenders and subverters of the society are equally deserving. The questions grow in number and urgency when it is asked, as it must be, what reasons might be good enough to count against the egalitarian assumption. If differences in morality, reasonability, law-abidingness, and citizenship count, then virtually nothing remains of the assumption since the great and undeniable differences among people in these respects constantly contradict it. And if these differences are said not to count, then what would justify a society in ignoring them in the distribution of good and bad things at its disposal?

The balanced view is that the time has come to consign the egalitarian view of justice to the dust heap of history, where it will join other passionately held follies of other ages, such as the divine rights of kings, classless society, possession by the Devil, planned economy, damnation outside the church, and an idyllic prehistoric society from which civilization has caused us to fall farther and farther. What should take the place of this absurd belief about what people deserve is the recognition that different people deserve different things and any claim that people deserve this or that must be backed by reasons.

I have been arguing that the reasons must be derived from the conventions that prevail in a society. The reasons are good if the prevailing conventions are free of mistakes in fact, proportion, in the identification of good and bad things, and do not miss the central importance of individual differences. It must be recognized, however, that even if good reasons of this kind are given in support of conventions about what individuals deserve, the conventions may still fail because they may themselves be defective. The view of justice I am defending does not deny that the generally accepted conventions in a society may be unjust because they may lead to people not having what they deserve or having what they do not deserve. The conventions, therefore, need to be justified, and it is not a sufficient justification that they prevail in a particular society.

7.3 The Justification of Conventions of Justice

The view of justice I am defending is not committed to the mindless perpetuation of conventions that happen to prevail in a particular society. It is, rather, committed to the perpetuation of conventions that have endured because people have voluntarily adhered to them; and they did so because conformity to them have made their lives better. I will say that conventions that meet these criteria (endurance, voluntarily conformity, and contribution to well-being) are justified because they have stood the test of time. Conventions endure if they last for a considerable length of time, measured in decades rather than months, and if they are so widely known as to be taken for granted by the vast majority of people in that context. In the appropriate situations, they naturally and spontaneously follow the conventions and they rightly expect others to do the same. If this expectation is not met, and it may not be, then its violation is widely regarded as blameworthy or as requiring an excuse.

Conventions may endure as a result of coercion that makes the failure to conform too costly for most people. One indication of voluntary conformity is that people conduct themselves according to the conventions in the absence of coercion. Another indication is that although there are political, legal, or social avenues for challenging and attempting to change the conventions, the avenues are not followed. A further indication is that even though people could leave the society in which the conventions prevail, they do not and they continue to follow them in appropriate circumstances. None of this requires a conscious, articulate approval of the conventions. Most people who conform to them voluntarily may do so without having or wanting to give the matter serious thought. Voluntary conformity, however, may just indicate habit, indoctrination, or that it is easier to go with the current than to swim against it. There may be a good reason for it, however, even if this reason is not uppermost in the minds of those who conform. The good reason is that people believe that their well-being depends on it. They do not question or feel the need to justify the conventions because they can afford to take them for granted.

There are, of course, deplorable, coercive, unfair, exploitative, ignorant, and stupid conventions, and they fail the test of time. Since justice consists in people having what they deserve and not having what they do not deserve, and since conventions that fail the test of time fail to distribute good and bad things according to what people deserve, justice requires abandoning or reforming unjust conventions and perpetuating just ones only if they have stood the test of time.

One crucial task in justifying conventions, therefore, is to provide reasons for thinking that conforming to them contributes to human well-being. These reasons emerge from reflection on life in a good society, by which I understand a society that protects the political conditions in which people can make good lives for themselves. Or, to put it in another way, if individual lives go badly in a good society, it is not because of adverse political conditions but because of personal failure or misfortune. Good societies are cohesive and enduring partly because their members largely agree about what they owe one another, what sorts of lives are good or bad, and what many of the political goods are that tend to make lives good or bad. These political goods have endured and people in a society believe, often only tacitly, that the political conditions ought to protect these political goods.

One of the political goods is order. It enables people living together in a society to have reasonable expectations about each others' conduct. These expectations rest on the justified assumption that most people most of the time will be guided by the same evaluations that follow from the prevailing conventions. Thus they know what counts as kind or cruel, routine or exceptional, appropriate or inappropriate, in countless different contexts, such as marriage, child raising, employment, competition, joking, electioneering, quarrelling, and so on. This knowledge comes from a shared moral education, which is the usually informal initiation into the shared evaluations. If successful, people in a society will be able to count on each other because there is a social bond between them. They recognize each other as having the same allegiances. Their social identity is partly defined by their shared adherence to the same variable conventions.

Consider as an illustration how this description fits American society. Here is a randomly compiled list of some of the prevailing conventions. Parents are responsible for their children, breaking a promise requires an excuse, politicians speaking in their public capacity should not lie, eating people is wrong, parents should not have sexual intercourse with their children, disagreements should not be settled by violence, people ought to be allowed to express unpopular views, it is wrong to spread malicious lies about one's rivals, permission must be asked before borrowing anything, white lies are permissible, deliberate cruelty is wrong, one should be loyal to friends, confidential information should not be made public, courage, honesty, and fairness are good and their opposites are bad. This list is not exhaustive or representative. Many of these conventions are uncodified, held unconsciously, and conformity to them is usually habitual. People may act contrary to them, but if they do, they can normally be shown, in a cool moment, the wrongness of their actions.

All societies have conventions that are in need of improvement. All conventions should be open to change, and they are always likely to be changing in one respect or another. But there must also be continuity because the reasons for deliberate reform depend on criticizing a prevailing convention by appealing to other prevailing conventions, which are thought to be deeper or more important. In American society, for instance, there is currently much controversy about abortion and voluntary euthanasia. A significant feature of these controversies is that both sides try to justify their position by appealing to conventions they rightly assume to be generally shared, even by their opponents. Supporters of abortion and voluntary euthanasia appeal to liberty; opponents appeal to the importance of protecting life.

7.4 Objections Considered

One objection likely to be made is that this attempt to justify conventions fails. Justice is said to consist in people having what they deserve and not having what they do not deserve; what is or is not deserved is taken to depend on the prevailing conventions; but how could it be decided whether the conventions are themselves just? How could conventions be deemed unjust if what is just follows from them? The answer, however, is obvious, and follows from what has already been said.

Conventions are unjust if they prompt evaluations that involve some mistake of fact, proportion, identification of good and bad things, or a failure to recognize relevant individual differences. Such mistakes prevent people from having what they deserve or not having what they do not deserve, and that is what makes the conventions unjust. Master-slave relationships are prejudice-ridden because they wrongly suppose that slaves are inferior to masters. Marriage contracts in which the husband acquires control over the wife's property are unfair because they falsely deny the wife's capacity to make reasonable decisions. The punishment of theft by cutting off an arm is deplorable because of its disproportionality. Depriving people of the fruits of their work in order to benefit those who could but do not work is wrong because it ignores the difference in what they deserve. In all these cases, the conventions governing the distribution of benefits or burdens are unjust because they lead to people having more or less than what they deserve. The bases for these criticisms are the mistakes the conventions appealed to prompt.

It must be acknowledged, of course, that there may be serious disagreements about whether or not a particular convention is adequate. These disagreements, however, concern the question of what is deserved. They arise only because those who disagree accept that justice depends on people having what they deserve and not having what they do not deserve. The existence of such disagreements strengthens, rather than weakens, the essential connection between justice and what is deserved. The right view of justice, therefore, is not that what people deserve depends merely on the prevailing conventions. What they deserve depends, first, on conventions that have passed the test of time by being enduring, voluntarily followed, and contributing to the well-being of people in a society, and, second, on the applications of these conventions being mistake-free. I think this is a view of justice that reasonable people are likely to share.

Another objection made by more than one critic is that the distribution of good and bad things on the basis of what people deserve is impractical because in American society there is no agreement about what human well-being consists in. There are many conceptions of it, what people are thought to deserve depends at least in part on which conception is accepted, consequently there is bound to be much disagreement about what people deserve. The problem is exacerbated by the fact that what people deserve depends on their beliefs and efforts, and these are not open to observation. It is unrealistic to suppose that political decisions about the distribution of good and bad things could take such subjective factors into account.

This objection rests on two assumptions that have led to misunderstanding the view of justice I am defending. One is that what people deserve depends on their personal qualities. The other is that the distribution of deserved good and bad things is the responsibility of the government. Both assumptions are mistaken, but neither is totally mistaken. Personal qualities may provide reasons why people do or do not deserve something, but they are merely one possible kind of reason among many. And the government does have responsibility for distributing some deserved good and bad things, but there are many others distributed by agencies that function independently of the government.

The reasons I have given for the distribution of what people deserve were derived from the prevailing conventions governing relationships, agreements, and actions affecting security. Personal qualities—virtues and vices, for instance—may be reasonably added to these conventions. But even if it were true that there are great practical difficulties in ascertaining what virtues and vices people have, this is not true of their relationships, agreements, and actions. The latter are open to public observation, and there is no greater practical difficulty in identifying them than there is in identifying countless other features people have.

It adds to the implausibility of this objection that it is often possible to ascribe to people virtues and vices. This is routinely done by families, teachers, coaches, selection committees, employers, and countless other people who are charged with making judgments about the personal qualities of some people. These judgments, of course, can be mistaken. But if they are not mistaken, then the alleged practical difficulties have been overcome. And if they are mistaken, it need not be because practical difficulties stand in the way.

This last rejoinder, however, will be regarded as irrelevant because of the second mistaken assumption on which the objection rests. If the distribution of deserved good and bad things were the responsibility of the government, then the success of individuals in identifying personal qualities would be irrelevant. The question is whether governments, not individuals, can succeed in formulating policies about the distribution of good and bad things on the basis of personal qualities. The answer is twofold. First, as we have seen, the distribution of deserved good and bad things is not based exclusively on personal qualities, but also on the relationships, agreements, and actions of the recipients. Second, their distribution is not the exclusive prerogative of the government, numerous non-political agencies have a very large role in it.

These agencies are families, schools, universities, corporations, athletic competitions, small businesses, orchestras, museums, quiz shows, honor societies, foundations, committees that award prizes, parole boards, neighborhood groups, arbitration panels, and many other more or less formal associations of people that stand between the private concerns of individuals and the political responsibilities of the government. They distribute money, honors, status, prestige; they distinguish between excellence, mediocrity, and deficiency; they set standards and evaluate performance by them; they assign rewards and mete out punishments; they have ways of rectifying violations of their procedures and standards; and they continually face and resolve disputes among their members about these matters. Non-political agencies, therefore, routinely identify personal qualities relevant to their concerns, and, of course, they do the same with the relevant relationships, agreements, and actions of those who come under their jurisdiction.

Even if it were true, therefore, that practical difficulties prevent the government from knowing what the deserved distribution of good and bad things is, the same would not be true of non-political agencies. But, of course, the government can also do what these agencies do. The government has no practical difficulty in identifying some requirements of relationships, such as marriage, parenthood, or citizenship; of agreements, such as taking out a mortgage, enlisting in the army, buying a car, or being a patient in a hospital; and of actions affecting the security of others, such as driving a car, having a fight, or owning a gun. All these cases may constitute reasons for the distribution of good and bad things. There is, therefore, no convincing reason to suppose, as this objection does, that distribution based on what people deserve is vitiated by great practical difficulties.

An entirely different kind of objection is that this view of justice is unrealistically optimistic. It supposes that if the conventions of justice have stood the test of time and their applications are mistake-free, then justice will prevail because there will be no obstacles left to people having what they deserve and not having what they do not deserve. This supposition is false, it is objected, because it ignores that vices often lead to unjust actions, that resources are often scarce, that people often suffer undeserved misfortune, and that these are often obstacles to justice.

There is a great deal to this objection. Vices, scarcity, and contingency have an important effect on how justice should be understood. The account of justice I have given is not of justice as it is any existing society, but of what a society would be like if it were just. It is perfectly compatible with this description to acknowledge that vices, scarcity, and contingency are likely to be permanent obstacles to a society's actually being just. This, however, does not make this view of justice impractical. On the contrary, it provides an impetus for trying to make one's own society as just as possible in the face of these obstacles. In order to come closer to this highly desirable goal, it must be recognized that justice has two aspects.

One is the distribution of good and bad things, which is what I have been discussing up to now. The other is the rectification of injustice that is bound to occur in distribution as a result of vices, scarcity, and contingency. The standard to which just distribution and rectification should aim to conform is that the good and bad things in life should be proportional to the goodness or badness of their recipients. The fact remains, however, that this standard is unattainable. Scarcity limits just distribution through the insufficiency of available resources. No matter how strong is the commitment to just distribution, if there is not enough money, food, medicine, prison space, police protection, or hospital care available, people cannot have what they deserve. Rectification is concerned with correcting unjust distribution to the extent to which this can be done. Its purpose is to make good and bad things more proportional to what is deserved.

Disproportionality, however, is often an insurmountable obstacle to rectification. Some forms of injustice cannot be rectified. Nothing could compensate people who sacrificed their lives for a noble cause, who were blinded or disfigured in an accident for which they were not responsible, or who were forced to spend the best years of their lives in a concentration camp on trumped-up charges. Nor is there a proportional punishment for mass murderers, torturers, or fanatics who destroy great works of art. No punishment could be commensurate with what is deserved by these evildoers. Disproportionality, therefore, unavoidably limits efforts at rectification.

Vices are also obstacles to justice. The same familiar ones recur throughout recorded human history. Cruelty, greed, destructiveness, selfishness, malevolence, envy, fanaticism, racial, religious, tribal, and ethnic prejudice have motivated people in very different times, places, and circumstances. There is no reason to suppose that in this respect the future will be different from the past. No doubt, the forms in which these and other vices are and will be expressed are bound to change, but they will be expressed and they will cause much injustice to innocent victims. There are, of course, also virtues, but they coexist with the vices in any given society and often in the same person. If vices are part of human nature, as virtues are, then they cannot be eliminated from the human repertoire. The best we can do is to limit their scope.

But even if scarcity and vices could be overcome in some way, the contingency of life will remain and be responsible for much misfortune befalling undeserving victims. Lightning will strike, buildings will collapse, volcanoes will erupt, earthquakes will occur, cancer will strike, metal fatigue will make bridges collapse, viruses will mutate and invade the human immune system, cars, ships, and airplanes will collide because of heart-attacks, and so on and on.

Justice, therefore, does not have the unattainable aim of making society perfectly just, but the much more modest aim of making society as little unjust as scarcity, vices, and contingency allow. The aim is to decrease imperfection, not to achieve perfection. This is a realistic aim that cannot be convicted of undue optimism.

7.5 JUSTICE AS HAVING WHAT ONE DESERVES

I hope it will not be thought that in presenting this view of justice I have offered a theory. What we need is not a theory but a reminder of what we already know: justice prevails in a society when people have what they deserve and do not have what they do not deserve. That we do know that this is what justice requires is shown by the fact that virtually everyone prefers the ordered society to the random one. We prefer it because it is just, whereas the random society is unjust. We all think that our imperfect society would be better if the good and bad things of life were proportional to the goodness or badness of their recipients. Justice aims to make our society less imperfect. Working for this aim does not call for an ideology, a revolution, radical reform, or a theory. It calls for small, everyday efforts, political and personal, to correct injustice. We can do that because we all know in our society what injustice is in a very large number of cases. That in some cases we are not sure, or that people in Timbuktu, Teheran, or Tianjin might disagree, affects what we know as little as the occasional optical illusion affects the reliability of what we see. This is behind the claim I made at the beginning that reasonable people already hold the view of justice I have been defending.

This view of justice is not new. That justice has an essential connection with what is deserved was already a generally accepted view in Plato's time, as we know from Book I of *The Republic*. There always were, of course, controversies about justice, but they were about who deserves what, not whether people should have what they deserve. But if this is the right view of justice, then certain implications follow. One is that justice is essentially inegalitarian because what people deserve varies with their very different relationships, agreements, and with how their very different actions affect the security of others. Justice certainly requires treating equals equally and unequals unequally, but what makes people equal or unequal is what they deserve. It happens only rarely and exceptionally that different people deserve the same things. This view of justice is thus incompatible with egalitarianism. If there is an essential connection between justice and what people deserve, and if different people deserve different things, then egalitarianism, ignoring the essential connection and the differences, is fundamentally mistaken.

Yet another implication of the present view is that the content of justice is likely to differ from society to society, or indeed, with the passage of time, within one and the same society. A society aiming to be just is committed to its members' having what they deserve and not having what they do not deserve. But what is and is not deserved depend on the prevailing conventions. In different societies different relationships, agreements, and actions affecting the security of others are likely to prevail, and these conventions are likely to change with time in all societies. Commitment to justice, therefore, is not commitment to conventions that can be set universally or with finality. It is commitment to treating people as they deserve to be treated, while recognizing that what they deserve depends on variable and changing conventions that have passed the test of time and prompt mistake-free applications. It is necessary for justice that there be such conventions, but it is not necessary that these conventions should have the same content.

The last implication of this view of justice I will mention here concerns reform. All societies need reform because the conventions to which people have to respond change. A society cannot endure unless it adjusts itself to new circumstances. Having some control over change requires asking and answering the question of when reform is desirable and what consequences are likely to follow from it. My view is that reform is desirable if a prevailing convention no longer passes the test of time or prompts mistaken applications. The reason for reform, therefore, is to remedy a specific dissatisfaction with a specific convention. And the reform should be incremental, specific, and no more than is needed for removing the dissatisfaction that prompts it.

Part of the significance of this attitude to reform emerges by noticing that it does not involve reform according to the theory, overall design, general plan, or the distant goal of an ideology; it does not involve wholesale reform, or abandoning conventions that have no discernible shortcomings, or reform simply to try something new. The balanced view is that unless there is dissatisfaction, there is no reason to reform, and when there is no reason to reform, there is reason not to reform. And that reason is that the prevailing conventions enable people to get on with their lives by protecting the political good they need for their well-being. To reform these conventions unnecessarily is to jeopardize them and thus to endanger the well-being of those who live together in a society.

It may happen, of course, that the bulk of the conventions prevailing in a society is seriously defective. In that case, defenders of the balanced view would not be in favor of maintaining them. Societies may be rotten through and through, as we know well from history, and then they should go under. To admit this is damaging only for a view that favors maintaining conventions simply because they have endured. But this is not the balanced view.

Nor is the balanced view committed to holding that justice is the most important political good. Justice is certainly a political good but there are many other political goods, and they may conflict with one another and with justice. It may or may not be reasonable to resolve some of these conflicts in favor of justice. Justice should not be done at all cost. There may be circumstances in which the claim of equality, or liberty, or order, or stability, or health should override the claim of justice. This is true of all political goods, and justice is no exception. How a particular conflict between two political goods should be resolved depends on how the resolution would affect the evaluative framework of a society. It may be reasonable to resolve the same conflict differently in different circumstances.

The justification of the balanced view is simply that if the prevailing conventions regulating agreements, relationships, and actions affecting the security of others, pass the test of time, are tried and true, command the allegiance of people, and prompt mistake-free evaluations, then they have advantages that ideological theories, overall designs, distant goals, and new possibilities lack.

The upshot of this chapter, then, is that the view that justice consists in people having what they deserve and not having what they do not deserve is one of the political goods the balanced view is committed to defending. In conjunction with the other political goods I have already identified it deepens the account of the balanced view. In subsequent chapters I will attempt to deepen it further.

CHAPTER EIGHT

✦ ✦ ✦

THE RIGHT TO PRIVATE PROPERTY

For when men ... have observ'd, that the principal distur-
bance in society arises from those goods, which we call exter-
nal, and from their looseness and easy transition from one
person to another; they must seek for a remedy.... This can
be done after no other manner than by a convention enter'd
into by all members of the society to bestow stability on the
possession of those external goods, and leave every one in the
peacable enjoyment of what he may acquire by his fortune
and industry. By this means every one knows what he may
safely possess ... which is so necessary to their well-being ...
as well to our own.

DAVID HUME
A Treatise of Human Nature

THE SPHERE OF JUSTICE is wide, covering many different areas
of distribution and rectification. One of these areas is the ownership of private property. The aim of this chapter is to consider how
owning it may be justified.

8.1 WHAT IS PRIVATE PROPERTY?

Suppose my hobby is to buy discarded bits and pieces of metal at
junk yards, take them home, weld them together to make various

figures, and then spray paint them. I do it only for my own amusement. I have a Don Quixote, a Zeus, the Devil, and I am now doing an elephant. An art dealer happens to see my handiwork and offers to sell them for me. It turns out that people are eager to buy. I quit my boring job, and make a lot of money by continuing what used to be a hobby. People buy stuff only if it pleases them, the art dealer gets a commission, I become rich, everybody involved is better off and no one is worse off. What could be more innocent?

The figures I make and the money I earn are my property. I think I am entitled to them and that I have a right to do with the figures and the money whatever I want, provided I harm no one. Many people, however, would disagree. They would say: property is theft; it is shameful to enjoy riches when people are starving elsewhere; I ought to be heavily taxed to help raise the living standard of my worse off my fellow citizens; it is immoral to benefit from economic arrangements that perpetuate inequality; it is frivolous to amuse oneself when others live in misery; I am voluntarily participating in a corrupt capitalistic system; and so on. These are often-heard judgments. Yet we are all attached to our property and do not want to be deprived of it. Are we justified? Am I just callous in enjoying my new found wealth? I am going to argue that we are justified, it is not callous to enjoy legitimately acquired property, and these critics are mistaken. For property is essential to our well-being and we have a right to it.

I begin with some assumptions. The first is that the starting point of the justification is where we presently are. The "we" are people living in America. There is a not very long list of political goods we agree about valuing, among them are education, justice, liberty, order, peace, prosperity, public health, security, and stability. Private property is one of these goods. I am assuming that a justification of private property must explain why it is reasonable to value it both in itself and in relation to the other political goods.

The second assumption is about rights. They may be basic or special. Basic rights derive from human nature, and, in that sense, may be thought of as natural. They have also been called universal or human rights. There are some basic needs, for food and sleep for instance, whose satisfaction is a minimum condition of human well-being. Basic rights are the rights we have to pursue such satisfactions. They impose a corresponding obligation on others not to interfere with us as we try to satisfy our basic needs. But neither the rights nor the obligations are absolute or unconditional because, as we have seen in the chapters on liberty and toleration, there are limits on what we may do to obtain the satisfactions and there are justifiable interferences with them. Special rights are attached to our many different positions, relationships, agreements, or activities. They vary with contexts but in a particular context they give rise to specific and restricted rights and obligations. Parents, teachers, employers, patients, consumers, and so forth have such rights and obligations. They derive from legal, political, or moral traditions, rather than from human nature. In that sense, therefore, they may be called conventional.

The third assumption concerns property. The core idea is the ownership of some material object, such as a car, a violin, or a computer. But the idea is often extended to include money, patents, undeveloped resources, shares, future payments, abilities, options, ideas, reputation, and so forth. I will understand property in a relatively narrow sense to include only material objects and money. The issue of justification is difficult enough, and I want to avoid the complications that follow from intangible possessions. If the justification works, it may be extended beyond the narrow sense.

It is also necessary to distinguish between possessions and property. I may possess a car because I stole it or bought it from someone who stole it. It is in my possession, but it is not my property because I came to possess it illegally. Property is legal possession. Nor should property be confused with wealth. I may own property and be poor. Wealth is to have property in abundance. The justification of property, therefore, is not the justification of wealth. Furthermore, property need not be privately owned. It may be owned jointly by several people; or by some collectivity, such as a cooperative, a church, or a labor union; or by a state, as are roads or parks. The justification of the right to private property must do more, therefore, than justify the right to property. It may be that a collectivity or a state has a right to property but individuals do not. My concern, then, is with the justification of the right to the less than abundant legal possession of private property.

The right to private property, understood in the light of the above assumptions, is then a special, conventional right, not a basic, natural one. A basic right is to the satisfaction of a basic need but the need for private property is not basic. Basic needs may be satisfied by distributions from collective or state property and many people (sworn to poverty for one reason or another) may enjoy well-being without owning anything. There may be a basic right to seeking private property, but, if there is, it is a right to liberty, not to property. The right to private property is to owning it, and that always depends on the specific requirements of the relevant laws, which differ from context to context. That is why the right to private property is special and conventional, rather than basic, universal, general, natural, or human. But what precisely is the right to private property a right to?

It is the right to possessing and using material resources within legally defined limits. Each constituent of this right—possession, use, and limits—is in turn constituted of several more specific rights. The right to private property, therefore, is a bundle of rights, not a single one. And the more specific rights that constitute the bundle typically vary with societies, legal systems, and changes in specific laws. Reference to the right to private property, then, is nothing more than a convenient shorthand. Two societies may each be committed to the right of private property but interpret the right quite differently.

The right to possessing private property includes having exclusive control of it; deriving income from it; holding it without time limit; having legal protection against its expropriation, theft, or unwanted destruction; and so forth. The right to using it includes deciding whether, how, or when to use it; permitting others to use it; consuming, modifying, or destroying it; selling, exchanging, bequeathing it, or giving it away as a gift; and so forth. And the limits include not having acquired it in a legally impermissible way and using it in ways that do not harm others.

8.2 THE IMPORTANCE OF PRIVATE PROPERTY

The importance of private property is that it enables us to control how we live. A good society must be committed to the protection of the right to private property because a society is made good by protecting the conditions on which the well-being of its members depends. And, I am supposing, having control of one's life is one of these conditions. Private property, according to this view, is an indispensable means of control. By control I mean directing how one lives: forming intentions, having the opportunity to carry them out, and then doing so. The intention must be uncoerced by external or internal pressures that are irresistible or unacceptably costly to resist. The opportunity to carry them out depends on favorable external conditions, such as order, prosperity, peace, and so forth, and on possessing the necessary resources. And the resulting action must be judged by the agent as an acceptable way of achieving the intended result. Private property is a necessary part of this process because it provides the needed resources.

By control, therefore, I do not mean domination. It does not involve lording it over others, subjugating nature, imposing one's will, or being obsessed with the minute details of daily life. To control one's life is to be one's own master, not to be at the mercy of the will or kindness of others, to make decisions for oneself, and to live with the consequences. Private property is a means to this kind of control because the intentions we form, the opportunities we seek, and the activities we engage in are centrally concerned with the satisfaction of our needs.

Some of these needs, as we have seen, are the basic needs of subsistence but, of course, we have many different needs beyond subsistence. Among them are the needs for psychological and financial security; relief from drudgery; interesting and rewarding work; a good marriage; possessing the tools of one's trade, such as a first-rate instrument for a concert violinist, books for a scholar, a well-lit studio for a painter, a good stove for a chef, reliable equipment for a rock climber; we all need some privacy and enjoyable distraction from work; we need a car to travel to work and shop, decent housing to live in, a computer to keep records and communicate with others; and so forth. I will refer to these needs jointly as secondary.

Basic and secondary needs are alike in their satisfaction being a requirement of our well-being, but they also differ because all human beings have the same basic needs, whereas we differ in what secondary needs we have. Calling these needs basic and secondary is not intended to suggest that the former are more important than the latter. Soul-destroying work, being prevented from pursuing our chosen profession, an unhappy marriage, or prolonged insecurity are as incompatible with well-being as starvation or sleeplessness. The satisfaction of both basic and secondary needs is essential for our well-being but we can satisfy them only if we have the required resources, and that is why the right to private property is indispensable for controlling how we live.

There still remains the point that recognizing the importance of property for well-being is not the same as recognizing the importance of private property for it because property may be owned by a collectivity or by the state. Why should the private ownership of property be important? Because it allows us to control how we live, whereas collective or state ownership would take control from us and transfer it to others. If this happened, forming and executing intentions would no longer be up to us but become subject to the approval or disapproval of those who distribute the resources we need. This would be an unacceptable interference with liberty and destroy our well-being, since no one acting on behalf of a collectivity or a state could possibly know nearly as well as we ourselves do what secondary needs we have and what would be an adequate satisfaction of them. No society committed to the well-being of its members could be in favor of depriving them of the control of how they live. Since that control depends on the right to private property, collective or state ownership is not a viable option, as we know from the dismal failure of all Communist regimes.

The reasons against collective or state ownership are not reasons against a society limiting in various ways the right to possess and use private property. There is obviously need for such limits because a society must coordinate the endeavors of its members to control how they live. Appropriate limits make it illegitimate to possess and use material resources in ways that prevent others from doing the same. The scarcity of resources necessitates additional limits because resources often have to be competed for and this has the unavoidable consequence that the acquisition of one person prevents the acquisition of others. The terms of legitimate competition must be set, and this further limits what individuals can do to obtain and use resources they need to control how they live. We inevitably chafe under such limits but if they are reasonable and no more extensive than what is needed to make the possession and use of private property secure, then we should recognize their necessity and stay within them.

It would be a mistake to think that the just-completed explanation of the importance of the right to private property is also an adequate justification of it. For the explanation tacitly presupposes one or another much too simple and far too problematic justification, as I will now proceed to show. I will not examine their details because what I find problematic are their overall strategies. These justifications are based on interest, entitlement, and utility.

✦ ✦ ✦

8.3 SIMPLE JUSTIFICATIONS AND THEIR PROBLEMS

The interest-based justifications proceed in the following way. We have needs and it is in our interest to satisfy them. Doing so depends on having the necessary resources and on being able to use them as we see fit. The right to private property is the right to having and controlling the use of resources we require for satisfying our needs. The justification of this right is that it serves everyone's interest. Since a good society must protect its members' well-being, and since the right to private property is essential for their well-being, a good society will provide legal protection for that right.

The problem with this attempted justification is a consequence of human fallibility. We may be wrong to have a need we rightly feel we have (e.g. for murdering a rival); or to feel a need we in fact do not have (e.g. as hypochondriacs do for medical treatment), or not to feel a need we should feel (e.g. as the ignorant do not for education). Individual well-being, therefore, does not depend on satisfying the needs we feel we have but on satisfying the needs we really have. If the justification of the right to private property is that our interest depends on it, then a good society will not leave it to our discretion to control our resources since we may use them contrary to our interests. Why should a good society protect a right to misuse scarce resources? Much more needs to be said, therefore, to justify the right to private property than merely that it enables us to satisfy our needs. But the more is said, the less control will be left to us, and the more tenuous the right will become. A good society, therefore, may well conclude that the collective or state ownership of property better serves the interests of its members than private ownership, or that there are often good reasons for interfering with the right to private property.

This problem is not unsolvable of course. My point in calling attention to it is to show that much more is required than a simple appeal to needs and to the importance of satisfying them. For needs and satisfactions must be limited, and setting reasonable limits unavoidably appeals to considerations other than our judgments about our needs and interests. There are complex moral, economic, legal, and psychological issues that must be considered and their respective importance must be weighed in order to decide what limits are reasonable. The interest-based justification is much too simple for that. It founders on the problem of limits.

The entitlement-based justification of the right to private property has several versions, distinguished mainly by what they base entitlement on. According to the earliest version, individuals are entitled to a piece of property if they mixed their labor with generally available resources and after they have done so enough is left of the resource for others to do likewise if they wish. Those who acquire the right to a piece of property in this manner can sell, exchange, or bequeath it. Other people, then, may acquire a right to it if they receive it from the original owner by one of these means.

There is no doubt that this justification holds good in some cases, but a little thought shows that it does not hold in many others. Suppose I hire a person to build a house for me and he does. He mixes his labor with it and he may do it very well but he certainly does not acquire the right to the house. The house is mine even though I have neither mixed my labor with it nor have I acquired it from someone who did. The builder is entitled to payment for his labor but not to anything more. Take another case. I buy a lottery ticket, win a sum of money, invest it in a mutual fund, and the money grows. I am clearly entitled to the proceeds but I have done nothing remotely resembling mixing my labor with the money I won. For these reasons, among others, contemporary defenders of an entitlement-based justification tend to back away from the emphasis on mixing labor with property and concentrate on present possession.

They also begin with intuitively appealing cases, such as that of a fictional Wilt Chamberlain. He is a great basketball player and people willingly pay again and again a lot of money to see him practice his artistry. He becomes wealthy and he is entitled to his wealth. He cheated no one, he delivered what people expected, everyone was better off, and no one was worse off. He has a right to do what he pleases with the money he has earned: he can spend it, invest it, give it away, leave it to his children, use it to support a cause he believes in, and so forth. Who could reasonably doubt that he has the right to possess and use what he has acquired in this way? A critic could.

A critic might say, to begin with, that the case has intuitive appeal only to those who share the conventions on which the case rests. But these conventions are deplorable, sharing them is a sign of corruption, and a society would be better off without them. One of these conventions is the commercialization of sports. It is a bad thing for a society that a great athlete, like Wilt Chamberlain, sells his talent for money. He does with basketball what prostitutes do with sex. People should be free to pay money for either, but surely a society should not encourage it and it should not model the right to private property on such dubious cases. And it is not just Wilt Chamberlain who demeans himself. Those who pay to watch him also do so because by finding enjoyment in the passive observation of an endlessly repetitive activity, they betray a great vacuum in their inner lives.

Now my point is not that these critics are right to condemn commercial sports. The point is that they are right to claim that the Wilt Chamberlain case rests on conventions it presupposes but does not justify. This entitlement-based justification simply takes the conventions for granted. The acquisition of possessions in conformity to prevailing conventions does not by itself entitle people to what they possess. A less obviously biased case will strengthen this point.

After the collapse of Communism many ex-Communist nations privatized previously state-owned enterprises. The states came to own them by expropriation when the Communists took power. After the collapse, laws governing privatization were enacted and the expropriated enterprises went up for sale. But the only people who had the money to buy them were members of the Communist elite who expropriated them in the first place. Thus the old discredited Communist elite transformed itself into the new super-rich capitalist elite. They acquired their new possessions in accordance with the recently established conventions. There is surely something wrong with these new conventions if they allow such blatant injustice. No reasonable person could say that the Communist elite have a right to such possessions.

The problem with this entitlement-based justification is that the conventions that entitle us to our possessions need to be examined and justified. But they cannot be justified on the basis of entitlement because that would simply assume that the conventions appealed to have been justified and that, of course, is precisely what is in question. The justification of the conventions, therefore, must proceed in some other way. Regardless of what that way is, the need for it is a conclusive reason for thinking that the entitlement-based justification is insufficient. We do not and should not have a right to all of our possession. But to draw a reasonable distinction between possessions to which we ought to have a right and those to which we ought not is a complex question that cannot be settled appealing to prevailing conventions. Perhaps the prevailing conventions should not prevail. The entitlement-based justification, therefore, is too simple to solve the problem of legitimate possession.

The utility-based justification postulates a good it takes to be essential for human well-being and then argues that the protection of the right to private property is necessary for the efficient pursuit of the postulated good. The versions of this justification differ because they postulate different goods. The version I will discuss has liberty as the good. The argument has a constructive and a critical component. The constructive one aims to show that liberty is necessary for our well-being because it enables us to decide how we want to live and allows us to choose without interference between the available alternatives. Liberty should be curtailed only to prevent interference with the liberty of others. By protecting the right to private property a society enables its members to enjoy the resources needed for the meaningful use of liberty. The critical component of the argument shows that collective or state ownership of property leads to an unjustifiable restriction of liberty.

In my opinion, the utility-based justification is correct in both its constructive and critical claims, but nevertheless falls short of providing an adequate justification of the right to private property. The fundamental reason for this is that, although it is undoubtedly true that liberty is necessary for our well-being, it is also true that there are other goods necessary for it. Liberty and these other goods routinely conflict, and there may be strong reasons for curtailing liberty in order to secure the other goods. Some examples of the other necessary goods are education, justice, order, peace, prosperity, public health, security, and stability.

It is one of the most obvious features of contemporary politics that liberty can be used and prosperity can be pursued in ways detrimental to these other necessary goods. It is similarly obvious that protecting these other goods may require curtailing liberty and prosperity. Goods we rightly recognize as necessary for our well-being often conflict. The reasonable resolution of these conflicts is to balance the conflicting goods so as to have as much as possible of all the goods we need. It cannot be reasonably supposed that when liberty and prosperity conflict with one or more of these other necessary goods, then liberty and prosperity should always take precedence over them. The circumstances in which it is reasonable to curtail liberty and prosperity are those in which it is reasonable to curtail the right to private property.

What are these circumstances? They are, for example, those in which the right to private property is used in ways that endanger public health, such as the discharge of industrial waste into rivers, advertising cigarettes to adolescents, or selling unsafe cars. Or when it threatens security, such as selling sophisticated weapon systems to terrorists, or using scarce resources needed for defense to produce more profitable luxury goods. Or when it puts stability at risk, such as resulting in great inequalities between those who possess private property in abundance and those who barely have enough for subsistence. These examples, of course, can be multiplied.

Defenders of the utility-based justification may respond by acknowledging the necessity of these other goods for human well-being, but arguing that liberty should still take precedence over them because these other goods can be pursued only by people who have and can make choices freely. And these are the conditions that liberty provides. I think this response is correct but it still fails to show either that liberty should have precedence over the other goods when they conflict, or that the right to private property should not be curtailed. For just as the pursuit of other goods presupposes liberty, so the pursuit of liberty presupposes, among other things, education, justice, order, peace, prosperity, public health, security, or stability.

In our complex contemporary circumstances, liberty cannot be meaningfully pursued unless there is a general understanding of the alternatives among which we can choose. This presupposes education. In an anarchic society, everyone is at risk, liberty is severely curtailed by the necessity of self-protection because no one's private property is safe. The liberty we cherish is possible only because there is adequate order and security in our society. When we use liberty to make choices, we make predictions about how the various alternatives would be likely to affect us in the future. These predictions presuppose stability. In the midst of war and epidemic, everyone's well-being depends on commandeering resources and severely restricting the liberty of choices about medical care, travel, and providing necessary services. Our enjoyment of liberty is possible only because public health is protected and peace is maintained.

These rather obvious observations make it clear that the goods necessary for our well-being are interdependent and mutually presuppose and strengthen one another. The utility-based justification is correct to insist that the right to private property must be protected if we are to have a free and prosperous society. But it is mistaken in forgetting that the pursuit of these important goods conflicts with pursuit of other important goods, that the reasonable resolution of such conflicts requires balancing the important goods, and that achieving a reasonable balance is possible only if we resign ourselves to having less liberty than we would like in order to secure other important goods, albeit they too to a lesser extent than we would like. This is the problem of balancing goods, and the utility-based justification of the right to private property is too simple to cope with it.

I conclude that the attempted justifications of the right to private property based on interest, entitlement, and utility are inadequate. I say inadequate, not wrong, because they are right to stress the importance of the interest we all have in satisfying our needs, of having resources to which we are entitled, and of enjoying liberty. And they are right also to stress the importance of private property for all this. But they nevertheless fail to justify the right to private property because they cannot cope with the problem of how to set reasonable limits to that right, how to identify legitimate possessions, and how to balance important goods. We need a complex justification for that.

8.4 A COMPLEX JUSTIFICATION

The complex justification I will now defend combines what I take to be right in the three simple justifications, overcomes their inadequacies, and replaces a shared assumption that leads them astray with a more realistic one. The fundamental reason why the justifications of the right to private property based on interest, entitlement, and utility are too simple is their assumption that there is some one thing—perhaps a canonical principle, or a conclusive theory, or a highest good—that makes the justification adequate. They disagree about what that thing is but they agree that an adequate justification must be based it. The complex justification I will now propose and try to defend rejects this assumption for three reasons.

One is that the right to private property is a bundle of rights and the components of the bundle need to be justified differently. These components are the possession, use, and limits of private property. The second reason is that the various rights to private property must be justified differently in different contexts. It is highly unlikely that its justified possession, use, and limits would be the same in feudal, revolutionary, post-Communist, ex-colonial, tribal, impoverished, affluent, agrarian, industrial, authoritarian, and democratic societies. And the third reason is that an adequate justification must cope with the problems of setting reasonable limits, identifying legitimate possessions, and balancing goods. These problems, as we have seen, introduce serious complexities. I will proceed by showing how possessions, uses, and limits may be justified in our context, that is, in contemporary, affluent, industrial, and democratic societies.

The justification of the possession of private property begins with accepting much of the entitlement-based justification. Possession, as opposed to use within limits, is justified if a piece of private property has been acquired legitimately. And the legitimacy of its acquisition depends on conformity to prevailing conventions. The problem with the entitlement-based justification is that it presupposes but does not justify the prevailing conventions, which, of course, may be unacceptable for numerous reasons. The complex justification, therefore, must do what the entitlement-based one fails to do. How, then, can the prevailing conventions be justified?

The first step is to remind ourselves of just how plausible are at least some of these conventions. Take those involved in agreements, for example. Two parties make a formal or informal agreement to the effect that one will do a job, lease an apartment, or sell a car and the other will pay wages, rent, or the purchase price. The performance of the first creates an entitlement to a possession that the second should transfer to the first. Or consider conventions involved in relationships. Parents should pay for a decent upbringing of their children, married couples should pool their resources, investors should get a share of the profit. Such relationships create entitlements to what their explicit or implicit terms specify. A large part of these entitlements is constituted of the unspoken conventions in the background. And these conventions are obvious and well-known to people of normal intelligence who live together in the context of a society. The obviousness of the conventions, however, may just show that they are customary and prevalent in the context, but not that they are justified.

The second step is to show what would justify them. My claim is that they are justified if they have stood the test of time. And by that I mean, as I have explained in the preceding chapter (7.3), that they are enduring, people conform to them voluntarily because they are important for their well-being.

There is, of course, no society in which all prevailing conventions about the ownership of private property are in this happy state. Some of the conventions are routinely questioned and then they need to be justified, reformed, or abandoned. This is what happened to primogeniture, to a husband controlling his wife's property, or to imprisoning those who have defaulted on a debt. And this is what seems to be happening now to inheritance and capital gains taxes. It may also happen that most of the conventions are being questioned and their justifications are found wanting. Then the society in which this happens is disintegrating and it is on the brink of revolution, as France was in 1789 and Russia in 1917.

The essential point is that according to complex justification, the possession of private property is legitimate if it has been acquired in accordance with enduring conventions to which voluntary conformity continues to be widespread because it is rightly assumed to be a condition of the well-being of those who live together in a particular society. This justification resolves the problem of legitimate possession on which the entitlement-based justification foundered. But it is nowhere near the end of the matter because it says nothing about the justified uses and limits of legitimately possessed private property.

The Right to Private Property

I turn next to the problem that arises in the context of the utility-based justification of the right to private property. That justification is, it will be remembered, that liberty is an important good because it is necessary for our well-being. But liberty requires the protection of the right to private property because it is the right to the resources that enable us to control how we live. Making use of the right to private property, therefore, is one way in which we enjoy the advantages of liberty.

The problem with this justification is not with any of its claims, which I think are correct, but with its failure to take into account other no less plausible claims. As we have seen, these other claims are made on behalf of goods other than liberty that are also necessary for our well-being. Some of them are education, justice, order, peace, prosperity, public health, security, and stability. The problem is that the enjoyment of these goods often requires limiting liberty and thereby limiting the right to private property. We need to know what limits are reasonable and how to balance the conflicting claims of all the important goods we need for our well-being. In this way, the problems of balancing goods and setting reasonable limits to the claim of each good are closely connected. If the complex justification is to be an improvement over the utility-based justification, it must resolve both problems. How may this be done?

It is clear, I hope, that it would be arbitrary to resolve such conflicts by assuming that one or two of these goods is always more important for our well-being than any of the others. For there are reasonable disagreements about the respective importance of acknowledged goods and they should not just be ignored. There may be, and have been, numerous circumstances in which order, public health, or security, for instance, justified some restrictions of liberty. But if the conflicts cannot be reasonably resolved by attributing overriding importance to one of the goods we obviously need for our well-being, then how could they be resolved?

Their reasonable resolution depends on bearing in mind three considerations. The first is that their resolutions rarely involves an all-or-none decision. Usually it is a matter of deciding how much of each we can have, so we will typically have to make a decision about the extent to which we can have one without endangering the other. The protection of security may require restricting liberty by requiring everyone to carry forgery-proof identification. Or the protection of public health may require stringent curbs on pollution. The decision, then, does not usually involve choosing one or the other but deciding how much of each we should have.

The second consideration is that what makes a resolution arbitrary is to decide once and for all which good or goods should have priority over the others. The avoidance of this arbitrariness does not mean that we could not or should not decide that one good is more important than another in a particular context. Arbitrariness enters only if we decide to maintain the same order of priority in other, not yet encountered, contexts. It may be that security is more important than liberty in a context where liberty is already extensive and the threats against security are serious. But if in another context liberty is already curtailed and the threats to security are negligible, then their priority should be reversed. Reasonable conflict-resolutions vary with contexts. They exclude only context-independent resolutions and acknowledge the necessity of assigning temporary priority to one of the conflicting goods in a particular context.

The third consideration is that at any given time in a society there are many goods whose necessity for well-being is generally recognized. These goods, together with the conventions that protect them and the traditions from which they are derived, form the evaluative framework of a society. And this framework is always more important than any of the particular goods that are part of it. Reasonable conflict-resolutions, therefore, have a standard to which they can appeal. This standard is the respective importance of the conflicting goods to the protection of the evaluative framework. Whether a particular conflict-resolution is reasonable does not, then, depend on which of the conflicting goods is more important for well-being in a particular context. It depends, rather, on deciding which of the conflicting goods is more important for the protection of the evaluative framework. Thinking only about the respective importance of the conflicting goods is bound to go wrong because it fails to take into account the effect of the resolution on the other goods that form the evaluative framework. This is just what the utility-based justification failed to do. The complex justification involves thinking about how the whole framework would be affected by a particular conflict-resolution. It is just as concerned with well-being as the utility-based one but it recognizes that at any time in any context well-being depends on the protection of many goods, not just on one or two of them.

The complex justification, therefore, resolves the problems of finding a reasonable balance of goods and setting reasonable limits to the pursuit of goods in the same way: by appealing to the standard constituted of the evaluative framework of a society. Reasonable balance is one that best protects the framework in a particular context and a reasonable limit is one that restricts one, or perhaps both, of the goods in order to protect the framework. Liberty and the right to private property may be reasonably limited if doing so is necessary for securing the other goods on which well-being also depends.

It may be objected to the complex justification that it does precisely what it criticizes the utility-based justification for doing: arbitrarily assigning priority to a particular good and resolving conflicts in its favor. But this objection rests on a misunderstanding of the standard to which the complex justification appeals. The standard is not a particular good but all the goods, conventions, and traditions that form the framework. And the appeal to it is not arbitrary because the goods that form the system are recognized as necessary for well-being in the context of a particular society. No one can reasonably suppose that education, justice, order, peace, prosperity, public health, security, and stability, to which we may add liberty, are arbitrarily regarded as goods. The serious question about them is not whether they are really good but which of them should have priority when they conflict. And it is the serious question that is answered by the complex justification.

We have now seen how the complex justification justifies the possession of private property and the limits on its use. From this it is but a small step to providing a justification for the remaining component of the right to private property: its actual use. Private property provides resources we can use to satisfy our needs. As the interest-based justification rightly claims, it is in our vital interest to have a right to the use of private property. What the interest-based justification fails to note is that we may misuse the private property we have by satisfying needs that should not be satisfied and by not satisfying needs that we should satisfy. What specifically constitutes the misuse of private property and how can it be avoided?

The number of ways in which we can misuse private property is large and depressing. We may be led to it by self-deception, stupidity, addiction, neurosis, vindictiveness, fanaticism, taking unreasonable risks, and so on and on. Legal and political strictures against misuse cannot possible take into account such subjective ways of wasting our resources by using them contrary to our interests. Protection of the right to private property must proceed, therefore, by thinking of interests in impersonal terms, that is, as interests that any normal adult in a particular context is going to have. The misuse of private property, then, may be understood as using it in ways that violate other people's interests impersonally conceived.

We can go a step further in specifying the ways in which the interests of others may be violated by drawing on what I have already said about justified possessions and limits. The misuse of private property is to use it in ways that prevents others from trying to acquire private property legitimately or from using it in ways that does not interfere with how others use their legitimately acquired private property. Another approach to specifying its misuse is that it prevents others from using their private property within reasonable limits, that is, in ways that are not contrary to the evaluative framework on which everyone's well-being depends in a particular context. Legitimate acquisition and reasonable limits, then, define an area of discretion within which we should have the right to use our private property in any way we see fit. If we use it within our area of discretion, we may still misuse it of course, but we can blame only ourselves if thereby our interests suffer. The proper business of politics and law is to protect our rights to private property, not to protect us from harming ourselves.

In summary of this account of complex justification, it may be said that the justification of the right to private property depends on justifying its possession, use, and limits. Possession is justified if it has been acquired legitimately in accordance with prevailing conventions that are enduring, voluntarily adhered to, and serve the well-being of those who conform to them. Limits are justified if they are set by the evaluative framework on which everyone's well-being depends. And uses are justified within our area of discretion. This explains the importance of private property by interpreting it as the means of controlling resources we need for our well-being. It avoids the problems that beset the entitlement, utility, and interest-based justifications. And it offers a separate justification of the possession, use, and limits of private property.

8.5 THE RIGHT TO PRIVATE PROPERTY

The complex justification is limited in a number of ways. It follows from its conventional character that the justification is context-dependent. For the justification of the possession, uses, and limits of private property depends on the conventions that prevail in a particular context. But these conventions may be quite different in contexts other than contemporary democracies. The question of whether the right to private property is as important in other contexts as it is in ours may well be reasonably answered differently in other contexts.

The complex justification is limited also because the right to private property conflicts with one or more of equally important other goods and it is not a foregone conclusion that it should take precedence over the others. The complex justification, therefore, is conditional on the absence of such conflicts, or, if the conflicts occur, then on its being reasonable to resolve them in favor of the right to private property.

A further limit is that I interpreted property to include only tangible goods and money and to exclude intangible goods, such as patents, abilities, reputations, options, and so forth. The complex justification may be extended to include these intangible goods as well, but I have not done so. This leaves the possibility of its successful extension open.

Lastly, the complex justification treats private property as a means necessary for controlling how we live. But we often possess private property far in excess of the means necessary for control and far in excess even of what is needed as a margin of safety. I have said nothing about the justification of the right to excess private property. I think it can be justified but I have not done so.

If we bear these qualification in mind, we can say, I think, that we have very good reasons for protecting the right to private property in American society. For that right is a condition of our well-being. We can, then, add the right to private property to the list of political goods that the balanced view is committed to defending: reason as prudence, the plurality of goods, the necessity of limits, limited liberty, toleration within reason, and justice as having what one deserves.

CHAPTER NINE

+   +   +

EQUALITY AS
THE EXCLUSION OF
ARBITRARINESS

*Democratic nations are at all times fond of equality, but
there are certain epochs at which the passion they entertain
for it swells to the height of fury. . . . [It] penetrates on every
side into men's hearts, expands there, and fills them entirely.
Tell them not that by this blind surrender of themselves to an
exclusive passion, they risk their dearest interests; they are
deaf. Show them not freedom escaping from their grasp, whilst
they are looking another way: they are blind—or rather, they
can discern but one sole object to be desired in the universe.*

ALEXIS DE TOCQUEVILLE
Democracy in America

OF ALL THE BASIC POLITICAL GOODS equality is perhaps the
most controversial. The reason for this is not that its importance is
doubted but that egalitarianism threatens to become the dominant
ideology in America and it inflates the importance of equality at the
expense of liberty, justice, and right to property. The controversies
about equality center on where its reasonable limits lie. If a society
values limited liberty, justice aimed at people having what they
deserve, and the right to private property, then the inevitable outcome will be unequal possession of resources, including not just
tangible goods and money but also diet, education, health care,

housing, and other conditions of well-being. Inequalities in these respects would emerge even if a society were to assure what no society could: the equal social conditions of all its members. For people differ in their characters, talents and weaknesses, capacities and incapacities, virtues and vices, in their religious, moral, political, and aesthetic views, in their attitudes to work, authority, sex, death, money, comfort, and so forth. As a result of these internal differences, they will differ in what they make of their social conditions, even if their conditions were identical. Egalitarians regard the resulting inequalities unacceptable and they are committed to limiting liberty, justice, and property rights in order to reduce the inequality of resources. The aim of this chapter is to defend equality against the egalitarian inflation of it. Equality is an important political good, but it is only one of the important political goods. A good society needs to balance all the important goods in order to assure the optimal enjoyment of all of them.

9.1 EQUALITY VS. EGALITARIANISM

It is possible that the fame of the Texas Rose Rustlers Society has not yet reached readers of these words. They may want to know then that its members prize roses that survive unattended in the wilds of Texas, having eluded the benevolent attention of gardeners. As all respectable societies, the Texas Rose Rustlers has bylaws stating the principles that unite its members. Here are some of them: there is more than one way of being beautiful; good climates are in the eye of the beholder; if you are attacked by disease, abandonment, or a bad chain of events, do not despair, there is always the chance that you were bred to be tough; and everyone should not smell the same. I mention these admirable principles because they reflect a vision profoundly at odds with the egalitarian one.

If we reject this vision because we think of the roses that perished that they were not bred to be tough enough to flourish when beset by a really bad chain of events, then we will want that benevolent gardener, the government, to step in and arrange matters so that everyone will smell, perhaps not as well as wild roses do, but well enough not to stink of misery. For this, however, there is a price to be paid. As Tocqueville said, there will be "an innumerable multitude of men all equal and alike. . . . Above this race of men stands an immense tutelary power, which takes it upon itself to secure their gratifications, and to watch over their faith. . . . For their happiness such a government willingly labours . . . it provides for their security, foresees and supplies their necessities, facilitates their pleasures, manages their principal concerns, dictates their industry, regulates the descent of property, and subdivides their inheritances—what remains, but to spare them all the care of thinking and all the trouble of living."

There is a choice to be made between these two visions but it is not as stark as these visions have it. Perhaps it is possible to keep apart impersonal contexts in which equality should prevail and personal contexts in which it should not. In the personal one roses could flourish. And if the impersonal one is not allowed to swallow up the personal, then a government could protect some of the conditions in which flourishing is possible without relieving us of "all the trouble of living." It was this possibility, I think, that Jefferson had in mind when he memorably wrote that "all Men are created equal . . . endowed . . . with inalienable rights . . . among these are Life, Liberty, and the Pursuit of Happiness."

It is not a trivial point that Jefferson wrote about equal rights to the pursuit of happiness, not to happiness. He thought, and America was founded on the assumption, that the government should protect —impersonally and equally—the rights of citizens to life, liberty, and the pursuit of happiness, but it should be left to their discretion what they may do with the rights they are guaranteed to have. And what they may do with them is likely to vary because of their very different personal qualities and preferences.

The impersonal context includes politics and the law. Political and legal rights and obligations are the same for all citizens regardless of their personal differences. The personal context includes moral, religious, economic, and aesthetic preferences; personal attitudes toward significant areas of life; and choices and cultivation of styles of life. The impersonal context of politics and the law is the proper sphere of equality. Any attempt to extend equality to the personal context must be at the expense of individual liberty and responsibility. But this is just the extension that egalitarians favor.

The principle that guides equality in the impersonal context is that in respect to their political and legal rights and obligations citizens ought to be treated alike unless there is a relevant difference between them. This requirement has two crucial implications. One is that it is wrong to treat people differently if in the relevant respects they are alike. Slavery was wrong because in the relevant respect of the capacity for human agency slaves were no different from those who were free. The other is that it is right to treat people differently if there are relevant differences between them. Depriving criminals of their liberty is right because in the relevant respect of law-abidingness they differ from other citizens.

According to the balanced view, the political good of equality requires that citizens should have equal political and legal rights and responsibilities. According to the egalitarian view, equality requires that the resources citizens need for their well-being should be equal. Egalitarians, therefore, understand equality to include not just equal political and legal rights and responsibilities but also equal resources. And they claim that equality thus understood is not just a political good, but the most important of all the political goods.

What is the justification of this egalitarian claim? What is the reason for supposing that the most important political good is that a society should protect equally the well-being of moral and immoral, law-abiding and criminal, reasonable and unreasonable people? Why should this be the most important good, especially if we bear in mind that the protection requires very costly systems of security, health care, education, and law enforcement? These systems must be paid for by taxation. Egalitarians require that the taxes be used to benefit equally those who maintain and those who violate the basic conditions of other people's well-being, or of those who have shown themselves to use well and those who have systematically misused the basic conditions of their own well-being? Why is the equal protection of these conditions more important than liberty, justice, and the right to private property? Egalitarians recognize that these questions require answers, and they give several, which I will discuss in the next three sections.

9.2 Unequal Resources

It is obvious and common ground shared by friends and foes of egalitarianism that in all known societies there are people who are better off and others who are worse off, and often there is a great difference in the resources the better and the worse off have available for their uses. On the basis of this truism, egalitarians go on to make a number of controversial claims. One is that the mere existence of a difference between the better and worse off is morally objectionable. Another is that morality requires the redistribution of resources from the better to the worse off. And a third is that the elimination or at least the reduction of the difference between the better and the worse off is the most important political good and it overrides the importance of any other political good that may conflict with it. I think that none of these claims is defensible.

That the mere existence of a considerable difference between the better and the worse off is not morally objectionable is quickly shown if the better off happen to have an annual income of $200,000 and the worse off merely $100,000. There is nothing morally wrong with that sort of inequality. From which it follows that inequality as such has no moral implication. What egalitarians find morally objectionable is that many of those who are worse off are much lower down on the economic scale. They think that reducing this difference is politically more important than protecting liberty, justice, private property, or any other political good. And the way to do that is to take resources from the better off and give them to the worse off.

I am going to argue that this is an unreasonable and morally unacceptable view, but before I give reasons against it I want to show that I am not attacking a straw man, that leading egalitarians actually hold this view. One example is Ronald Dworkin's claim that "a distribution of wealth that dooms some citizens to a less fulfilling life than others, no matter what choices they make, is unacceptable, and the neglect of equality in contemporary politics is therefore shameful." (Many further examples and references are in the Notes to this chapter).

Two considerations will show just how repugnant these views are. The first is to stress the central relevance of a question egalitarians conspicuously do not ask, namely, how the better and the worse off came to be in their positions. The second is to point at the likely consequences that would follow from doing what egalitarians claim should be done. I begin with the first.

It clearly makes a considerable moral difference whether the better off became better off by means fair or foul. Suppose their resources were acquired criminally. There is good reason, then, to deprive them of their ill-gotten gains, but that reason has nothing to do with equality. Justice requires that people should not benefit from crimes they have committed. Suppose, however, that the better off acquired resources legitimately, say as a result of having found a way to satisfy needs people have. They have designed and built cheaper, better, more lasting housing than what was previously available. They became better off by benefiting others. They worked by the rules, they are entitled to their earnings, they have done nothing wrong and much good. There is here nothing morally objectionable.

Consider now why the worse off might be in that position. One possibility is that misfortune befell them through no fault of their own. They were seriously injured in an accident for which no one could be blamed, or they contracted a disease that ruined their health, or they lost their job as a result of foreign competition and are too old to compete successfully with younger applicants for the available jobs. There is certainly a moral case for helping such people, but that case, once again, has nothing to do with equality. It has to do with pity, fellow-feeling, sympathy that decent people living together in a society feel toward those who have suffered unmerited misfortune. Another possibility is that it is the fault of the worse off that they are in that position. They took stupid risks and lost, or they cannot hold a job because they lack sufficient discipline, or they live thoughtlessly and waste the resources they have. Such people are worse off as a result of their irresponsibility. Their irresponsibility does not make others responsible for doing for them what they could but fail to do for themselves. The self-created inequality of those who are worse off through their own fault imposes no obligation on anyone to alleviate the hardships they have brought upon themselves.

Egalitarians, however, are unimpressed by the obvious moral differences I have just described. They think that it ought to be the highest priority of a decent society to eliminate or reduce the difference between the better off and the worse off regardless of how they came to be better or worse off because the mere fact that one has more than the other is morally objectionable. It makes no difference if the worse off are responsible for their position or if the better off earned what they have. Egalitarians condemn all societies as immoral unless they recognize that overcoming inequality is the highest political good to which all other political goods must be subordinated. Consider now in concrete terms two possible cases in which the egalitarian view prevails.

Take two high schools drop-outs, both from poor families. One starts to work in a low-paying job in a firm and slowly, over the years, rises through the ranks. He now has a decent middle-class existence, owns a house, pays the mortgage, saves to send his children to college, although his wife also has to work. The other has never held a job, supports a drug habit by petty crimes, bets on horses and gambles in other ways, although not very successfully, and maintains a hand-to-mouth existence. The egalitarian view is that the highest moral obligation of a society is to take resources from the worker and give them to the non-worker.

In another case, two homeowners live side by side in a housing development. They have comparable well-paying jobs, but one is profligate and the other is not. The first takes expensive vacations, runs a fancy car, wears tailor-made suits, and accumulates large debts. The other lives much more modestly, within his means. The first goes bankrupt, cannot meet the payments on his house and car, loses his job, house, car, and becomes poor and unemployed. The egalitarian view is that a decent society will take resources from the first and give them to the second.

These are outrageous implications of egalitarianism and no reasonable person could accept them. They violate the most elementary requirements of justice; penalize people who make good use of their liberty and reward those who misuse it; and they do this while self-righteously claiming that proceeding any other way is immoral. What justification do egalitarians offer in defense of their view? The answer is that they offer none, and admit it. Once again, this is such an amazing view that I feel I must document it. Isaiah Berlin, for instance, tells us: "Equality is one of the oldest and deepest elements in liberal thought and it is neither more nor less 'natural' or 'rational' than any other constituent in them. Like all human ends it cannot be defended or justified, for it is itself which justifies other acts." From which it follows that egalitarianism is based on a rationally indefensible article of faith. (Additional examples and references are in the Notes to this chapter).

On the basis of their admittedly unjustified view egalitarians advocate the redistribution of resources from the better to the worse off. They do this regardless of whether the better off are entitled to what they have and the worse off are responsible for their position. And egalitarians advocate this as a requirement of morality that overrides the requirements of liberty, justice, private property, or of any other political good. I hope to have shown that this is an unreasonable and morally unacceptable view. But I do not want to leave at this. I want to offer a hypothesis about what drives egalitarians to advocate and so many people to accept this indefensible view. I think that behind egalitarianism is the belief that the better off are rich and live in luxury; the worse off are poor and cannot satisfy their basic needs; and this is morally offensive. What should we think about this belief behind egalitarianism?

Strictly speaking the belief is false: most of those who are better off are neither rich nor live in luxury and most of those who are worse off are not suffering and can satisfy their basic needs. But ignore these exaggerations. The core of the unexaggerated belief is true. A good society should not allow that the basic needs of some of its citizens are unsatisfied, while some other citizens live in luxury; and let us not haggle about precise numbers of the best and worst off. The important point is that holding this belief does not commit one to egalitarianism: to regarding equality as the most important political good; to finding the mere existence of differences in economic positions morally objectionable; to violating elementary requirements of liberty, justice, and private property; and to setting up a perpetual redistributing machinery. The belief commits one only to the recognition that people living together in a society should help those in serious need if they can without great sacrifices. If the society is affluent, no one in it should be allowed to fall below the level at which basic needs can be satisfied.

This, however, is not a matter of equality, but of decency, compassion, or solidarity. Most people in American society share this attitude, and it is to their credit. Egalitarians, however, abuse people's good nature and make political capital out of it by emotional blackmail and moralistic bullying. They condemn all past and present societies for their inequality and preach the radical transformation of their society that goes far beyond the simple requirement of not allowing anyone in an affluent society to fall below the level at which basic needs are satisfied. Using taxation to meet this simple requirement is justified. Using it as a permanent device for redistributing resources from those who earned them to those who have not is unjustified.

As to the endlessly repeated condemnation of our society, egalitarians should bear in mind that contemporary democracies have achieved unprecedented stability, affluence, liberty, justice, and equality. These achievements make it the envy of the world. Their political arrangements are very far from perfect, but they are better than any past or present alternative to them. Its many shortcomings should certainly be improved. Doing so, however, must be done cautiously, so as not to endanger what we already enjoy. The radical transformation egalitarians advocate would be to abandon the hard-won achievements of centuries in order to pursue a practically impossible, morally undesirable, and rationally unacceptable goal.

Egalitarians would not be impressed by these objections. They would concede that people have different merits but they would deny that the possession of resources should depend on merit. They would argue that regardless of differing merits people have the same worth, and that is why they should have equal resources.

9.3 WORTH AND MERIT

According to the egalitarian distinction between worth and merit, merit depends on how well people follow the requirements of morality, law, and reason. This obviously varies, so merit tends to be unequal. Worth is said to be independent of merit because everyone has a basic worth simply in virtue of being human. Since people are equal in their humanity, they are equal also in their worth. This ought to be recognized, egalitarians say, and recognizing it means that all human beings ought to be accorded a basic respect, an elementary dignity on account of being moral agents who can distinguish between right and wrong, make choices, and use reason. Following the Kantian tradition, egalitarians call these capacities jointly the capacity for autonomy.

Autonomy is more than the mere capacity to choose, it is the capacity to choose between alternatives that have been understood and evaluated in the light of reason and morality. All human beings are supposed by egalitarians to be equal in respect to the capacity for autonomy, and they are supposed to remain equal even if they misuse it. No matter how great may be their demerit, their worth remains the same because it derives from their capacity for autonomy, not from the use they make of it. And it is because of their equal capacity for autonomy that they have equal rights to resources, and to be protected from the violation of the conditions necessary for their autonomous functioning. The reason, then, why equality is not just one political good among others but the most important political good is that the use of autonomy is presupposed by all the other political goods. For if people were not guided by reason and morality in making choices, they could not recognize and would not pursue any of the political goods. This has been an extraordinarily influential line of thought. It is the basic assumption on which much contemporary moral and political thought rests, and it is from it that egalitarianism follows. The assumption, however, is mistaken for several rather obvious reasons. Only the reluctance to question it stands in the way of recognizing how weighty are the reasons that tell against it.

To begin with, the capacity for autonomy is complex. It is composed of many other capacities that are involved in understanding and evaluating available alternatives, such as intelligence, memory, conceptualization, imagination, concentration, control of desires and emotions, and so forth. The extent to which people possess these other capacities is variable and unequal. Since the capacity for autonomy depends on these unequally possessed capacities, the capacity for autonomy is also possessed unequally. If worth depends on the capacity for autonomy, then worth is unequal.

Egalitarians may say in response that what they have in mind is just a minimal capacity for autonomy, and that all normal human beings possess. This, however, does not help their case. For children, drug addicts, alcoholics, the mentally ill, those with subnormal intelligence, and the senile typically lack even a minimal capacity to make reasonable and morally acceptable choices. They have diminished capacity for autonomy, and hence less worth than those whose capacity is undiminished. But egalitarians cannot accept this implication of their own position because it commits them to the view that human beings have unequal worth.

Another reason against the equality of worth is that people have many capacities and autonomy is only one of them. There are capacities for aggression, devotion, envy, friendship, generosity, love, procreation, rage, self-sacrifice, and so on. Why should worth depend only on the capacity for autonomy? Why do these other capacities not affect people's worth? What conceivable justification could egalitarians have for singling out one capacity among many and building their moral and political edifice on it? Proceeding as egalitarians do requires a grotesquely narrow view of the human capacities that influence the choices people make. Egalitarians simply assert that the fundamental purpose of political arrangements is to foster people's capacity for autonomy. But they do not say why it is not just as important for understanding and evaluating choices to foster people's capacities for altruism, generosity, or love, or to hinder their capacities for aggression, envy, or hatred.

If egalitarians accept the political importance of these other capacities, they cannot reasonably derive equal worth from them. For the extent to which people possess these other capacities varies greatly. And the variation is even greater because interdependence leads capacities to strengthen or weaken each other, depending on people's very different genetic inheritance, upbringing, and adult experiences.

A further problem for egalitarians is to justify their concentration on a capacity. Why do they make worth depend on a capacity rather than on what people do? Why stress a capacity for action rather than actual actions? Employees are paid for the work they do, not for what they could do. People are punished for crimes they commit, not for their capacity to commit crimes. Why, then, should people's worth be thought to depend on a capacity rather than on the use they make of it? After all, actions, not capacities, affect others. Furthermore, the actions people perform cannot be predicted merely from the capacities they have. A capacity may be misused, unused, rarely used, or be overwhelmed by another capacity. Different capacities may lead to the same action and the same capacity to different actions. The mere capacity for autonomy, therefore, cannot be a reasonable basis for acceptable political arrangements, whose purpose is to protect conditions of human well-being. Well-being depends not just on having the capacity for autonomy, but on using it in accordance with reason, morality, and the law.

The distinction egalitarians draw between equal worth and unequal merit, therefore, is untenable. Worth depends on merit. It is absurd to claim that a teacher in a slum high school who inspired and equipped hundreds of children during a forty-year career to seek a better life and a drug dealer who enticed hundreds of children into a life of addiction have, on some basic level, equal worth. Only an ideologue in the grip of a dogma would claim that the Stalins, Hitlers, Maos, and their henchmen have the same basic worth as artists, writers, and scientists who have greatly enriched human lives. Only self-imposed blindness can commit egalitarians to the moral judgment that terrorists and their hostages, mass murderers and their victims, torturers and the tortured should have the same share of scarce resources and should enjoy the same protection. Political arrangements that distribute benefits on the assumption that people are equally worthy of them do not protect but endanger the conditions of well-being. For they provide benefits for people regardless of whether they are likely to use them unreasonably, immorally, and illegally.

Egalitarians will indignantly reject this conclusion. They will say that their commitment to equal worth is unaffected by the acknowledged fact of unequal merit. They agree that political arrangements should take into account merit. But that does not mean, they will say, that anything can be done to those with demerit. There are moral limits to what may be done to human beings and the limits are set by equal worth. I certainly agree that there are moral limits to what can be permissibly done to people, but I do not think that the limits depend on equal worth.

The limits are set by what is beyond the pale of civilized life. There are primitive, barbaric, evil possibilities that ought not even occur as candidates for action to people who are committed to reason and morality. This is not because evildoers might not deserve to have terrible things done to them or because they are entitled to some basic respect and recognition of their dignity. Many evildoers have forfeited their entitlement to such considerations. The reason for staying within civilized limits has to do with us, not with them. Trespassing the limits, even in extreme cases, corrupts the trespassers and transforms what ought to be unthinkable into a possibility that might be realized in some exceptional cases. And then indignation, passion, horror at the evil that has been done leads to seeing more and more cases as exceptional, thereby giving barbarism a beachhead in civilized life. This is what should be avoided, this is what sets limits to what we may do to people even if they deserve much worse. But this does not commit one to the absurdity of regarding benefactors and scourges of humanity as having equal worth.

I conclude that the egalitarian claim that equality is the most important political good cannot be justified by appealing to equal worth because worth is not equal. It is possible, of course, that egalitarianism could be justified in some other way, and I will now discuss one of them. It should be remembered, however, that showing that egalitarianism is indefensible shows only that equality is not the most important political good, not that it is not a political good.

Equality as the Exclusion of Arbitrariness

9.4 MORAL RULES AND EXCEPTIONS

We have seen that egalitarianism cannot be justified on the basis of equal worth or the immorality of the unequal distribution of resources. It has been suggested, however, that it follows from the very nature of moral rules that equality is the most important political good. The argument for this is roughly as follows. Moral rules apply universally. If an action, like murder, is wrong, then it is so always, everywhere, for everyone, regardless of time, place, or context. It is irrelevant to its wrongness where, when, and by whom it is done. This is true also of morally right actions, such as kindness. The wrongness or rightness of an action, therefore, does not depend on who performs it. A direct consequence of the supposed universality and impersonality of moral rules is that they apply equally to everyone. Equality is thus presupposed by all moral rules and that is why it is the most important political good. Egalitarianism, therefore, is not a political ideology to which there could be morally acceptable alternatives. For any morally acceptable alternative must, by the very nature of moral rules, presuppose equality. There are political ideologies that reject egalitarianism, but by rejecting it they reject morality itself, and thus they are immoral.

This, I believe, is the line of thought that is behind the egalitarian charge that their critics are immoral. Here is one example from Ronald Dworkin: "we cannot reject the egalitarian principle outright, because it is . . . immoral that [the government] should show more concern for the lives of some than of others." And "a distribution of wealth that dooms some citizens to a less fulfilling life than others, no matter what choices they make, is unacceptable, and the neglect of equality in contemporary politics is therefore shameful." That makes it immoral and shameful not to equalize the resources of those who earned them and those who did not. (Further examples of such groundless charges are in the Notes to this chapter.)

I turn now to the reason why this last egalitarian attempt to justify the claim that equality is the highest political good fails.

189

This will also be a reason for regarding the egalitarians' treatment of critics as ill-tempered abuse, rather than justified condemnation. The basic reason is that this justification of egalitarianism rests on the assumption that moral rules are universal. But the assumption is false.

If moral rules were universal, there could be no morally justifiable exceptions to them because a universal rule would hold everywhere, always, for everyone, and in all contexts. I cannot think of a moral rule that meets this condition, but if there is one, it is surely extremely rare. The vast majority of moral rules holds, at best generally, most of the time, and thus allows morally justified exceptions. There are countless circumstances in which murder, for instance, is morally justified: in a just war, in self-defense, in the course of law enforcement, in preventing a terrorist from murdering many innocent people, in assassinating a vicious dictator, and so forth. The same goes for kindness, which can misplaced and morally unjustified, as in lying to save the guilty from punishment, preferring the undeserving to the competent for a job, meddling paternalistically, and so on.

It certainly should be recognized that there is a presumption against the violation of moral rules and in favor of meeting them, but overruling the presumption is often morally justified. Moral rules typically allow exceptions. The question is, of course, how to decide whether an exception would be justified in an actual situation. But this is not particularly difficult to do in many cases. Murder is normally wrong but it is justified, for instance, if it saves from murder many innocent people. Kindness is normally right but it is unjustified if it is likely to cause more harm than good.

Now apply this to the egalitarian moral rule that all people living in a society ought be guaranteed equal resources necessary for their well-being. There is, I think, a presumption in favor of meeting this rule, but there are many cases in which overruling it is morally justified. If some people use their resources to deprive others of theirs, to commit crimes, to acquire more resources fraudulently, to squander them imprudently, or if they are lastingly incapacitated cognitively or emotionally, then it is morally justified to withhold from them resources equal to those who are not going to misuse them criminally, immorally, imprudently, or incompetently. And the case for this morally justified inequality is especially strong if the resources are scarce, as they nearly always are.

If the egalitarian rule is not universal, if the unequal distribution of resources may be morally justified, then, it may be asked, what is the reason for the rule that resources ought to be distributed equally? This brings us back to the requirement that forms the basis of equality, namely that like cases should be treated alike. Egalitarians begin with human beings who are alike in needing resources for their well-being and then formulate the rule that they ought to be treated alike in the distribution of resources. This rule has two crucial features: contrary to what egalitarians assume, it is not a moral rule at all, and, even though it is not a moral rule, it can be overruled for moral reasons.

Why, then, is the rule to treat human beings alike in the distribution of resources not a moral rule? Because it is a characteristic of all rules, moral and other, that like cases that come under their jurisdiction ought to be treated alike. The characteristic is part of the nature of rules. A rule says how the cases it covers should be treated, so of course the cases it covers should be treated as the rule says. This is as true of rules about sorting apples or appraising antiques, as of rules about the distribution of resources. The rule, treat like cases alike, expresses a semantic requirement. There cannot be a rule that fails to conform to this semantic requirement because if it failed, it would not be a rule.

The rule, however, covers only cases that are alike, and cases may not be alike. It often happens that a case that seems to be like the cases that are properly covered by the rule is in fact not like them. If it is thought that this is true of a case, then reasons must be given why the case is unlike the others. Such reasons may be good or bad. Good reasons point at relevant differences, bad reasons at irrelevant ones. What reasons are relevant depends on the purpose of the rule. If the rule is about sorting apples, then the relevant reasons have to do with the characteristics of the apple in question, not with who wants to buy or sell it, or whether it is domestic or imported. If the rule is about appraising antiques, then the relevant reasons have to do with the provenance and condition of the piece, not with the profit margin of the appraiser or with who owns it.

What is true of rules in general is also true moral rules in particular. If a moral rule is about the distribution of resources, then its purpose is to protect conditions of human well-being. Whether resources should be distributed equally to a number of people depends on whether the people are alike or whether there are relevant differences among them. Relevant differences have to do with whether the resources will be used in a way that is conducive to human well-being. Cases where the resources are used immorally, illegally, imprudently, or incompetently are unlike cases where the resources are used morally, legally, prudently, or competently. In such cases unequal treatment is justified. What justifies it is that the two cases are relevantly different. Treating these cases differently does not violate the semantic requirement that like cases should be treated alike. The justification of treating them differently are the relevant differences between them. This justification is moral, but only, as it were, incidentally because the rule happens to apply to human well-being. Exactly the same justification would hold for treating apples or antiques differently, but then, of course, the justification would not be moral.

The deep confusion of egalitarians is to mistake a semantic requirement for a universal moral rule, then quixotically rise to its unnecessary defense, and follow it by heaping abuse on their critics. There is a moral rule about the distribution of resources, but it is not universal. It creates a presumption for equal distribution, but the presumption can be overruled in case of relevant differences. Egalitarians are unwilling to recognize that there may be relevant differences between human beings because they confusedly think that the semantic requirement is a universal moral rule. They compound the confusion by supposing further that the moral rule allows no exceptions. And on the basis of this double confusion they conclude that it is morally impermissible to distribute resources unequally because it involves not treating like cases alike.

9.5 EQUALITY AS THE EXCLUSION OF ARBITRARINESS

We have now examined three ways in which egalitarians attempt to justify their view that equality is the highest political good and that it should override any other good that may conflict with it. I have given reasons for thinking that each of these attempts fails. Worth is unequal if merit is unequal; the possession of unequal resources is not morally objectionable if the better off have acquired the resources they have legitimately and the worse off have fewer resources as a result of irresponsibility; and moral rules allow the unequal distribution of resources, if there are morally relevant differences among the recipients. There is thus no good reason to suppose that equality is the highest political good. Defenders of the balanced view nevertheless believe that it is a political good. What is the basis of this belief?

The beginning of the answer is the semantic requirement that like cases should be treated alike. Human beings are certainly alike in respect to being human, so there is a presumption in favor of treating them alike. But there is also a presumption in favor of treating them differently because of obvious differences in how reasonable, moral, prudent, responsible, competent, and law-abiding they are, and in why they are better or worse off. There is no general formula for deciding which of these contrary presumptions should prevail in particular cases. The decision can be made only on the basis of the concrete examination of actual differences and weighing the reasons for and against their moral relevance. There are, however, three general remarks that defenders of the balanced view can make about equality.

One is that the distribution of resources on the basis of morally irrelevant differences is morally objectionable. Equality is a political good because it requires that differences between the better and the worse off not be arbitrary. They are not arbitrary if morally relevant reasons can be given for them and they are arbitrary if there are no such reasons. There will be disagreements, of course, about the moral relevance of the reasons that are adduced. But these disagreements can be resolved, at least in principle, because the moral relevance and respective importance of reasons depends on whether and how much they affect the well-being of all those concerned. According to the balanced view, equality is a political good because it excludes arbitrariness in how people are treated.

A second general remark is that the very exclusion of arbitrariness that makes equality a political good points to the need to balance the conflicting claims of equality and other political goods. For one of the morally relevant reasons for the unequal distribution of resources is that justice requires that people should have what they deserve and should not have what they do not deserve. And surely people deserve to have the resources they have earned and those who have not earn them do not deserve to have a share of the resources of those who have earned them. Another morally relevant reason against the redistribution of unequal resources is that people who acquired their resources legitimately ought to be free to dispose of them in any legitimate way they see fit. The political goods of liberty, justice, and private property, therefore, limit the extent to which the political good of equality prevails. But this limit is not absolute. For just as liberty, justice, and private property limit equality, so equality limits liberty, justice, and private property. Political goods often conflict, their reasonable claims must be balanced, and that means that none of the conflicting claims can be fully met, that each of the claims is reasonably limited. This is a direct consequence of the non-ideological component of the balanced view. The most important consideration whenever political goods conflict is not which and to what extent should be given precedence over the other, but how the resolution of the conflict, in one way or another, would affect the evaluative framework that the people of a society have historically found reasonable to prize. This is just the consideration that egalitarians and other ideologues ignore by insisting that there is a highest political good that must always override any other political good that conflicts with it. The result is that they endanger the prevailing system of political goods.

The third general remark about equality is that defenders of the balanced view hold that, liberty, justice, and private property notwithstanding, there is a limit to how great the morally acceptable difference may be between the resources of the better and worse off. In American society people should not be allowed to fall below the level at which their basic needs are unmet, not even if they are responsible for their predicament. This level is not one that assures a comfortable life, but merely one that prevents lasting damage as a result of starvation, illiteracy, physical abuse, or lack of elementary health care. The reason for such a safety net follows from the balanced view, according to which there are many political goods and none is the highest. Unequal resources are justified if they are based on morally relevant differences, but that justification may be overridden by other considerations, such as decency, compassion, solidarity, and so forth. The balanced view recognizes that people living together in a society owe one another a basic concern. But egalitarians cannot reasonably derive from this basic concern that equality is the highest political good and the mere existence of differences between the better and worse off is morally objectionable.

The upshot of this chapter is that we can add yet another political good to the account of the balanced view that I am developing throughout the book: equality as the exclusion of arbitrariness.

CHAPTER TEN

✦ ✦ ✦

POLITICAL DEMOCRACY

*Democracy is the worst form of government, except for all
those other forms that have been tried from time to time.*

WINSTON CHURCHILL
in a speech to the House of Commons

THE POLITICAL GOODS I am discussing in this book are connected in a variety of complex ways: they conflict, they overlap, and
they reciprocally strengthen and limit one another. The connection
between the goods I discuss in Chapters 9–11—equality, democracy, and authority—is especially close. I argued in the preceding
chapter that equality is a political good provided it is limited to the
political and legal equality of citizens. I argue in the present chapter that democracy is also a political good, partly because it aims
to protect the political and legal equality of citizens. And I will
argue in the next chapter that authority is also a political good that
American society must protect; that this requires limiting equality
to political and legal contexts and excluding it from personal contexts; and that the legitimacy of democracies depends in part on the
extent to which they succeed in achieving this aim. This is how,
according to the balanced view, equality, democracy, and authority
overlap. But they also set limits to one another. For, as I will argue,
the democratic tendency to extend equality beyond the political
context is contrary to the well-being of the citizens that democracies are meant to serve.

✦ ✦ ✦

Political Democracy

10.1 Two Types of Decision

There is a type of decision that needs to be made in political contexts. Suppose, for instance, that the cost of health care has dramatically increased and it must be decided how it should be financed in a particular society. It may be done publicly by the government and paid for by taxation; or privately by non-governmental organizations or individuals and paid for by the purchase of insurance policies; or it may be some mixture of public and private financing, which is what is being done presently in America.

There is another type of decision that needs to be made in a personal context. Say I was born and raised a Catholic but gradually lost my faith. I wonder whether I should just leave it all behind or continue to participate in the appropriate practices even though I no longer believe in them. I consult my priest and he tells me that crises of faith are frequent and the best way to overcome them is to continue to participate even without faith. But I have come to doubt the priest's authority as well. Part of the decision I have to make is whether to trust him or my own doubts. Take another case. I am a struggling young artist. I think I have serious talent but I am not sure. I am tired of being poor and I am offered a lucrative job as a commercial artist. I consult a trusted older friend, a successful artist who has advised me in the past, and he tells me to turn down the job offer. I know that, being an artist, that is just what he would say, and I wonder whether to accept his advice.

Why is it reasonable to make the decision democratically in the political context but absurd to make it democratically in the personal context? The simple answer is that political decisions affect all citizens and they are entitled by their political and legal equality to have a say about them. Personal decisions concern how particular individuals should live their lives and what authority, if any, they should accept. Democracy and political and legal equality are irrelevant in personal contexts because individuals have a privileged position in making such decisions.

The distinction between these two types of decision is intuitively obvious, I hope, but further examples will reinforce it. Laws specifying what constitutes felony or misdemeanor; those that formulate policies concerning defense, welfare, the infrastructure, domestic and foreign trade, and education; and yet others adjudicating conflicts concerning these laws should be made democratically because they involve political goods that affect all citizens.

The personal context includes activities and preferences in religion, art, science, sports, personal projects, hobbies, literature, fashion, sex, travel, and family life. Decisions about such matters involve personal goods, beliefs, and interests, and they concern only those who prize the goods and share the relevant beliefs and interests. The majority of citizens is unaffected by and indifferent to what decision individuals make, and, in any case, they lack the facts and interests that would enable them to decide reasonably for others. It is reasonable, therefore, to let people decide for themselves.

The broad outline of the difference between these two contexts will be obvious to any normally intelligent person who has lived for an extended period in American society. What is not at all obvious, however, is how political and personal goods can be distinguished and how unavoidable disputes about the limits of the government's authority and of the discretion of individuals are to be resolved. How far can the government legitimately go in deciding what is and what is not a purely religious matter, an acceptable sexual practice, a proper way to raise a child, a criminal action, and so forth? And, since decisions made in the personal context often have effects that reverberate throughout the society, at what point do religious, scientific, child-rearing, and like decisions become the legitimate concerns of the whole society?

In a democratic society, controversies about such matters abound and there is no generally accepted principle for resolving them. Beliefs and interests unavoidably differ and, although reasonable resolutions can be and need to be found in particular cases and conflicts, they will vary. Reasonable resolutions must take into account changing circumstances and the varying importance of the conflicting political goods. That is why the balanced view is preferable to resolving the controversies by the imposition of some ideology that disregards circumstances and ascribes overriding importance to one of the many political goods. The viability of a democratic society requires, however, that there be generally known and accepted procedures for resolving such conflicts. Having and following procedures is part of the responsibility of a democratic government.

Distinguishing between contexts in which democratic political authority is legitimate and contexts in which it is not is therefore crucial but notoriously difficult. A clue to it, however, may be found in Tocqueville's distinction between the political character and the laws of a country, on the one hand, and its civil society, on the other. He is not sufficiently clear about what he means by civil society but I think it is close to what I have called the personal context in which individuals and the associations they form should be left free to make whatever personal decisions seem fitting to them without political interference, provided they do not violate the laws. We might say, then, that in the political context a democratic government's authority is legitimate, whereas in the personal context it is not. In the political context, a democratic government ought to be guided, among other things, by the political and legal equality of the citizens. In the personal context, however, democracy, equality, and political authority are out of place. Drawing this distinction, however, requires knowing what makes a government democratic.

10.2 WHAT MAKES GOVERNMENTS DEMOCRATIC?

The answer to this question cannot be purely descriptive because the forms of government that have claimed to be democratic are extremely varied. Nor can the answer be merely prescriptive because that would arbitrarily exclude candidates that do not fit a particular evaluative standard. Perhaps the best approach is to combine descriptive and prescriptive elements but the number of ways in which this has been done is very large. A recent article on democracy in the *Handbook of Political Theory* lists fifty-four different combinations.

The answer I propose is a description of a number of features that contemporary democracies actually have and a prescription that any government that deserves to be called democratic ought to have many of these features. I do not claim, however, that all democracies have or ought to have each of these features; none of them is necessary and various combinations of them may be sufficient to qualify a government as democratic. Furthermore, governments typically possess different features to different extents, and it is a matter of interpretation and judgment what the minimum required extent is for the possession of a particular feature. There is, therefore, no precise answer to the question of how many and which of these features must a democratic government have and to what extent it must have them. It is pointless to seek a definition because democracy has no essence. There will be disputed cases about which reasonable disagreements, conflicting interpretations, and contrary judgments are possible. To strive here for logical clarity and individually necessary and jointly sufficient conditions is futile. Politics is complex, and it is a strength, not a weakness, of political thought if it reflects the complexities.

Having said this, I must now consider what the actual features are whose possession—in various combinations and to various extents—justifies calling a government democratic. The order in which I consider them has no significance. But I must begin somewhere, and I begin with majority rule. It consists in a form of government whose political power—legislative, executive, and judicial —ultimately derives from the vote of the citizens, as expressed in regularly held elections. Contemporary democracies are large and populous. The political decisions their governments have to make often require knowledge and experience that most citizens lack.

This makes it impracticable that citizens should vote directly for or against possible decisions. What usually happens is that citizens express their preferences indirectly through elected representatives who are supposed to be best qualified to serve the citizens' interests. Political power is thus delegated, and contemporary democracies are representative, not direct. It is a further feature of contemporary democracies that all citizens have the right to vote, unless there is good reason to disqualify some segment of the population, such as children. We can say, then, that contemporary democracies are partly characterized by majority rule, representative government, universal suffrage, and regular elections.

These features taken together are compatible, however, with forms of government that no reasonable person could call democratic. For, given only what I have said so far, no limits have been set to how the majority or its representatives may use political power. History amply shows that unlimited political power is likely to be abused. Stable or shifting majorities will make decisions that violate the legitimate interests of those in permanent or temporary minority: their liberty will be curtailed, or they will be treated unjustly, or their legitimate interests will be frustrated in other ways. This will destabilize the society because no one can be sure of not being part of some future mistreated minority. Basic rights will not be protected, and insecurity will spread. This is a well-known danger of majority rule. Numerous political thinkers committed to democracy have repeatedly warned against it.

Democracies, therefore, have to set limits to how the majority may use its political power. And this is what the constitutions of contemporary democracies do. A constitution is normally a written document. The great exception is the English one, which is embedded in traditions, conventions, habits, and precedent, and from which most other democratic constitutions have been derived. A written constitution, however, has the considerable advantage of clarity, general accessibility, and resistance to change when practical exigencies make adherence to it inefficient or inconvenient. But whatever form it takes, a constitution defines the legitimate and illegitimate uses of political power through procedural and substantive laws.

In its procedural aspect, a constitution defines the various offices, functions, and branches of government; sets some requirements of how legislative, executive, and judiciary activities should and should not be conducted; prescribes when and in what form elections and voting should occur; specifies the authority, duties, and privileges attached to various political offices and branches of government; and so forth. Generally, the constitution contains the basic laws governing how political activities should and should not be conducted, but it leaves largely open what particular aims political activities may have.

The constitution also defines the substantive basic rights and responsibilities of citizens. They are basic in the triple sense of being general because each citizen has them equally; presumptive because they hold normally and can be legitimately violated only in exceptional circumstances in the absence of reasonable alternatives; and minimal because citizens usually have many other rights and responsibilities as well, which may or may not be general and presumptive. Basic rights, for example, are to life, liberty, security, and property. And basic responsibilities include respecting the basic rights of fellow citizens and conforming to properly enacted laws.

A constitution, then, limits political power by prescribing what it must and must not be used for. But it leaves ample scope for many other uses political power may legitimately have within these constitutional limits. Good constitutions combine stability and flexibility by setting basic requirements that can be changed only slowly and with difficulty and by defining only a narrow range of basic requirements that enable citizens and political office holders to pursue an enormous variety of aims in continually changing circumstances. Good constitutions also limit political power by dividing it among the legislative, executive, and judicial branches of the government and by assigning to each a sphere of authority which limits how the other branches may use their political power. The resulting separation of powers and checks and balances are among the most significant developments in modern times affecting how a good society ought to be governed.

A constitution may be thought of as embodying the primary laws of democracies, but there need to be many secondary laws as well that spell out in detail procedures, requirements, and penalties concerning torts, taxation, welfare, defense, the infrastructure, education, trade, and so forth. These secondary laws are like the primary ones in being general and presumptive, but they are unlike them in not being minimal. The legitimacy of secondary laws requires that they be enacted in accordance with the procedures specified by the constitution and that they conform to all the other relevant requirements the constitution has laid down. The combination of primary and secondary laws is the legal system of a democracy. A further feature of contemporary democracies is that political power must be exercised in accordance with the legal system. This feature is the rule of law, not of men, meaning that the authority and power of office holders is specified by law and what they may or may not legitimately do depends on the relevant laws, not on their preferences. Their rights and responsibilities are attached to the office they hold, and do not vary with the particular individuals who happen to occupy the office.

The rule of law is not mere legality that could be met by following whatever procedures are specified in the constitution and secondary laws. The legal system also lays down substantive entitlements to specific rights—to life, liberty, security, and property, for example—that all citizens have. The rule of law, therefore, does not merely limit political power but also enables individual citizens to enjoy the benefits provided by the laws and necessary for their well-being. The rule of law as it occurs in a particular democracy is justified if it serves the citizens' interest by protecting them from the abuse of political power and by safeguarding their rights. If the legal system of a democracy provides these benefits, it is the best guarantee of such political goods as prudence, pluralism, limits, liberty, toleration, justice, property, and equality.

The last feature of contemporary democracies I will mention is the accountability of office holders to the citizens. Some office holders are elected directly, others indirectly, and yet others are appointed for shorter or longer fixed terms by those who hold elected offices. The simplest form of accountability is to have to run for re-election, which involves being held responsible for the decisions that the official has made or supported. Appointed office holders may not need to be re-elected but they may have to be re-appointed, and even if their appointments are for life, they can be impeached for dereliction of duty. Accountability, therefore, is another way in which political power is limited.

The features I have ascribed to contemporary democracies—majority rule, representation, universal suffrage, regular elections, constitution, rule of law, and accountability—are possessed by them imperfectly. The less imperfect they are, the better they are at preventing the abuse of political power and at protecting the political goods on which the well-being of citizens depends. Although all democracies are more or less imperfect, they nevertheless constitute notable achievements. They are perhaps the best political systems that have so far emerged in human history. I am in complete agreement with John Dunn's moving words that "Human beings have done many more fetching and elegant things than invent and routinize the modern democratic republic. But, in the face of their endlessly importunate, ludicrously indiscreet, inherently chaotic and always potentially murderous onrush of needs and longings, they have, even now, done few things as solidly to their advantage." This is why democracy is one of the political goods to which defenders of the balanced view are committed—provided it is kept in its place. There is, however, a dangerous tendency not to keep democracy in its place but to extend it from the political to the personal context and thus to insinuate politics into areas of life that should be left to the discretion of individuals and their associations.

10.3 AGAINST POLITICIZATION

I call this dangerous tendency politicization. In democracies it involves the political invasion of personal life. Tocqueville presciently warns that a democratic government may "cover the surface of society with a network of small complicated rules, minute and uniform, through which the most original minds and the most energetic characters cannot penetrate.... The will of man is not shattered, but softened, bent, and guided; men are seldom forced by it to act, but they are continually restrained from acting. Such power does not destroy, but prevents existence; it does not tyrannize, but it compresses, enervates, extinguishes, and stupefies people, till each nation is reduced to nothing better than a flock of timid and industrious animals, of which the government is the shepherd."

Consider now some cases in the American context indicating that the danger Tocqueville warned against is upon us. All adult citizens are legally required to pay income tax every year. The US tax code contains 3.4 million words; counting 60 lines per letter-sized page, it fills 7,500 pages. Few taxpayers can prepare their own income tax forms. Most people rely on professionals who do it for a substantial fee, but even they rely on software programs whose directions they often cannot follow without consulting other tax experts. The completed forms are submitted to and then reviewed by government officials, who, if they find anything questionable, require taxpayers to present themselves for an audit at which they have to document and justify the claims that have been made on their behalf by experts to whom they turned in the first place because they found the tax code incomprehensible. If the auditors find taxpayers at fault, they have to pay the taxes they supposedly owe, as well as a considerable penalty, or appeal to a tax court where they can defend themselves by using the tax code they cannot understand and contesting the decisions of the auditors against whom they stand no chance. Taxpayers can hire experts for an even more substantial fee than before to represent them at audits or tax courts, but they have no hope of judging whether they have been adequately represented, or, indeed, whether the charge against them was well-founded. Sooner or later most taxpayers give up and like sheep are herded by the government.

Take another case: a family of four, where husband and wife work and the two children are just beginning school. They employ both the young daughter of a neighbor as an occasional housecleaner and babysitter and another local teenager to mow the grass around their house. They are required by law to pay the same minimum wage to both as is paid by large firms to adult laborers and service employees. If the payments to either teenager exceed in the course of a year a fairly low figure, the family is legally required to pay into the teenagers' social security account (which they are legally required to have) a specified percentage of their wages. If the teenagers accidentally injure themselves while in their employ, the family may be sued for damages and negligence by the insurance company with whom the parents of the teenagers are forced by the outrageously high cost of health care to insure them. If you think these absurdities are not taken seriously, recall that numerous people being considered for important appointments were disqualified because the FBI investigation of their background found them in violation of these absurd legal requirements.

These cases are not exceptional aberrations but typical of the enervating and stupefying intrusion of the law into personal lives. Here are some further examples. Suppose you own the house you live in and the land on which it stands, and want to add a room to it. You must apply to the local authorities for a permit. The permit is given only if you submit a blueprint drawn by a licensed architect; your own blueprint is unacceptable. The local authority must ascertain that the added room constitutes no environmental hazard and does not endanger wildlife, even if there is no wildlife where you live. Once the permit is issued, the regulations specify the number and positions of the electric outlets in the room, the size and the position of the windows, the number of fire and smoke detectors that must be installed, the distance between the floor, ceiling, and wall beams, how close the nearest stairway must be, and so on. Once the actual building has begun, it cannot go on from one stage to the next unless an inspector employed by the local authority inspects it and certifies that it conforms to the requirements. When the addition is complete, you cannot inhabit it until the inspector gives his consent. Then the taxes you pay on the house are raised to reflect the increase in its value as a result of the addition. If you employ a builder to do the work, you must make sure that the workmen are insured because if they are not and are injured in the course of doing the work, you are legally liable for damages.

If you have a garden and want to use chemicals to fertilize it or to protect it from insects, the government prescribes the chemicals you can and cannot use. If you want to rent a room in your house, you cannot rent it to whomever you prefer as a tenant. You are charged with discrimination if you prefer heterosexuals to homosexuals, men to women, whites to Hispanics or blacks, although, interestingly enough, not if your preference is the reverse. If you tell a joke in which blacks, Orientals, Jews, homosexuals, women, or Hispanics come off badly, you are liable to be prosecuted for hate speech. If you use words like nigger, kike, wop, and so forth, even as a joke, you can be fired from your job and, if you are prominent enough, be investigated and vilified. Some years ago an official almost lost his position because he incautiously described a budget provision as niggardly. Countless people are legally required as a condition of their employment to join a labor union, pay substantial monthly fees for the unwanted membership, parts of which union officials routinely use to support political causes even if the member is opposed to the causes. If a community decides to build a meeting place, the government mandates that it must be accessible to wheelchairs, regardless of cost, even if no one in the community needs it. To these examples countless others could be added.

These are examples of politicization: the government's intrusions into personal affairs that should be left to the discretion of individuals. But the effects of politicization are much worse than mere bureaucratic absurdities that the management of large systems unavoidably produces. Politicization is stifling, strangles initiative, dooms effort, dampens the spirit, and shrinks the area in which people can control their lives. Its effect is like sinking slowly in a swamp. There is nothing to grasp onto, there is no appeal, there is no one to blame, no one to hold responsible. Faceless, impersonal officials politely follow the rules it is their job to follow, they may even sympathize with the absurd situations in which their clients find themselves, for the officials are also individuals who find themselves helpless in similar predicaments, and everyone is slowly suffocating in the swamp. Why is life like this in democracies?

The cause is not ill will. Legislators generally make laws they intend to serve the interests of citizens and those charged with executing the laws usually feel no animosity toward the people into whose lives they are obliged by their position to intrude. Why, then, does benign motivation result in an outcome that deprives people of the control of their lives? Because the underlying motive behind the examples I have given is egalitarian ideology.

Democratic governments have committed themselves to opposing inequalities in the personal sphere because they regard them as unjust discriminations against individuals or groups whose status is less desirable than the position of others. The tax system is intended to redistribute wealth; minimum wage, social security, and health insurance requirements are intended to diminish the gap between higher and lower earners; building codes are intended to extend equal protection to all citizens; laws about rentals, jokes, offensive words, and hate speech are intended to prevent discrimination against minorities; and compulsory membership in labor unions is intended to save employees from exploitation by employers.

All these laws extend the government's legitimate authority to enforce political and legal equality to the government's illegitimate authority to enforce equality in the personal sphere. The extension is motivated by egalitarian ideology that regards equality as the highest political good that overrides any other good that may conflict with it. This is what makes the extension of the government's authority illegitimate and the politicization of personal life the danger that it is. For by ascribing overriding value to equality the legitimate claims of prudence, pluralism, limits, liberty, toleration, justice, property, and democracy, and so forth are ignored. Of course tax fraud, unsafe housing, exploitation, and discrimination are wrong. But it is no less wrong to make and enforce laws against them that lead to the absurd and life-diminishing consequences I have described. The trouble with egalitarian—and any other—ideology is that it violates political goods that are just as important for human well-being as the one the ideologues regard as the highest. Because ideologues are blind to the need to balance the often conflicting claims of all the political goods and thereby protect the whole system of political goods, they actually endanger the political conditions on which the well-being of citizens in democracies depends.

Equality is one of the political goods and it has legitimate claims, but there are also other political goods whose claims are also legitimate. It is thoughtless moralizing to stress the importance of one of the goods at the expense of others. However satisfying is the expression of self-indulgent indignation, it is not a substitute for the reasonable acceptance of the complexities of life. There are deep and serious questions, for example, about how to make just tax laws, protect the environment while maintaining prosperity, prevent exploitation, and safeguard the rights of minorities. But approaching such questions with the presupposition that whatever is done must increase equality, while ignoring what it costs in the loss of other political goods guarantees that reasonable answers will not be found. One of the great dangers of democratic government is that it encourages this approach and thereby undermines the political goods that conflict with equality. As the government extends its authority from the political to the personal context, it diminishes the sphere in which individuals can make what they wish of their lives. The cost of this in human well-being is immense and paying it is contrary to the aim and justification of democracy in America.

10.4 IN FAVOR OF DISTINCTIONS

Political goods are important but not sufficient for human well-being. Individual lives may be miserable in a democracy even if it guarantees an optimal balance of political goods. The enjoyment of these goods is compatible with lives dominated by a sense of ennui, futility, meaninglessness, and triviality, by an inchoate, irritable wish that there be more to life than an unexciting job, watching TV, shopping for bargains, and the occasional pornography to add spice to life. I will call this widely shared sense boredom. Boredom shows that human well-being depends not just on hospitable political conditions but also on the use individuals make of these conditions. People may fail to take advantage of favorable political conditions, and then it is their fault if well-being eludes them. But it may also happen that what stands in their way are adverse social circumstances, such as repressive puritanism, ascetic religious orthodoxy, tyrannical family life, an ethos of self-sacrifice, or obsessive concern with personal or familial honor.

In American society such adverse social influences are rare and usually confined to small tightly knit sects or ethnic groups. What is not rare, however, is an atmosphere of deadening boredom devoid of aesthetic enjoyment, creativity, joyful engagement in personal projects, imaginative exploration of the possibilities of life, intelligent appreciation and admiration of great human achievements, the thrill of reading good literature, or the intellectual excitement of understanding unfamiliar aspects of the world. Boredom stifles sensibility, dulls the emotions, preempts life of the mind, dampens enthusiasm, and dooms people to a colorless, routine existence. It is the creation of this drab, life-diminishing atmosphere that is the danger inherent in the efforts of democratic governments to extend equality from political contexts to personal affairs.

Why is this so? Because it produces uniformity by a concerted moralistic effort to eliminate distinctions between higher and lower, better and worse, exceptional and routine, admirable and mundane. Inequalities of this kind are deplored in democracies but they need not be deplorable. They may indicate genuine achievements, rather than unjust discrimination; excellence, rather than taking unfair advantage of others; deserved recognition for enriching human lives, rather than invidious comparisons. The only way equality can be achieved in the personal sphere is to level down rather than up. For achieving what is higher, better, exceptional, or admirable depends on talents, capacities, and dedication that most people lack. Increasing equality in the personal sphere requires, therefore, fostering conditions that prevent some from rising above the many. If some rise because of their achievements, then the unavoidable cost of greater equality in the personal aspect of life is fewer achievements and fewer distinctions. And that is just what leads to mediocrity and life-diminishing boredom.

Some, of course, may rise above others undeservedly by luck, manipulation, deception, or crime. Distinctions are often not based on merit, and the balanced view does not favor distinctions as such. But the reason why unearned distinctions are questionable is not that they confer unequal status on those who are wrongly favored but that they constitute reward for merit when merit is lacking. If, however, some have higher, better, exceptional, or admirable status because of genuine achievements, then their unequal position is not only deserved but also beneficial to all those whose lives are improved by their achievements. Genuine achievements make life better and those who are rightly credited with them deserve recognition and respect.

Genuine achievements may make life better directly or indirectly.

Direct improvements have immediate and concrete effects, as do the discovery of cure for a dreaded disease; a labor-saving and cost-cutting invention; a negotiated treaty that honorably avoids war; legislation that puts an end to some glaring injustice; an acting or musical performance that moves countless people; a feat of heroism under terrible circumstances; a poem, drama, or novel that articulates previously inchoate sentiments widely shared at a certain time and place; a courageous stance that inspires others to resist forces of darkness; a book that alters the prevailing climate of opinion; and so forth.

Indirect improvements are slower to be felt, less tangible, but no less important than direct ones because they enlarge the possibilities of life, lift the spirit, open people to the non-utilitarian appreciation of the finer things in life, and thereby alleviate boredom. They make life more enjoyable, more hopeful, or, if life does not go well, they make it easier to bear adversity by allowing people to get out of themselves, achieve a distance from their troubles, and be consoled by the reminder that life holds out possibilities better than what they experience in their plight. This is vague and requires explanation.

Most people are not active participants in areas of life where direct or indirect achievements are made. They are not scientists, artists, writers, inventors, actors, musicians, diplomats, or moral exemplars. They are, at most, amateur participants, but few are even that. They are, to be sure, active agents but their activities focus on their work, family, church, neighborhood, ethnic group, clubs, hobbies, causes, and pastimes. The indirect improvement that may result from genuine achievements is not that it inspires people to leave everyday life behind and embark on a career as an aspiring scientist, artist, or whatever. It is rather to allow them to participate in creative endeavors by appreciating excellence in them. By seeing what excellence consists in, they can make distinctions between higher and lower, better and worse, exceptional and routine, admirable and mundane. The importance of appreciation and of the corollary distinctions is not that they make people informed spectators of the activities of others but that they add a dimension to their own enjoyment of life. The achievements they may come to appreciate are fine. They may come to see them as moving examples of the workings of human spirit: of the power of the intellect, of the precision and acuity of feeling, of the discipline and dedication of the will, and of the use of creative imagination.

These achievements give hope for the human prospects, they make those who appreciate them understand deeper and feel better about the human condition, even if, and especially if, they are beset by adversity and misfortune. They console and uplift. The great ages of the past we celebrate—Athens in the fifth century B.C., Augustan Rome, Elizabethan England, Renaissance Italy, France during Louis XIV, the Scottish and the French Enlightenments, for example—are notable for these achievements. They go a little way toward redeeming man's inhumanity to man and the ignorant armies wreaking havoc throughout the mostly dark epochs of human history.

The soul of man shrivels and boredom becomes pervasive in democracies if in the name of misplaced equality the personal is politicized, distinctions are stifled by moralistic bullying, and the achievements of the few are denied the recognition and respect they deserve. It is a dangerous mistake to suppose, as egalitarian ideologues do, that since equality is good in politics it is also good in personal life. The betterment of life depends on the achievements of the few who are the best hope for the future.

10.5 POLITICAL DEMOCRACY

All forms of government are imperfect, but their imperfections can be greater or smaller. I think that the imperfections of democracies are the smallest of all. But the imperfections exist. Those who live with them are not consoled by the knowledge, if they have it, that life is much worse elsewhere. One measure of imperfection is the dissatisfaction of citizens with the political conditions under which they live. If these dissatisfactions are felt widely and acutely, then something must be done to cope with them. Proposing specific policies to cope with specific dissatisfactions is problematic because the conditions in American society are complex and interdependent. The effects of a specific policy reverberate throughout the prevailing conditions and it is hard to foresee how these effects may change the conditions. This is one main reasons why it is reasonable to think systematically but cautiously about how to cope with prevailing dissatisfactions. Political thought, as I have been understanding it throughout this book, aims at such thinking.

If political thought is conceived as I have conceived it, its success depends on reaching three kinds of understanding. One may be thought of as sociological. It involves understanding the present political conditions and the strength, extent, and causes of dissatisfactions with them. A second kind of understanding may be characterized as historical. It has to do with how and why the political conditions have become what they are. The third kind of understanding may be called political. It concerns what can and cannot, should and should not be done to cope with the dissatisfactions. Each kind of understanding combines descriptive and interpretive elements. The descriptive one has to do with getting the facts rights. The interpretive one is concerned with judging the significance and the comparative importance of agreed upon facts. Reasonable political thinkers will agree about the facts but they will often disagree about their judgments because their judgments reflect different ideological commitments, or, if they reject ideologies, different non-ideological approaches.

My concern has been to show how the non-ideological approach of the balanced view yields the three kinds of understanding on which the success of political thought depends. My claim has been that this view is better than any other. The full support for this claim will emerge only at the end of this book but by way of an interim report I can indicate the progress we have made toward reaching the three kinds of understanding.

The sociological understanding I have offered is that our present political condition is that we have reached a consensus about a fairly short list of political goods that we should aim to secure. Our dissatisfactions are the result of conflicts among these goods. We never have as much of any of them as we wish because the more we have of one, the less we can have of the others.

The historical understanding I have been proposing is that our consensus about the political goods we prize is the outcome of a long historical process in the course of which some goods have survived, stood the test of time, and continued to attract the allegiance of many citizens of our society. The great aid in this process has been the constitution, which has proved remarkably successful in combining the defense of some of our political goods with sufficient flexibility to allow for changes in their interpretation, thus making them fit our changing circumstances. The political understanding I have argued for is that coping with our dissatisfactions requires finding an optimal balance among the conflicting political goods. This, however, is a never-ending task because our circumstances continually change and the comparative importance of political goods changes with them. The most serious threats to our efforts to maintain an optimal balance are ideologies as such, quite independently of their content. For all ideologies cause imbalance by their insistence that a particular political good should always override any other political good that may conflict with it. However, since the dominant ideology in our present circumstances is egalitarianism, I have been directing many of my criticisms of ideologies in general against it in particular.

The outcome of this chapter is, then, that we can add democracy, limited in the way I have described, to the other, previously identified political goods defended by the balanced view. We can thus say that the balanced view is committed to reason as prudence, the plurality of goods, the necessity of limits, limited liberty, toleration within reason, justice as having what one deserves, the right to property, equality as the exclusion of arbitrariness, and political democracy.

CHAPTER ELEVEN

✦   ✦   ✦

LEGITIMATE AUTHORITY

*Of all the consequences of the steady politicization of our
social order, of the unending centralization of political power,
and of the accelerating invasion of the social order by the
adversary mentality . . . the greatest . . . is the weakening and
disappearance of traditions in which authority and liberty
alike were anchored.*

ROBERT NISBET
Twilight of Authority

IN AMERICAN SOCIETY resistance to authorities is widespread.
They are thought to interfere with liberty and toleration and
coerce people to act contrary to their own wishes. They are suspected of being pretentious phonies, moralistic bullies, or sinister
dogmatists bent on imposing their will on others. There are such
authorities, and they should be resisted. But there are also others
who help us do what we want to do but could not without their
help. It is crucial, therefore, to distinguish between legitimate and
illegitimate authorities. I will consider two kinds of authority:
political and personal; discuss the very different conditions of their
legitimacy; and argue that legitimate authorities are indispensable
to our well-being and having them is a political good.

✦   ✦   ✦

The Art of Politics

I will discuss only authority that may be possessed by individuals, not by laws, institutions, customs, precedents, treaties, and so forth. But this is still ambiguous because the authority of individuals may mean the individuals themselves who are authorities, such as a judge or surgeon, or it may mean a position, like Chief of Police, or an excellence, like deep knowledge, that makes individuals an authority. In order to avoid this confusion, I will use authorities in the plural to refer to individuals and when I refer to the position or excellence that makes them authorities I will say that their authority, in the singular, is derived from that source.

Political and personal authorities alike involve a relation between authorities, subjects, and contexts. Authorities and subjects are individuals who live and act in a shared context. I will consider political authorities only in the context of contemporary democracies but there are political authorities and subjects in all forms of government. The contexts of personal authorities and subjects are the traditions that partly constitute the evaluative framework of a society. Authorities are legitimate if they have acquired their position by following accredited procedures or if they actually have, not just claim to have, the required excellence. Their position or excellence entitles legitimate authorities to guide their subjects' actions and their subjects have good reasons to follow their guidance.

The relation between political authorities and their subjects is impersonal because political authority is derived from an office, not from the personality of its temporary occupant. And being subject to the authority of the office is similarly independent of the personalities of those who come under its jurisdiction. Personal authorities, by contrast, stand in an essentially personal relation to their subjects because it is in virtue of their personal excellence that they can guide others and their subjects seek their guidance. Lastly, being the subject of political authorities is not a matter of choice but a condition of living in a democracy, whereas being the subject of personal authorities involves choice twice over. Subjects must choose whether to accept the guidance personal authorities may give and personal authorities must choose whether to provide guidance, and, if they do, what form it should take.

In order to avoid misunderstanding, I stress that I am not claiming that authorities must be either political or personal. They can be both and this is important. It is important also to recognize that authorities differ in degree so that two people may have the same position or excellence, and yet one may have more authority than the other. I will now consider in greater and more concrete detail the legitimacy of each kind of authority.

11.2 POLITICAL AUTHORITY

In 1974 Richard Nixon resigned as President, and the Vice President, Gerald Ford, became President. Nixon resigned when it became likely that he would be impeached as a result his role in the Watergate scandal. One of the earliest presidential acts of Ford was to pardon Nixon for any crimes he may have committed while being President. Ford announced the pardon in a widely televised speech. Nixon's resignation and Ford's succession and pardon of Nixon were momentous political events. They tested the rule of law in American democracy, but it stood up to the challenge. There was no doubt that the Constitution provided for Ford's succession and gave him the right to pardon Nixon. Ford thus became President, acquired legitimate political authority as a result of a legal procedure, and he acted within the clearly defined rights of his office when he issued the pardon.

Although the legitimacy of the pardon could not be reasonably doubted, its wisdom and justice were widely questioned by those who thought that Nixon ought to have been tried for his actions and convicted if found guilty. But there was also much support for Ford's view that, since the country has been lurching for many months from one political crisis to another, the time has come to put the Watergate scandal behind us and tackle increasingly urgent political matters that have been neglected. A reasonable case could be and was made both for and against the pardon.

The significant point I want to stress in the context of this chapter, however, is that the legitimacy of Ford's authority was not thrown into doubt by questioning the advisability of the pardon. His decision may have been unwise and unjust but he was within his rights as President to make it, even if it was wrong. The legitimacy of political authorities depends on whether they have acquired their position in accordance with legally prescribed procedures and whether they exercise their authority within the rights and responsibilities that the law also prescribes. Ford had met these conditions. At the same time, there is good reason to suppose that he did not use his authority well. Perhaps he did as well as he could but that left much to be desired. He was a legitimate and a poor President.

It is important to recognize that political authorities can be legitimate and yet perform poorly. This is what made some Presidents, like Wilson and Carter, bad. Good Presidents not only have legitimate political authority but they also use it well, as I think Truman and Eisenhower had done. There were also great Presidents, like Washington and Lincoln, who had been not only legitimate and good but also possessed personal authority that allowed them to guide Americans at difficult times when guidance was badly needed. It is, of course, highly desirable to have great or good Presidents but the fact remains that the legitimacy and good performance of political authorities are only contingently connected in democracies. Political authorities may use their authority poorly and yet remain legitimate.

The good use of political authority depends on discharging of the responsibilities of a political office reasonably. This involves accurate estimate of the seriousness of the prevailing dissatisfactions, historical knowledge of how well or badly similar dissatisfactions were handled in the past, knowledge also of the feasible policies that are available in particular circumstances and of the likely costs and consequences of the adoption of these policies. Political authorities need good judgment about political matters. The extent to which they have it is the extent to which their legitimacy and good performance coincide.

It is a serious problem in democracies that the majority of citizens who vote for or against various candidates for office neither have nor need good political judgment. They tend to be busy with their own affairs, lack adequate information and experience in formulating and comparing the merits of alternative policies. As a result, they often cannot tell whether the candidates have good judgment. It is, therefore, a constant danger in democracies that less deserving candidates are preferred to more deserving ones. As far as I can see, this is an unavoidable problem in contemporary democracies.

Political authorities can be voted out of office of course, but this does not solve the problem. For few citizens are in a position to know whether they are dissatisfied with an elected official because he or she is incompetent or whether the official did as well as possible by pursuing the least unsatisfactory policy in coping with genuine difficulties. And even if poor performance were obvious and the responsible official was voted out of office, the newly elected replacement may turn out to be as poor as the previous one. The problem is that the skills required for winning an election are not the skills required for doing well once elected. Winning an election depends on appealing to the electorate's dissatisfactions and proposing simple, easily understandable ways of removing them. This is precisely what ideologues do. Their rhetoric stresses the importance of a political good and ignores all the other political goods that are no less important than the one they favor.

Doing well once elected, however, depends on coping with dissatisfactions by balancing the conflicting claims of many different political goods and privileging none of them. This is a complicated task and understanding its complexities depends on detailed knowledge of concrete circumstances and of the comparative merits of available policies. Most citizens lack such knowledge. If in doubt, think of the complexities involved in the judging the safety of nuclear reactors, the consequences of various proposals for tax reform, the costs and benefits of possible trade agreements, or the ways in which ever-rising costs of health care could be controlled. The reasonable balanced approach to politics, therefore, tends to be hard to understand and unpopular, while simple-minded populist sloganeering is a permanent threat in democracies.

The source of these problems is the contingent connection between the legitimacy and competence of political authorities. Many of our dissatisfactions are the result of the poor performance of legitimate office-holders. Yet living with these dissatisfactions is preferable to making the legitimacy of political authority depend on good performance. For the distinction between poor and good performance can be reasonably drawn only by those who know and understand the complexities political authorities face. Since few people have this knowledge and understanding, the electorate in democracies cannot draw the distinction. The choice, therefore, is either to live with the contingent connection between legitimacy and good performance, or to replace democracy with some other form of government in which legitimacy depends on good performance. The choice is not hard to make because, as history so amply shows, many other forms of government have been tried but none has been found that could succeed where democracies fail. We must put up with democratic politics in which we forever have to choose between greater and lesser dissatisfactions. Democratic politics is the politics of imperfection.

To summarize: political authorities are legitimate if they have been elected or appointed to legislative, executive, or judicial offices in accordance with accepted procedures and if they stay within their rights and discharge their responsibilities. These procedures, rights, and responsibilities are defined by law. There is, therefore, a necessary connection between the legitimacy of political authorities and the rule of law. Political authorities may perform their official tasks better or worse but their legitimacy does not depend on how well they do them. They can be impeached in rare circumstances, but only if they are found guilty of gross misuse of their rights or grievous neglect of their responsibilities.

American society could not function without political authorities. There must be laws defining permissible and impermissible conduct, the laws must be enforced, and disputes about their interpretation must be settled. Countless policies concerning defense, security, the economy, foreign relations, health, taxation, the infrastructure, education, and so forth have to be formulated. Forms and conditions of contracts, licenses, immigration, employment, and welfare must be defined. Dates for public holidays and elections must be set. Births, marriages, and deaths must be officially certified. Political authorities are needed to coordinate the activities of people living together in a society and this makes them indispensable.

11.3 PERSONAL AUTHORITY

Confucius is thought to have lived between 551 and 479 B.C. For more than 2000 years he was recognized as the most important personal authority in China. The work known as *The Analects* is a compilation of his supposed, often cryptic, utterances directed toward particular persons in a context whose details are obscure. It is never easy to understand the full significance of what Confucius is reported to have said. It complicates matters further that unlike comparable Western figures, such as Socrates, Confucius does not offer reasons for what he says. He addresses his remarks to particular persons, and his aim is to make them see matters in a better light than their own and thereby become better human beings.

One instance of this is an exchange between Confucius and Zigong about the ceremony of sacrificing sheep on the first day of the month. The ceremony was meant to be a meaningful occasion on which the ruler announced the tasks of the month to the responsible officials. The sheep was sacrificed as a way of asking the powers that be to help with these tasks, expressing piety toward the natural order of things, reminding everyone of that order, and reaffirming it. The ceremony, however, has become an empty ritual. Sheep were sacrificed, but piety was neither felt nor expressed through the ceremony. The significance of the ceremony as the celebration of the natural order was lost. Against this background Zigong asks whether it would not be better to do away with what has become the meaningless sacrifice of the sheep. And Confucius says to him: "you begrudge the sheep used in this, but I begrudge the ritual."

What Confucius says indicates several significant features of the exercise of personal authority. Confucius responds to a question that is put to him. He speaks because he was asked. He does not issue a command, impose his will, or tell Zigong what he should do. He rather shows how he, Confucius, thinks about the matter. In thinking as he does, Confucius mediates between a tradition that he and Zigong share and a defect in it. Zigong's question is prompted by this defect. It is a question they both want to answer because they are committed to the tradition. Confucius thinks that the defect is that the ceremony no longer expresses and affirms important attitudes in the lives of those who share the tradition. This is a loss that matters. The question Zigong puts to Confucius is difficult. There is no simple answer to how to cope with a serious defect that people recognize in a tradition they value and to which they are committed. Should they reaffirm the old attitudes that are being forgotten or should they try to form new attitudes toward changing circumstances? Finding an answer requires understanding both the tradition and the new circumstances, judging the importance of the old attitudes, and weighing whether possible new attitudes would be adequate substitutes for the old ones. It is unlikely that most people, kept busy by the demands of their lives, would have the understanding, judgment, sense of proportion, and seriousness to answer these questions. That is why they need the guidance of personal authorities who have what they lack.

In these remarks about why personal authorities are needed I have referred to a tradition Confucius and Zigong share. I have given an account of moral traditions earlier (see 3.2) but perhaps a brief reminder of its salient points is in order. There are universal, social, and personal goods required for living a good life. Universal goods are the same for everyone; social goods vary with societies; and personal goods vary with individuals. A society's views about these goods and conventions are embedded in its legal, moral, religious, aesthetic, educational, and other traditions. The system formed of all the recognized goods, conventions, and traditions is what I have called the evaluative framework of a society. It is in this sense that I am talking about a tradition that Confucius and Zigong share.

Traditions, the three kinds of goods, and the required and variable conventions exist in a state of tension. There are unavoidable disputes about their interpretations and comparative importance in particular situations. People's allegiance to them is weakened or strengthened by comparisons, criticisms, successes, and failures. And both the evaluative framework and particular traditions have to be adjusted in response to ever-changing circumstances. The well-being of people living in a society requires coping with these difficulties. Personal authorities are those whose excellence consists in a deep understanding of their tradition that gives them good judgment about how to cope with these conflicts. Zigong's question is a request to Confucius to use his personal authority to mediate between their tradition and a problem that arises in it. Zigong asks for his mediation because he recognizes that his own judgment has become inadequate. He, and of course others, encounter an increasing number of situations in which the simple connection between hitherto acceptable attitudes and a particular problem at hand has been broken. They no longer know what their attitude should be, how they should see the problem.

Is the sacrifice of sheep just an act of cruelty? Is it a waste of livestock? Is it a hypocritical show of piety? Is it a stalwart adherence to old attitudes in a changing world? There is no obviously persuasive answer because the old attitudes are no longer generally held. Those who value their tradition no longer know whether they should stop the sacrifice, or continue to express the old attitudes even as they are being widely abandoned, or just do as they please because they can no longer rely on their tradition for guidance. Their state of mind is not unlike that of contemporary Americans toward marriage. It is called into question by secularization, countless unmarried people living together, the frequency of divorce, single-parent families, and homosexual unions. It is in just such cases that individuals need to turn to personal authorities to help them cope with the problem they face in the no longer clear light of their tradition.

To see how personal authorities can provide the needed help, it is important to remember that they offer a judgment, not a command. They do not say: do this, rather than that. They say: if you look at the problem in this way, it will become clear to you what you should do. Their judgment is not a decision they hand down as a judge might, but an interpretation of a complex situation formed of a particular case, changing circumstances, attitudes of uncertain relevance, and a valued tradition in the background. Do not begrudge the sheep, says Confucius, begrudge the ritual. What matters, he suggests, is that human lives should be meaningful, not the life expectancy of sheep or the cost of the ceremony. Or, as it might be said in response to our uncertainties about marriage, what matters is that two people should form a lasting intimate relationship, face the world together, and be united by love, appreciation, and delight in each other. To focus on the legalities in changing circumstances and attitudes is to misjudge what is important. The guidance of personal authorities is based on a deeper understanding of their tradition than what other people have and on their excellence in dealing with complexities that bedevil others.

In our everyday lives we often encounter such complexities. We have grown uncertain about what we owe our parents, children, and ourselves; how to respond to corrupt practices; whether we should get out of an unsatisfactory marriage; what risks are worth taking in support of an unpopular cause; how to allocate our time and energy between private pursuits and public causes; how we should think about abortion, assisted suicide, welfare programs, capital punishment, or pornography; what really is our attitude toward religion, race, sex, money, death; and so forth. We are routinely perplexed about such matter but nevertheless have to make choices and act on them. In such situations we need the guidance of personal authorities and we would willingly follow it if we could trust it. This is not because we are unreasonable, craven, deceived, or indoctrinated but because we want to make the right choice and personal authorities may help us make it. They can do so because they have thought more deeply about our shared tradition and they know better than we how to deal with its complexities. Personal authorities are legitimate if they in fact know better. Their legitimacy depends on their excellence, not on their office or title, for they need not have one.

The problem is that there are many false personal authorities who pretend to an excellence they in fact lack. Here we encounter the same problem as we have found in discussing political authorities. How can those who turn to authorities because they lack the excellence the authorities claim to have know whether the claim is true? I said that in the case of political authorities the voters cannot know before they vote whether a candidate will be worthy of an office and that this is an unavoidable problem in democracies. It is otherwise with personal authorities. It is possible to know whether they have the required excellence or merely falsely claim to have it because legitimate personal authorities have observable signs of excellence.

The first of these signs is a thorough understanding of a tradition. This is not particularly hard to acquire. Experience and living in a society are normally sufficient for it. Those who have this understanding know how to distinguish between simple and complex, routine and controversial, banal and surprising cases. They know what it is to treat someone fairly or unfairly, harshly or indulgently, generously or meanly. They know what counts as negligence, scrupulousness, diligence, efficiency, or going beyond the call of duty. They know when they can trust their intuitions and when they have to stop and think. They are skilled in applying the vocabulary of their tradition to evaluate relevant conduct. Anyone with sufficient motivation, moderate ability, and long enough practice will meet this elementary, but by no means only, sign of personal authority.

That this understanding is not sufficient for personal authority becomes obvious once it is seen that having it is compatible with rejecting or being indifferent toward a tradition. Anthropologists studying it or hypocrites violating it whenever they can get away with it may be familiar with a tradition and be skilled in mediating between it and difficult cases. They may know what the tradition prescribes, but they need not accept its prescriptions. They may act according to them, but only because expediency dictates it.

It is necessary therefore to add a second sign required by legitimate personal authorities: commitment to the tradition. They believe that they ought to live and act according to the conventions of the tradition, and they endeavor to do so. This, however, is still an insufficient sign of legitimacy because much depends on how the understanding and the commitment are acquired and acted on. The lives and actions of some people may just reflect rigorous training in the course of which their minds and hearts are so thoroughly influenced as to make it psychologically impossible for them to regard any other tradition or basic dissent from their own as a live option for themselves. They know of course that other people at other places have different commitments, but they know it only intellectually. There are cannibals, samurai, shamans, men with harems, and women with bordellos, but what has that got to do with them? They are immersed in their lives, have no doubts about their tradition, they see the world from its perspective, and their motivation has no contrary sources.

We need to add, therefore, a third sign of the legitimacy of personal authority: reflectiveness. Reflectiveness involves understanding the vision at the core of a tradition. The vision is of human possibilities and limits and of how best to pursue the first and recognize the second. Reflectiveness involves penetrating to the deepest level of a tradition and to understand what motivates it. For Christians, it is the imitation of Christ; for Jews, the covenant with God; for liberals, individual autonomy; for utilitarians, the happiness of humanity; for Plato, the transformation of the self as guided by knowledge of the Good; and so on. If the prevailing form of a tradition is seen as the concrete expression of the underlying vision, then there will be a principled way of justifying, criticizing, or changing it. Traditions change with times and circumstances. Reflectiveness allows legitimate personal authorities to evaluate the changes and the advisability of future ones by comparing the prevailing state of the tradition with the underlying vision. The evaluation may be unfavorable, and personal authorities may be critics of the *status quo*.

A further sign of the exercise of personal authority is to make vivid to their subjects the vision that lies behind the commitments that they have made. The vision may fade; commitments may weaken; limited energy, lack of emotional agility, and the demands of everyday life often make it hard to bear the vision in mind; wickedness, weakness, and love of comfort frequently act as countervailing motivational forces; and the inevitable defects in the tradition further cloud the original vision. People turn to personal authorities for help when they find themselves beset by such conflicts, doubts, and weakening commitments. The way they can be helped is to remind them of what they already know but tend to forget under the pressure of their lives and circumstances: the vision that provides the rationale for living as they do.

Implicit in this account of reflectiveness is a further sign of the legitimacy of personal authorities: articulateness. Personal authorities can make simple the situations others find complex because they have reflected more deeply on their tradition than those who turn to them for help. But they could not help them if their reflectiveness merely enabled them to see clearly what appears to be obscure for others. They must also be able to communicate what they have seen in a way that would make those who have not seen it see it too. Personal authorities must be teachers, and they must know how to bring those who want to learn from being lost in complexities to the point where their own efforts to cope with them will suffice.

There is one further sign. Its necessity emerges if we bear in mind that the subjects' recognition of personal authorities is always a matter of trust. It involves the belief that the judgments of personal authorities are better than their own. What is it about personal authorities that make it reasonable for people to trust their judgments more than they trust their own? It must be some readily observable sign, and it is that the conduct of personal authorities is exemplary as judged the conventions of their tradition. The trust placed in personal authorities is warranted, therefore, by the way they live. They are recognized as authorities because they have shown how to live well according to the tradition they and their subjects share. Their authority derives from the admired examples they set to those who want to live that way. This bridges the gap between being a legitimate personal authority and being recognized as such. Articulateness alone is insufficient because it is unclear whether verbal facility is a sign of understanding, commitment, and reflectiveness, or merely of rhetorical talent. But if the lives and actions of putative personal authorities are of a piece with the vision they articulate, then they demonstrate in the most convincing way possible that they mean what they say, that it is reasonable to trust them, and that they are indeed legitimate personal authorities.

Legitimate personal authorities, therefore, are essential to the viability of the traditions of a society, and the traditions are essential constituents of the evaluative framework of the lives of people in that society. Traditions provide many of the possibilities of life that individuals find attractive and strive to realize and many of the limits they must observe in order to live with others. From their traditions people derive ideals about how to live and their efforts to live that way give meaning and purpose to their lives. As the epigraph to this chapter says, it anchors their liberty, not by providing mere choices, but by providing worthwhile possibilities among which individuals can choose some to make their own. Lives are made good by the goods they contain, and traditions are the repositories and protectors of many of those goods. This is what legitimate personal authorities help to sustain, this is why they are indispensable, and this what makes personal authorities one of the political goods.

11.4 IMPLICATIONS

The political goods I am discussing in this book are, of course, among the goods of our evaluative framework. They are important goods because they are necessary conditions of our well-being. But they are only necessary conditions. Our well-being depends also on other goods, and they are non-political. They are goods that make our lives interesting, enjoyable, creative, reflective, compassionate, adventurous, loving, learned, or conscientious. They are derived from personal relationships and from the understandings, feelings, imaginative constructions, and sympathies involved in the practice or the appreciation of science, history, the arts, literature, religion, music, or philosophy. I call them collectively personal goods because their recognition, pursuit, and enjoyment vary with individual character, education, and experience. They are not personal in the sense of being subjective, as opposed to objective, nor in being private, rather than communal. What makes them good are not our attitudes toward them, but that they actually enrich the lives of those who can enjoy them. And their enjoyment may depend either on participation in the activities of a community of like-minded people, or on the private cultivation of an innate or acquired ability.

Our evaluative framework contains both political and personal goods and both are conditions of our well-being, but they are different conditions. Political goods are instrumental, whereas personal goods are good in themselves, not as means to something else. Personal goods are intrinsically enjoyable, political goods are not. If equality, justice, liberty, and the other political goods were not needed for the enjoyment of personal goods, they would be dispensable. Given our nature and the world, these and other political goods are important and necessary means to the enjoyment of personal goods, but their importance and necessity derive from the ends to which they lead.

I stress that political goods and personal goods are related as means are to ends because it follows from their relationship that the ideological approach to politics is incorrigibly mistaken. It is an essential feature of ideologies that they are committed to regarding a particular political good as the highest of all goods. Whenever the enjoyment of any personal good conflicts with the highest political good, ideologues resolve the conflict in favor of the political good. What makes a society good, ideologues claim, is that equality, or justice, or liberty, prevails in it, and to this highest of all goods all personal goods must be subordinated. The political, according to ideologues, takes precedence over the personal. The incorrigible ideological mistake is to subordinate the ends, namely personal goods, to a means, namely the favored political good, that leads to them. Ideologues are doctrinally committed to reversing the natural order of importance between means and ends. They lose sight of the fact that we value political goods only because we could not have personal goods without them.

This is not a mistake that could be corrected by amending the details of the ideological approach, say by substituting one political good for another as the highest, or claiming that not one but two or three political goods jointly are the highest. For the mistake is to regard any political good as the highest and to subordinate all personal goods to it. Only by abandoning the essential ideological commitment to the elevation of some political good to the highest status could this mistake be avoided. That, however, would be to abandon the ideological approach.

Recognizing that the subordination of personal goods to a supposedly highest political good is a mistake should not lead us to make the opposite mistake of subordinating political to personal goods. For political goods remain necessary means to the pursuit of personal goods. If the pursuit of personal goods involved the violation of political goods, it would doom itself by undermining the conditions of its own success. The way to avoid both mistakes is to avoid attributing the highest status to any good, regardless of whether it is political or personal. And this just what the balanced view does. According to it, there is no good of any kind that always overrides the claims of any good that conflicts with it.

Defenders of the balanced view can consistently acknowledge that in the case of particular conflicts one good may override another. But which should override which depends on the context of the conflict, and the contexts change as historical, cultural, economic, technological, and other conditions change. There is nevertheless an objective standard to which we can appeal in deciding in any particular context which of the conflicting goods should take precedence. The decision should be guided by the need to protect the evaluative framework of a society formed of all the recognized goods, conventions, and traditions. The protection of that framework is always more important than the protection of any of its constituents.

This does not reduce the balanced view to just another ideology that is committed to yet another highest good as the standard. For the evaluative framework is not a good but a continually changing system of goods, protected by changing conventions, and incorporating particular moral traditions formed out of some of these changing goods and conventions. An evaluative framework is a standard but it is a forever changing one that lacks the universality ideologues require of the highest good. It makes reasonable conflict-resolutions possible but it recognizes that what is reasonable in one context may not be reasonable in another. The art of politics is to cope with conflicts within an evaluative framework by maintaining an optimal balance among all the conflicting goods, conventions, and traditions in the midst of continually changing circumstances.

It may be objected that the balanced view simply assumes that the evaluative framework that constitutes the standard of reasonable conflict-resolution is acceptable. The assumption is unwarranted, it may be said, because an evaluative framework may be unacceptably narrow, vicious, discriminatory, dogmatic, and so forth. If the standard is the evaluative framework, then how could the standard itself be reasonably justified or criticized? How could disagreements about the acceptability of an evaluative framework be reasonably settled?

The answer is that if people living in a society are by and large able to enjoy the universal, social, and personal goods they need, and if the required and variable conventions have, with appropriate changes, stood the test of time and continued to attract general allegiance, then there is good reason to believe that the evaluative framework is acceptable. And if the evaluative framework is defective, as all of them are to some extent, because its participants lack some of the goods they need or because they keep violating some of the conventions, then there is good reason to criticize and try to improve it. It may also happen that serious efforts at improvement fail. Then there is good reason to abandon the evaluative framework in favor of another with fewer defects. But there is no reasonable alternative to trying to live according to one evaluative framework or another because that would mean trying to live without the evaluative dimension of life, and such a life would not be human.

If the account of political and personal authority I have been giving is even approximately correct, it implies that the personal, as opposed to the political, sphere of life in democracies is necessarily committed to the inequality of its participants. For traditions form a large part of the personal sphere and the distinctions between good and bad and better and worse lives and actions are essential features of a tradition. These distinctions are based on the extent to which the participants' lives possess universal, social, and personal goods and actions conform to the required and variable conventions. The vast majority of lives and actions obviously differ in these respects and the differences are important. It matters, for example, how just or unjust, prudent or imprudent, tolerant or intolerant, law-abiding or criminal individuals and their actions are. It is important whether they strengthen or weaken the evaluative framework on which everyone's well-being depends. Individuals and actions systematically differ in these respects and the differences make them morally better or worse. If a society has an evaluative framework, the inequality of its participants will inevitably follow. And if a society lacked an evaluative framework, it would be disintegrating.

This is not to doubt that equality is a political good. It remains a good in the political and legal spheres of life. It is right and proper that the citizens of a democracy should have equal political and legal rights and responsibilities. If political authorities have more extensive rights and responsibilities than others, it must be because those who have less granted them to the political authorities in accordance with constitutional procedures. But equality is not a good in the personal sphere of life. The egalitarian insistence that it should be recognized as a good in that sphere is incompatible with the distinctions that an evaluative framework requires drawing. Since our well-being depends on our evaluative framework that provides the goods, conventions, and traditions we need for our well-being, egalitarianism is incompatible with our well-being.

The political implication of all this is that American society must be as committed to supporting inequality in the personal sphere as to supporting equality in the political sphere. Each is centrally important in the appropriate sphere. Any ideology that fails to acknowledge this is for that reason dangerously mistaken.

11.5 LEGITIMATE AUTHORITY

One conclusion that emerges from this chapter is that authority, in its political and personal forms, is an indispensable condition of human well-being. Political authorities coordinate and regulate the activities of people living together in a society and propose policies for coping with the prevailing dissatisfactions. Personal authorities protect the evaluative framework of a society by coping with the defects and finding ways of adapting our traditions, with their goods and conventions, to fit continually changing circumstances. A society cannot endure if these tasks are not performed successfully. American society ought to be committed, therefore, to recognizing authority as a political good and to maintaining the political conditions that enable it to exist and function. We can, then, continue to expand the list of political goods that the balanced view is committed to defending by adding legitimate authority to the other basic political goods.

Balancing political goods requires imposing on them both internal and external limits. The internal limits are set by narrowing the interpretation of the political good in question. All political goods lend themselves to unreasonably wide interpretations that make it possible to treat many other political goods as merely special applications of one of the goods. Reason may be interpreted as commitment to pluralism, limits, and justice. Equality may be thought of as guaranteeing justice and liberty for everyone. Democracy may be said to be the form of government in which pluralism, justice, and equality prevail. The result of such promiscuous interpretations is to ignore the essential differences among the political goods. But it is precisely in virtue of these differences that political goods continually conflict and the resolution of their conflicts constitutes a central political problem in contemporary democracies. Moreover, it is these conflicts that require imposing external limits on recognized political goods. The balanced view sets these limits by denying that there is any political good that always takes precedence over the others and by resolving their conflicts by limiting each good in order to optimize the extent to which all of them can be maximally enjoyed.

What is true of political goods in general is true also of political and personal authorities in particular. Both must be interpreted narrowly and not allowed to override all other political goods. I have argued that both requirements can be met by specifying what makes political and personal authorities legitimate. As we have seen, the legitimacy of political authorities depends on acquiring their position by following constitutional procedures and exercising the authority of their position within its rights and responsibilities. The legitimacy of personal authorities, by contrast, depends on their personal excellence as indicated by their understanding, commitment, reflectiveness, articulateness, and exemplary conduct within the context of their tradition.

CHAPTER TWELVE

✦ ✦ ✦

CIVILITY AS A SOCIAL CONDITION

The ... essential condition of stability in political society, is a strong and active principle of cohesion among the members of the same community ... a feeling of common interest among those who live under the same government, and are contained within the same natural or historical boundaries. We mean, that part of the community do not consider themselves as foreigners with regard to another part; that they set a value on their connexion—feel that they are one people, that their lot is cast together, that evil to any of their fellow-countrymen is evil to themselves, and do not desire ... to free themselves from their share of any common inconvenience by severing the connexion.

JOHN STUART MILL
A System of Logic

12.1 THE CONDITION AND ITS OPPOSITE

IF A SOCIETY WERE FORTUNATE enough to have and to have balanced the various basic political goods I have so far discussed, there would still be something missing. For the political conditions of the well-being of its members require more than just a large number of people pursuing side-by-side their individual interests. The porcupines in Schopenhauer's remarkable parable (see 6.3) do not merely learn to keep their optimal distance from one another. They also need to draw as close together as their quills permit in order to generate sufficient warmth to escape from the cold outside their circle. This centripetal warmth has been called by Aristotle civic friendship, by Hume and Adam Smith sympathy, and by Mill the feeling of common interest of which the epigraph speaks. I will call it civility, and claim that it too is one of the basic political goods.

In current usage, civility is often treated as a virtual synonym of politeness, but this is not what I mean by it. What I mean is well-said by Mill in the epigraph. This sense is also recognized by the *Oxford English Dictionary*, which lists, among others, "Senses connected with civilization, culture. . . . The state of being civilized; freedom from barbarity. . . . Behaviour proper to the intercourse of civilized people; . . . decent respect, consideration." And it also lists as one of the definitions of civil "In that social condition which accompanies and is involved in citizenship or life in communities; not barbarous; civilized, advanced in the arts of life." Civility, as I will understand it, then, is a social condition involved in citizenship.

By way of an initial account of this condition, here are two description of it. The first is of a context in which the condition holds optimally, and the second is when it has been destroyed. In his 1920 *Character and Opinion in the United States*, Santayana writes about the "omnipresence in America of this spirit of co-operation, responsibility, and growth. . . . Far from being . . . lost in the opposite instincts of so many alien races, it seems to be adopted at once by the most mixed circles and in the most novel predicaments. . . . Where individuality is . . . free, co-operation . . . can be all the more quick and hearty. Everywhere co-operation is taken for granted. . . . Together with the will to work and to prosper, it is of the essence of Americanism, and it is accepted as such by all the unkempt polyglot peoples . . . with the . . . manly purpose of beginning life on a new principle. Every political body, every public meeting, every club, or college, or athletic team, is full of it. . . . The general instinct is . . . to pull through somehow by mutual adaptation, and by seizing on the readiest practical measures and working compromises. . . . All meet in a genuine spirit of consultation, eager to persuade but ready to be persuaded.... It is implicitly agreed, in every case, that disputed questions shall be put to a vote, and that the minority will loyally acquiesce in the decision of the majority.... Such a way of proceeding seems in America a matter of course, because it is bred in the bone, or imposed by that permeating social contagion which is so irresistible.... But if we consider human nature at large and the practice of most nations, we shall see that it is a very rare, wonderful and unstable convention.... Impulses of reason and kindness ... under such circumstances can become effective; people can help one another with no great sacrifice to themselves.... The community prospers; comfort and science, good manners and generous feelings are diffused among the people, without the aid of the foresight and cunning direction which sometimes give a temporary advantage to a rival system." This is the condition of civility when all is well with it. We can only wish that the ideal were realized by us here and now. We may also doubt that it had been realized in the early years of the last century but these doubts do not affect the desirability of civility. It would remain an important political good even if the condition had never been realized.

Now contrast Santayana's description with the hell on earth created when the gap between civility and actual conditions has become an abyss. The contrasting description appears in a private letter the linguist, Olga Friedenberg, wrote in the 1930s in what was then the Soviet Union. "Wherever you looked, in all our institutions, in all our homes, *skloka* was brewing. *Skloka* is a phenomenon born of our social order, an entirely new term and concept, not to be translated into any language of the civilized world. It is hard to define. It stands for base, trivial hostility, unconscionable spite breeding pretty intrigues, the vicious pitting of one clique against another. It thrives on calumny, informing, spying, scheming, slander, the igniting of passions. Taut nerves and weakening of morals allow one individual or group rabidly to hate another individual or group. *Skloka* is natural for people who have been incited to attack one another, who have been made bestial by desperation, who have been driven to the wall."

It is clear, I hope, that civility is a condition worth pursuing and that it is crucial to avoid the state of *skloka*. But it is not clear what precisely civility involves; what its characteristics are; and what forms it takes. These are the questions I will now endeavor to answer. The answer needs to describe the relationship of civility that holds between individuals and the attitude of individuals who stand in that relationship. I will discuss the relationship first and the attitude next. I take for granted that the extent to which civility prevails in a particular society at a particular time is a matter of degree and that individuals routinely have many other relationships and attitudes than the ones involved in civility.

12.2 THE RELATIONSHIP

The relationship involved in civility holds between individuals, not between individuals and some collectivity, such as a church, a university, or a club. It is a *conventional* relationship, not a natural one like those between parents and children, patients suffering from the same disease, or people living in the same geographical area or at the same time. The relationship typically holds between adult members of the same society, but it may extend beyond its limits. Some examples of civility are relationships between co-religionists; fellow scientists; members of a fraternity, club, or university; professionals sharing a specialty; sports fans; neighbors; business partners; music lovers; chess players; gardeners; dog breeders; war veterans; bird watchers; and so forth. It may hold between professionals and amateurs, savants and dilettantes, leaders and followers, contributors and critics, active participants and passive spectators, rich and poor, young and old, and so on.

Civility is also a *voluntary* relationship. Individuals participate in it because they find it satisfying and they may sever it if it no longer yields the hoped for satisfactions or if they come to prefer some other relationship, which may or may not be a form of civility. Participation in the relationship may be based on explicit choice, such as membership in a club or practicing a profession, but this is not always so. People are often born into a form of civility, raised in it, and simply continue participating in it in adult life, as they may do with their religion or family business. The relationship is on certain terms dictated by the customs and the formal or informal rules that have emerged in the course of the history of that form of civility. Conformity to these conventions, however, is neither coercive nor enforceable. Participation is conditional on following the conventions and fairly regularly meeting the expectations of other participants. But if participants find conformity or the expectations onerous, they have an exit right.

It remains true, however, that it is difficult to exercise that right because the relationship is usually *meaningful* and severing it has the heavy cost of losing something that participants have found valuable. Abandoning a profession, giving up a cause, moving away from a long familiar neighborhood, losing religious faith, becoming unable to pursue a hitherto strong interest creates emptiness that was previously filled with significance and comfort. If this happens, the evaluative dimension of life is impoverished. This is the penalty for opting out of a form of civility, but it is self-imposed rather than meted out by an authority. No wonder, therefore, that people are reluctant to sever such relationships even though they could do so freely.

Civility is a *reciprocal* relationship but it is reciprocity of a particular kind. It is not one of intimacy, such as married couples, lovers, and close friends may have. For civility involves only casual acquaintance and those related by civility may know very little of each others' lives apart from what bears on the form of civility in which they jointly participate. Yet it is not an impersonal relationship either in which people participate merely for the mutual advantage they derive from their association, as do trading partners, lenders and borrowers, or plumbers and homeowners. Civility is less warm than intimacy but warmer than impersonal mutual advantage. It is based on the shared recognition of the participants that they have the same allegiance to a particular ideal, they are alike in their dedicated engagement in a valued activity, they conduct themselves, in the relevant respect, according to the same customs or rules, and they admire the same outstanding achievements that set standards of excellence in their common pursuit. The meaningfulness of civility derives precisely from this shared allegiance to an ideal, engagement in a valued activity, and admiration of the same achievements.

It follows that the participants regard their relationship as *prescriptive*, not merely as descriptive, as may be done by classmates, patients in a hospital, or candidates for the same job. Civility is prescriptive because the participants are committed to judging the same way in the relevant sphere of life by using the same standards to distinguish between excellence and deficiency, conformity and deviation, expertise and dilettantism, tradition and innovation, relevance and irrelevance, and so forth. It is this shared aspect of the evaluative dimension of their lives that makes civility a more intimate relationship than mere impersonal association for mutual advantage and yet less intimate than what may hold between masters and disciples, parents and children, or comrades. For the many areas of life that lie beyond the particular form of civility that the participants share are irrelevant to their relationship, whereas anything they care or not care about may be of interest and be shared by intimates.

As the foregoing imply, the relationship is essentially *performative*, by which I mean that people participate in it by what they do and how they do it. Being a professional, say a physician, is not just to have acquired a degree and a license to practice but also actually to practice it by diagnosing and treating disease, keeping up with new information and techniques, and consulting with other physicians about cases that are difficult or beyond their own expertise. Being a member of a club is not just to pay dues but to engage in the activities for which the club is formed, such as playing golf, dining with fellow members, going on bird-watching expedition, or whatever. Being a Catholic is not just to have been baptized in the Church but to go to confession and Mass, have a sense of sin, accept priestly authority, and so forth.

The relationship is thus *active* and *communal*. Active because it consists in doing what is appropriate in a particular form of civility. And it is communal because many of the things done are done with or in the company of other participants. The relationship centrally involves the participants in engaging in the same type of activity, following the same conventions, being aware of each other as they do it, and accepting the same standards as guides to how what they do is to be done.

Participation in the relationship tends to become part of people's second nature. A large majority of those who live in a society, which virtually everyone does, participate in several forms of civility: in professional societies; social clubs; neighborhood associations; churches; in groups of dedicated horticulturalist, chamber music lovers, sports fans, reading groups, private charities, literacy volunteers, vintage car restorers, scrabble players, martial artists, college alumni, and so on and on. Participation in such forms of civility has become a *habitual* part of many people's lives, and they need not be articulate or thoughtful about it. They are engaged because they find it satisfying. They feel no need to analyze why they are satisfied, nor do they feel the need to justify their engagement in it.

Forms of civility vary with societies and times. But in all societies where they exist—and it is important to remember that they may not—they form the substance of what may be called *common life* which occupies a space between the government and individuals. On one side of civility, there is the government whose business is politics, and part of politics is to make laws, enforce them, and adjudicate inevitable conflicts about the range, interpretation, and application of the laws. In a good society, the rule of law prevails and it sets limits to permissible forms of civility. These limits, however, are wide and a good society is hospitable to countless forms of civility. On the other side of civility, there is the private sphere of individual lives. It includes marriage, friendship, children, love affairs, earning a living, reading books, taking walks, handling investments, foreign travels, and so forth.

Politics, civility, and privacy are all important aspects of a good society but they are at once separate and overlapping. For politics through the rule of law provides the stable, orderly, and secure framework in which civility and privacy may prevail. Many of the ideals, conventions, and patterns of activity that individuals may adapt to their characters and circumstances are embedded in forms of civility. And privacy is the space left for individuals in which they can choose to participate in the various forms of civility from which they may derive meaning and comfort that satisfies their needs and warrants their allegiance.

In order to avoid misunderstanding the complex relationship between politics, civility, and privacy, I need to stress several points. First, in choosing to participate in forms of civility individuals need not be thoughtful or articulate. Their choices may just be made by default when they simply continue the familiar patterns in which they have been raised, which they could leave behind if they wish, but to which they nevertheless continue to adhere because they find them meaningful.

Second, although individuals derive part of their private concerns from forms of civility, the sphere of privacy is much richer than that. It also includes, among other matters, intimate relationships and attitudes to sex, work, leisure, death, illness, risk, money, and so forth. Their relationships and attitudes may be influenced but not determined by their allegiance to particular forms of civility. For it remains an individual matter what weight they attach to these influences. Third, while it is true that politics through the rule of law, and civility through conventional forms, set limits to privacy, the basic justification of both politics and civility is that they make the lives of individuals better. A substantial portion of what betterment consists in comes from the private sphere in which individuals make choices about how they think it is best to live, given their understanding of their characters and circumstances. Politics and civility provide the framework in which this can be done but the framework is for individuals, not the other way around.

Fourth, the relationship I have described between politics, civility, and privacy is of what it ought to be, not what it is in any known society. The political, civil, and private ought to be discrete and ought not impose their own concerns on the genuine and separate concerns of the other spheres. Yet what ought not happen happens all the time. Political considerations often intrude into civility and privacy. Purely private passions and preoccupations frequently corrupt civility and politics. And excessive civility may prevent the development of private life and divert much-needed attention from facing serious political problems. Each sphere is important and ought to be free from the unwarranted intrusion of the other spheres. But more important than any of them is the balancing of their respective claims. It seems to me that in American society ideological politics threatens to destroy civility. I will return to this point.

12.3 THE ATTITUDE

I have described the relationship of civility from the outside, from the perspective of an observer. I will now approach it from the inside, from the perspective of those who participate in it. Participants have a certain attitude toward one another, and no account of civility can be complete without recognizing the importance of this reciprocal attitude.

By an attitude I mean a complex psychological state that combines beliefs, feelings, and intentions directed toward the same object and, in normal circumstances, leads to appropriate action. The attitude involved in civility is composed of beliefs about the conventions, practices, and ideals of the form of civility in which the agent participates and about other participants holding by and large the same beliefs. The attitudes also include feelings about the importance, meaningfulness, and allegiance to the objects of these beliefs, as well as sympathy, fellow-feeling, warmth toward other participants who are believed to have similar feelings. These beliefs and feelings prompt intentions to follow the conventions, engage in the practices, try to approximate the ideals, and recognize those who share the beliefs and feelings as being moved by many of the same considerations. The intentions normally lead to appropriate actions, which participants not only perform themselves but see others performing often at the same time, place, and occasion. In this way, religious believers pray communally, fellow scientists pursue a shared research project, rock climbers roped together scale the face of a cliff, bird watchers delight in the sighting of a rare specimen, reading groups are moved by the victories or defeats of fictional characters, and defenders of a cause join forces to battle a common foe.

The significance of this attitude is not merely its possession by particular individuals but also their reciprocal recognition of one another as possessors of it, as participating in the same practice, respecting the same conventions, and admiring the same ideals. This enhances the significance of their own attitude, reinforces their beliefs, feelings, and intentions, and motivates their actions. They are thereby strengthened both in their individuality and in their sense of belongingness to the form of civility they share with like-minded others. Individuality and belongingness thus go together when individuals voluntarily participate in a form of civility because it satisfies their need for meaning and motivates their appropriate activities. In repressive societies the opposite happens because if individuals are forced to accept uncongenial conventions, practices, and ideals, then their individuality is expressed by resistance to being coerced in this way. But in American society such coercion is the exception, not the rule. This is not to say that all is well, only that our problems have different sources. Be that as it may, the widely shared belief that by belonging people are bound to compromise their individuality is mistaken. The contrary is true: people develop their individuality if they voluntarily participate in forms of civility they find meaningful.

A corollary of the shared sense of belongingness is that participants in a form of civility are not competitors but companions. They see each other as engaged in the same activity, having the same attitude, adhering to the same conventions, and being inspired by the same ideals. They naturally wish well for one another even though they may know little about the political views, private lives, or financial circumstances of other participants. What they share is an important part of their public lives. In that respect, they can count on a common understanding, on shared knowledge of what ought to be done on appropriate occasions, and on doing what ought to be done in the right way. They feel at ease in each other's company because they do not have to explain or justify why and what they do and how they do it.

If in a society the condition of civility is optimal, the shared feeling of good will extends beyond the context of particular forms of civility. In American society, there is a large plurality of different forms of civility. They are readily recognizable to normally intelligent citizens, even though they do not participate in many of the recognized forms. They are seen as available possibilities of life, as roads that may be taken in life's way, although they themselves chose to travel on other roads. If civility prevails, people will respect others who participate in forms of civility they recognize but do not share. Lutherans can wish well for creative artists, novelists for athletes, historians for philanthropists, priests for baseball players, musicians for arctic explorers, and vice versa.

What civility provides for those who live together in a society is a language of conduct. They all speak that language even though they use it to express very different things. Competent users readily recognize that meaningful commitments, dedication to ideals, individual perspectives on life can be expressed in many different ways, and they understand what is being expressed even though they themselves have different perspectives which they express in very different conduct. Yet all these people, expressing different things differently, share the language and recognize each other as competent users of it. They know when strong feelings are expressed and they can tactfully acknowledge the strong feelings of others even if they do not share them. When the condition of civility is optimal, the prevalent attitude is not toleration of disapproved forms of civility but accommodation of the wide variety of ways in which people can find meaning and purpose in their lives. If this desirable condition holds, people give each other the benefit of the doubt and they wish well for others who participate in other forms of civility.

Those who live together in a society share the surface activities of common life. They shop for groceries, balance their checkbooks, eat breakfast, go to work, have their cars serviced, ferry their children, gossip about their neighbors, and so forth. But if they are at all thoughtful, they realize that beneath this surface people have deeper allegiances to forms of civility, even if they do not call them by that name. Whether people are satisfied or frustrated by their lives partly depends on the forms civility in which they participate. For that is the commonest way in which they can find meaning and take comfort in their lives and have a reason for doing all the many mundane things that everyone is so busily engaged in. This reason, however, can be found only if forms of civility are available. And that is why I am saying that civility is one of the basic political goods on which the well-being of citizens in contemporary democracies depends.

It may be tempting to dismiss what I have been saying about the relationship and the attitude involved in civility as sentimental falsification of the actual conditions that prevail in contemporary democracies. This would be a just criticism if what I have been saying were meant as a description of what exists. But that is not how it is meant. It is meant as a description of what the optimal condition would be if it existed. American society approximates the optimal condition very imperfectly. Civility is seriously threatened. This is one cause of the prevalent sense of alienation in the midst of unprecedented prosperity, great personal liberty, and virtually unrestricted access to what is called higher education. I now turn to these threats.

12.4 INCIVILITY

Civility is a public and non-political part of life. Incivility threatens it by politicization, which is a consequences of the spread of ideological politics. The basic reason why ideology threatens civility is that ideology by its very nature is absolutistic, whereas civility is pluralistic. The more pervasive is the influence of ideology—any ideology—in a society, the less civility there is, and the more civility there is, the less scope does ideology have. An ideology (recall 1.4) combines a view of human nature and a hierarchical conception of political goods. The goods in the hierarchy are regarded as good because, given the ideology's view of human nature, they are thought to be necessary for human well-being. These goods form a hierarchy because one good, or perhaps the combination of a few, is taken to be the most important one for human well-being and therefore the highest, while other goods are said to derive their importance from their contribution to the realization of the highest good. Ideological politics, then, involves making and enforcing laws and pursuing policies that would make the realization of the supposed highest good more likely. Politics is thus regarded by ideologues as a moral enterprise since its aim is the improvement of human well-being. What improves it is good, what improves it most is best, and what detracts from or hinders its improvement is bad. The great merit ideologues always claim for their creed is that it authoritatively answers the questions of what is politically good or bad and why it is one or the other.

This makes the mere existence of forms of civility anathema to ideological politics. For their existence is a repudiation of the view that human well-being can be pursued only in the particular way ideology depicts. Human well-being partly depends on engagement in meaningful activities, and different people with different characters and in different circumstances find different activities meaningful. Religious worship, scientific research, historical understanding, artistic creativity, athletic endeavor, literary life, parachute jumping, public-spirited pursuits, dedication to a cause, connoisseurship in one of the arts, participation in bridge tournaments, fighting for justice, helping the poor, collecting first editions, and raising hostas are some of the countless activities that people find meaningful and in which they can participate only because the existing forms of civility create a hospitable conventional setting.

Ideologues cannot countenance this unregulated, undirected plurality. They are led by their commitment to evaluate conventional activities by whatever hierarchy of political goods is favored by their single-minded conception of human well-being. They criticize or justify existing forms of civility and the activities involved in them on the basis of their hierarchy of goods. And they condemn individuals, activities, and forms of civility if, according to the ideology, they contribute less than they should to human well-being.

These condemnations are moral, not political or prudential. For ideologues see people who participate in forms of civility that fail to conform to their ideology, not merely as wasting their time or being frivolous, but as immoral. By living as they do, they reveal their indifference or opposition to what is truly good. Against this, ideologues insist on the moral obligation to work for the enactment of laws and the implementation of policies that coerce people to participate in activities that their ideology deems good. They feel justified in this repudiation of civility because they believe that they are acting for the greater good by condemning intentional or unintentional enemies of human well-being and by coercing others to live and act as they would if they understood as well as the ideologies do the conditions of their own well-being.

This is the reason why some egalitarians malign their opponents as "beyond the pale of civilized dialogue," "immoral," "shameful," or as "Nazis"; why some utilitarians accuse those who fail to donate at least 10 percent of their after-tax income to relieve world hunger as "murderers"; why some impassioned do-gooders condemn those who do not share their promiscuous compassion as "dangerously rootless and hollow"; why some feminists insist that they ought not care about the truth but should concentrate on waging "intellectual guerilla warfare"; and why some radicals proclaim that "the goal of higher education should not be the pursuit of truth, which is both an illusion and an instrument of oppression, but social transformation . . . changing ideas, symbols, and institutions from tools of racist, sexist, capitalist, imperialist hegemony to instruments of empowerment for women, minorities, the poor and the Third World."

The result of this pervasive ideological mentality is the politicization of public life. Everything becomes a political issue, and since politics is seen in moralistic terms, everything becomes moralized as well. We are said to have a moral obligation not to buy groceries picked by non-unionized workers, not to eat meat, not to refer to God by the use of masculine pronoun; it has become a moral matter what we do with our garbage, what clothes we wear, where we pray or smoke, how we invest our money, what clubs we belong to, how we refer to people who are handicapped, what we use to heat our house, what jokes we tell; we must take a moral stand about whether utter strangers should or should not have an abortion, whether the suicide of sick old people should be decriminalized, whether felons should have the vote, whether illegal immigrants should be able to get a driver's license, whether goods should be shipped by trucks or trains, whether it is demeaning if men let women go first, whether corporations should pay more or less to their executives, whether school girls should have a wrestling team, whether it should be permissible to copulate with animals, and so on and on. Everybody's business has become everybody's business. We are thus forced to choose either to take a side in the shrill, intransigent antagonisms that ideologues have created by their misguided fervor or to shun the public sphere in order to escape the incessant, offensive bullying by the politicized moralizing of ideologues and their benighted followers. The choice is between participation in the public sphere whose forms of civility have been corrupted and withdrawal into private life impoverished by the lack of participation in forms of civility that used to make meaningful activities possible. One is as serious a threat to our well-being as the other. The mere fact that ideological intransigence forces us to choose, therefore, has grave implications.

The reason why we have to choose is that ideological politics is undermining the distinction between the private and the public spheres. What used to be private is increasingly forced into the public view and what used to be public increasingly intrudes into the private concerns of individuals. Historians of ideas have convincingly shown that the distinction between the public and the private is drawn very differently at different times and places. But the distinction has been drawn. The situation we face now is not that the dividing line is shifting but that the very distinction is being eroded. The hitherto widely shared sense is disappearing that each of us is sovereign master of a domain that contains some of our most private thoughts, feelings, and experiences. We may occasionally allow someone to whom we are exceptionally close to have a glimpse at our inner sanctum but otherwise, we used to feel, the world ought to be kept out. This is no longer so. The public more and more invades what used to be private and more and more what used to be private is exposed to the public.

Speaking of invasion is not an exaggeration. During a recent three-day weekend a friend of mine had to go to the emergency unit of a large hospital because she had severe abdominal pain and her physician was unavailable. A competent and friendly nurse took her history, part of which were the questions of whether she felt safe at home, whether anyone in her household uses—uses!—alcohol, and whether anyone has threatened her. When she protested that these impertinent questions have no relevance to the pain she is having, the nurse told her that the social service of the State mandated that they be asked. This is not an aberration but a symptom of the mentality that makes people's private concerns a matter of public interest.

There is no aspect of the life of public figures that escapes the minute scrutiny of the media. Casual sexual encounters that took place decades before are investigated; medical records are scrutinized; inquiries are made whether they smoked pot as college students; their neighbors are questioned about the comings and goings at their homes. The careers of journalists depend on unearthing what could be peddled as dirt to the prurient public. And all that sells is written up in newspapers or broadcast on radio or television. It is now obligatory for biographies to tell about their subject's sex life, religious practices or lack of them, divorces, fights and reconciliations with their spouses, friends, and children. Psychobabble about Oedipus complex, toilet training, birth trauma, repressed memories, anal retentiveness, and the like are taken seriously as politicians running for office and job applicants are scrutinized. Homosexuals are supposed to make public that that is what they are. The rehabilitation of alcoholics is taken to involve the repeated public admission that they are alcoholics. There is now an industry that specializes in the publication of the gory details drawn out of raped women, abused children, drug addicts, pornographic performers, tortured hostages, mental patients, and other unfortunate people of their humiliations and sufferings. Congressional hearings are dominated by ideologically motivated attempts to unearth possible past indiscretions of prominent judges, generals with distinguished service record, and dedicated private servants.

The justification offered for this grotesque, demeaning practice is that the public is entitled to know. But it is nonsense to suppose that the public is entitled to know the intimate details of other people's lives, details that have no conceivable relevance to how well those who are hounded may perform whatever their position requires. The real reason for the invasion of privacy is that ideologues allow nothing to escape their political scrutiny. Everybody is either a friend or an enemy; everything either helps or hinders human well-being. We all have to take a stand, declare our allegiance, and if we do not, we tacitly support the enemy, which is the status quo, the immoral state of affairs that it is the business of the ideology to remedy. If you do not publicly deplore racism, you are a racist; if you do not support the preferential treatment of women, you are a sexist; if you do not speak up for homosexual marriage, you are a homophobe; if you continue to use masculine pronouns in a gender-neutral sense, you support the oppression of women; if you do not send money to Amnesty International, you collude in the practice of torture; if you do not contribute to Oxfam, you choose self-indulgence over saving the lives of starving children; if you are not with us, you are against us.

The terrible consequence of the ideological polarization of the public sphere and the self-righteous invasion of private life is that it spreads like the plague. The public has come to mistake shrill moralistic rhetoric for genuine commitment. Effective opposition to it can no longer be moderate, measured, and civil. Like must be matched by like, otherwise reasonable voices are drowned out by the passionate intensity of benighted ideologues. If we respond in a like manner, we exacerbate the breakdown of civility and collude in destroying an essential condition of our well-being. If we fail to respond, we leave politics to those who are bent on destroying the plural forms of civility whose development has been one of the great achievements of American society. The plague is upon us and there are no good choices left.

The consequence is that Aristotle's civic friendship, Hume's and Adam Smith's sympathy, Mill's feeling of common interest,

Santayana's mutual adaptation, genuine spirit of cooperation, good manners, and generous feelings are disappearing from politics and their place is more and more taken up by *skloka*. Political opponents have become enemies and they no longer have decent respect and consideration of one another. The President of the United States is routinely compared to Nazis; Supreme Court decisions are described as "guided by no political or judicial principle" and "intellectually disreputable"; the Chief Justice is accused of the "continuing subversion of the American Constitution"; dedicated public servants are hounded out of office because congressional leaders dislike the policies they implement; the thousands of soldiers and police killed and wounded in the line of duty are unmentioned by the media but the handful of criminal acts committed in the heat of emergencies are front page news; and so on.

The enemies of civility are many and its defenders are hard pressed. I think that internal ideological attacks on civility are far more serious threats to American society than terrorism, Islamic militancy, and the emerging China. America has the means to defend itself against external enemies but it is an open question whether it can prevail against internal ones. Societies often disintegrate because of internal corruption and I regret to have to say that this has become a threat we should take seriously.

12.5 CIVILITY AS A SOCIAL CONDITION

I have been arguing in this chapter that civility is one of the basic political goods. The threat of incivility is serious because what it endangers is a political condition of our well-being. In closing, I will make explicit, first, two reasons why civility is important, and, second, why, its importance notwithstanding, the case for civility must be limited by considerations that have like importance.

If we were motivated only by rational self-interest, civility would not be particularly important. It would perhaps be like wit, charm, or a pleasing voice—a grace but a dispensable one. But we have motives other than rational self-interest. We want to have a sense of belongingness, we want companionship, approval, camaraderie, trust, and respect. We want to have closer relationships with others than mutually advantageous commercial transactions. Yet we want less than intimacy because it is demanding enough so that we could have it only with a few special partners. The intermediate nexus we want consists in friendly, casual, circumscribed, predictable encounters, solidarity and fellow-feeling, a shared sense of participation in some jointly valued activity, and the confidence that we can count on others to follow the shared rules. When these modest expectations are met in a society, we are connected with many others by reciprocal good will, such as may exist among neighbors, colleagues, worshippers, sports fans, opera lovers, joggers, and stamp collectors. We are like the porcupines, then, who have found the optimal distance not to be bothered by each other's quills and yet enjoy the warmth our contacts generate. This is just what civility provides. We would not die without it, but its lack would impoverish life and make it bleak and cold.

It might be thought that even if the public sphere were lacking in civility, it would not be as bad as I am supposing. We could still satisfy our emotional nature by nurturing the private sphere: the particular ways in which we develop our individuality, form intimate relationships, and try to realize whatever conception of well-being we happen to have. This, however, would not be possible without civility. For the contents of the private sphere are not created by us sui generis. We derive them from the public sphere, where we find possible ways of living and acting that have emerged in the course of the history of our society from successful experiments in living. Having an emotionally satisfying private life is a matter of choosing among the available possibilities ones that suit our particular character an circumstances. We can choose, however, only if there are possibilities available, and that is what forms of civility are. We make ourselves the individuals we end up being but we make it by imposing on the raw material of our inherited and acquired dispositions the forms we find in the public sphere. As the *Oxford English Dictionary* says, this is the "social condition which accompanies and is involved in citizenship or life in communities." It is a condition "not barbarous; civilized, advanced in the arts of life." Without civility, life would be barbarous, and, as it has been rightly said by Santayana, "the barbarian is the man who regard his passions as their own excuse for being; who does not domesticate them either by understanding their cause or by conceiving their ideal goal. . . . He is the man . . . who merely feels and acts . . . careless of its purpose and its form."

We must be careful, however, not to overstate the importance of civility. It is important but it is not all-important. There are other basic political goods that are just as important, and the often conflicting claims of these goods must be balanced in a way that allows the optimal enjoyment of all of them together. Civility, therefore, must be limited. There may be forms of civility that are contrary to human well-being. They may conflict with the rule of law, with the development of some conceptions of individuality, and with other basic political goods. The well-being of people in a society requires finding a reasonable balance between these conflicting claims, and finding it may involve reforming or even abandoning some forms of civility. It is a consequence of the balanced view of politics that all political goods are subject to limits that may vary with time, place, and context, and yet reasonable limits may always be found.

I conclude, then, that civility as a social condition should be added to the other political goods I have discussed, that is, to reason as prudence, the plurality of goods, necessary limits, limited liberty, toleration within reason, justice as having what one deserves, the right to private property, equality as the exclusion of arbitrariness, political democracy, and legitimate authority.

CONCLUSION

✦   ✦   ✦

*The nature of man is intricate; the objects of society are of
the greatest possible complexity; and therefore no simple disposition or direction of power can be suitable . . . to the quality of his affairs. When I hear the simplicity of contrivance
aimed at . . . I am at no loss to decide that the artificers are
grossly ignorant of their trade, or totally negligent of their
duty. . . . Political reason is a computing principle; adding,
subtracting, multiplying, and dividing, morally and not
metaphysically or mathematically, true moral denominations.*

EDMUND BURKE
Reflections on the Revolution in France

IT IS ODD THAT political dissatisfactions loom large in our consciousness but we pass over in silence the unprecedented prosperity, comfort, health, liberty, and stability we enjoy. We worry about
crime, pollution, terrorism, welfare, apathy, discrimination, drug
addiction, education, and about the approximately 15 percent in
our society who live below the so-called poverty level but who
would be regarded as prosperous in much of the rest of the world.
We forget that never before in human history has about 85 percent
of the population lived in greater or lesser affluence, that we live
longer, in better health, with less pain, in greater comfort, in a
more stable society than even the most fortunate aristocrats did in
the happiest historical epochs. We forget that the great changes we

are undergoing are not bloody revolutions, enraged uprisings of people with nothing to lose, nor foreign invasions, despotic dictators, or widespread starvation, but revolutions in birth control, medicine, communication, technology, travel, and the availability of information. We forget that these revolutions have made and are making our lives better. We forget that much of the rest of the world is trying to approximate what we have achieved, that tens of millions legally and illegally flock to our societies in the hope of sharing the life we have created for ourselves.

The key to our well-being is our political system, and the key to our political system is the balance of political goods that I have been discussing throughout this book. That balance has to be maintained actively because it is again and again disrupted by conflicting political goods, by ideologues who threaten it from the inside, by enemies who attack it from the outside, and by the unavoidable contingencies of life that unpredictably frustrate even our best efforts to cope with these threats. Maintaining the balance requires us to accept that the best will forever elude us and yet remain undeterred in our efforts to secure the political conditions of our well-being to the extent that is possible in our ever-changing circumstances in the face of unceasing threats. The ideological quest for the best undermines these conditions. We have learned from the bitter historical experience of religious fanaticism, Nazism, Communism, and other quests for the best that they have invariably ended up destroying the goods we need.

The political dissatisfactions that loom so large in our consciousness are caused not only by ideological crusaders and external enemies but also by the scarcity of our resources, not the least of which are honest politicians with adequate knowledge and good judgment; by our weakness of will and infirmity of purpose; and by the fact that we must create and maintain the political conditions of our well-being in a world that is at best indifferent and at worst hostile to whether we succeed. Our political dissatisfactions are real and numerous. The aim of politics is to cope with them, but as we do, we should not lose a sense of proportion. We should bear in mind that our satisfactions are no less real and numerous. In each chapter of the book I have tried to show the satisfactions we may derive from a particular political good and the dissatisfactions we may have to put up with because we cannot have as much of it as we would like.

It is obviously better to try to secure the political conditions of our well-being by relying on reason than on intuition, sentiment, faith, hope, and so forth. But reason in politics must typically proceed by making judgments based on imperfect knowledge, conflicting interests, and forever changing circumstances. Such judgments cannot yield certainty. For they are not about ascertainable facts but about the interpretation of shifting facts whose very relevance is often a matter of disagreement. There is, nevertheless, a reasonable judgment in every situation but it does not guarantee success, and even if it leads to success in one case, it cannot be generalized to other cases because the facts, the interests, and their comparative importance vary from case to case. Making reasonable judgments is an art, not a science.

We are impatient with lack of certainty. The attraction of ideologies is that they promise to make politics into a science, obviate the need for fallible judgments, and rely on universal principles that determine what ought to be done in all situations. I have argued throughout the book that this promise cannot be kept and the recurrent attempts to keep it lead to far more serious dissatisfactions than those caused by the fallibility of judgments. Reason requires us to accept that fallibility is part of our political condition. The refusal of ideologues to do so is a futile attempt to straighten the crooked timber of humanity.

In each chapter of the book I traced the contrary implications that follow from the acceptance of reasonable limits within which we can enjoy political goods and from the ideologically motivated urge to go beyond those limits. The plurality of goods we need for our well-being will conflict. Coping with their conflicts requires us to accept less of each of the goods than we would like. We gain from this the much greater benefit of having as much as possible of both goods. The unreasonable alternative is to opt for one good and neglect the other. Doing that would deprive us of the condition of our well-being that the neglected good would have provided.

If our motives were all benign and we were all reasonable, we would live together harmoniously and pursue goods without interfering with the attempts of others to do the same. Unfortunately we are also motivated by the darker urges of cruelty, greed, envy, hatred, aggression, and the like, and we are often unreasonable. This is why the imposition and enforcement of limits on human actions is a political necessity. We cannot have all the goods we would like, and those we can have we must pursue only in lawful ways.

Optimistic ideologues think that destructive motives and irrationality are the result of bad political conditions. They think that if the bad conditions were improved, we would have only benign motives and be guided only by good reasons. They adduce this optimistic illusion as one of the strongest reasons for following the dictates of their ideology. The temptation to think well of ourselves is strong but it should nevertheless be resisted. We must face the fact that political conditions are bad because those who are responsible for them are vicious or irrational; that there are benignly motivated and reasonable people even in bad political conditions; and that there are viciously motivated, unreasonable people even when the prevailing political conditions are good. The belief in the basic goodness of human nature is an illusion and a reasonable approach to politics must recognize that limits are necessary.

Within the necessary limits, however, liberty and toleration should be as extensive as possible. For liberty is the opportunity to make what we can of our lives. And toleration is the civilizing attitude that makes us refrain from interfering with others even if we find their lives and actions distasteful, unwise, misguided, foolish, or timid. But liberty and toleration must have limits and the limits must be justified. Some are justified because they protect basic goods we all need regardless of what our conception of well-being is. Other limits are justified because they protect the very existence of the evaluative framework that safeguards the basic goods and provides the possibilities of life we may try to realize. Although such limits are necessary, having them is compatible with changes in conventions about how basic goods are protected and what possibilities of life are recognized as feasible and desirable.

A great variety of conventions is necessary if we are to live together harmoniously. They make life orderly and predictable. They guide our conduct and expectations as we enter into relationships, make agreements, count on our security, and respect the security of others. These conventions establish what we do and do not deserve. But we often fail to get what we deserve and get what we do not deserve. This violates the prevailing sense of justice. Justice is the political good whose aim is to come as close as possible to people getting no more and no less than what they deserve. But as a result of immorality and irrationality, scarcity of resources, unavoidable practical obstacles, and the contingencies of life justice keeps breaking down. The aim of justice, therefore, is not the unreasonable pursuit of unattainable perfection but the realistic endeavor to minimize injustice as much as the prevailing conditions permit.

One of the things justice aims to protect is the right to legitimately acquired private property. Its protection is particularly important because private property provides the resources we all need to pursue our well-being. The right leaves it to our discretion how we use our property, provided only that we use it in conformity to the prevailing conventions that have stood the test of time and continue to be supported by the large majority of people in a society. The conventions are supported because they form a system of cooperation that aims to provide as great protection of our right to private property and as little interference with our liberty as is possible. One implication of this system is that significant inequalities will emerge in the quantity and quality of property we have.

For what we have and how we use it depends on inevitable individual differences in our abilities, circumstances, aspirations, and good and bad fortunes. These differences affect the resources we need for our well-being and lead to the difficult question of how much and what kind of inequality is acceptable.

The answer I have defended is that political and legal inequalities should be eliminated but economic inequality is unavoidable. Adults should have equal right to vote, unless they are disqualified by handicap or criminality, and the laws should apply equally to everyone. Economic inequality, however, is a consequence of people being at liberty to pursue their well-being. This liberty is the key to prosperity, to the betterment of our condition, and to people getting what they deserve and not getting what they do not deserve. Interference with it undermines both justice and liberty, and causes more harm than good. Egalitarian ideologues find this unacceptable and want to extend equality to the economic sphere. I have repeatedly pointed out the damaging consequences that follow. Egalitarianism involves depriving people of some of their property in order to benefit others. The supposed justification is that it is morally unacceptable for some to have more when others have less. But, since this so-called justification ignores the crucial questions of whether those who have more deserve it and those who have less are responsible for it, it is the supposed justification, not economic inequality, that is morally unacceptable. Egalitarianism is another misguided ideology that arbitrarily designates one good as the highest and makes it a policy to deprive us of other goods we need for our well-being. And yet it is the dominant ideology that threatens American society. I have argued that it is one of the most serious internal threats we face.

I have pointed out again and again the danger of sliding from the justified recognition of the importance of a political good to the unjustified assumption that since the good is good more of it is better. More is not better if having it is incompatible with having other just as important goods. This is the mistake egalitarians make about equality, and the same mistake is made by those who slide from the recognition that democracy is a political good to the assumption that it would be even better if it were extended to the personal spheres of life. The effect of this ill-advised extension is the government's invasion of privacy and interference with purely personal matters that should be left to the discretion of individuals. Our attitudes to family, intimacy, religion, illness, death, sex, work, recreation, exercise, money, art, and the like are essential components of our conception of well-being. In American society, the government's responsibility is not to shape our conceptions of well-being but to create the political conditions in which we can pursue whatever they happen to be so long as we allow others to do the same. Yet politically motivated interference with personal attitudes is ubiquitous. We are coerced by hundreds of state, local, and institutional rules and regulations to adopt attitudes others think we ought to have. This happens because the personal sphere is politicized by dedicated meddlers who make it their business to mind other people's business.

Implicit in the question of where democracy ends and the personal sphere begins is the nature and legitimacy of authority. The legitimate authority of democratic governments derives from the procedures specified in the prevailing laws and conventions. But the laws and conventions also set limits on how far its authority extends, and it does not extend to personal attitudes to religion, intimate relationships, aesthetic preferences, sex, work, death, illness, and so forth. This is not to say, however, that there can be no legitimate authority in the personal sphere. There can be and there is, but it is personal, not political. The legitimacy of personal authority derives from the many traditions—athletic, horticultural, scientific, literary, commercial, medical, aesthetic, educational, and so on—that form an essential part of the social identity of people in a particular society. Participants in these traditions are engaged in activities they find meaningful, activities that can be pursued more or less well, as judged by the standards that have emerged during the history of particular traditions. Personal authorities are legitimate if their performance is recognized as excellent by the prevailing standards and if they are articulate about why and how they do well what they do. Since other participants also aim to do well, they have good reason to appreciate and want to learn from those who excel. Personal authorities can help others to do better what they want to do. This is the key to their legitimacy.

The extension of political authority to the personal sphere reflects the failure to distinguish between the legitimate spheres of political and personal authority. The consequence is that personal authority is undermined, excellence at traditional activities becomes suspect, and a general leveling that is the bane of American society spreads. It is widely supposed that just as everyone's vote counts the same, so everyone's opinion is of equal value. But when there are standards of excellence, then the value of opinions depends on the standards and are not matters of taste or preference. To think otherwise is to impoverish life and undermine the traditions participation in which has made the lives of countless people meaningful. Widespread boredom, hunger for the cheap thrills of pornography, horror films, sensationalism, drugs, oriental cults, mindless television programs, and shopping as a favored pastime are some of the symptoms of this impoverishment.

Throughout the discussion of the various political goods we need for our well-being I have endeavored to show why they are good, why we need them, and what threatens them. The threats are numerous and mostly ideologically motivated, but I do not think that we need to despair over them. What we need to do is to guard against the threats and reaffirm our commitment to the goods. Whether we succeed or fail depends on many things, one of the most important of them is the persistence of civility, the spirit of cooperation and fellow feeling. If we lose the sense that we share our social identity, that we wish well and can count on each other, that we are committed to and are willing to defend the evaluative framework of our society, then, and only then, would despair be justified. Civility is certainly threatened. One of the most important things we can all do to protect it is to remain civil in our encounters with others, even when, and especially when, it is difficult.

NOTES

The notes that follow are meant to provide representative examples of the views I mention in the text, to suggest further readings, and to document that people really hold the views I attribute to them.

CHAPTER ONE: THE BALANCED VIEW

The non-ideological approach is followed by numerous conservative thinkers. Their views are often expressed casually, in criticism of ideologies, and appear scattered in several works. See Michel de Montaigne, *The Complete Essays of Montaigne*, (Stanford: Stanford University Press, 1588/1958), especially "Of Physiognomy" and "Of Experience." David Hume, *Enquiries concerning Human Understanding and Concerning the Principles of Morals*, ((Oxford: Clarendon Press, 1748–1751/1961), *Essays Moral, Political, and Literary*, (Indianapolis: LibertyClassics, 1777/1985). Edmund Burke, *Reflections on the Revolution in France*, (Indianapolis: Liberty Fund, 1790/1999). James Fitzjames Stephen in *Liberty, Equality, Fraternity*, (Indianapolis: Liberty Press, 1873/1993), and George Santayana in *Dominations and Powers*, (New York: Scribner's, 1951). Closer to our times, near contemporaries are Michael Oakeshott, especially in *Rationalism in Politics*, (Indianapolis: Liberty Press, 1962/1991) and *The Politics of Faith & the Politics of Scepticism*, (New Haven: Yale University Press, 1996). Elie Kedourie, *The Crossman Confessions*, (London: Mansell Publishing, 1984). Shirley Robin Letwin in *The Pursuit of Certainty*, (Cambridge: Cambridge University Press, 1965) and *The Gentleman in Trollope*, (Cambridge, MA.: Harvard University Press, 1982). The non-ideological approach is also followed by some liberals, such as are John Locke, *The Second Treatise of Government*, (Indianapolis: Hackett, 1690/1980). Albert de Montesquieu, *The Spirit of the Laws*, (New York: Macmillan, 1748/1949). Adam Smith, *The Theory of Moral Sentiment*, (Indianapolis: LibertyClassics, 1853/1969), and *An Inquiry into the Nature and Causes of the Wealth of Nations*, (Indianapolis:LibertyClassics, (1775–6/1981). Alexis de Tocqueville, *Democracy in America*, vols. I–II, (New York: Knopf, 1835, 1840/1945) and *The Old Regime and the French Revolution*, (New York: Doubleday, 1856/1955). Friedrich von Hayek, *Law, Legislation and Liberty*, vols I–III, (London: Routledge, 1973, 1976, 1979). Isaiah Berlin, *Four Essays on Liberty*, (Oxford: Oxford University Press, 1969). Jacob Talmon, *Origins of Totalitarian Democracy*, (London: Secker and Warburg, 1952). Leo Strauss, *Liberalism Ancient and Modern*, (New York: Basic Books, 1968) and *What is Political Philosophy?*, (Glencoe, IL.: Free Press, 1959).

Ideological thinkers are numerous, and I will mention only a few. Jean-Jacques Rousseau, *Discourse on the Origin of Inequality*, (Indianapolis: Hackett, 1754/1987) and *On the Social Contract*, (Indianapolis: Hackett, 1762/1987). Immanuel Kant, *Foundations of the Metaphysics of Morals*, (New York: Bobbs-Merrill, 1785/1959). Jeremy Bentham, *Introduction to the Principles of Morals and Legislation*, (Amherst, NY: Prometheus, 1781/1988). Karl Marx, *Manifesto of the Communist Party* in *Marx & Engels*, (New York: Doubleday, 1848/1959). John Stuart Mill in *Utilitarianism*, (Indianapolis: Hackett, 1861/1979), Ayn Rand, *Atlas Shrugged*, (New York: Dutton, 1957). John Rawls, *A Theory of Justice*, (Cambridge: Harvard University Press, 1974) and *Political Liberalism*, (New York: Columbia University Press, 1993).

Some ideologues committed to a highest good or a supreme principle are: Hobbes thinks that "the safety of the people" is the aim of government, see *Leviathan*, Part 2, Chapter XXX; Kant formulates the categorical imperative as the supreme principle of morality, see *Groundwork*, Preface; Bentham thinks that the greatest happiness is the guiding principle of morality and legislation, see *Principles of Morality and Legislation*; Mill gives liberty as the simple principle to which politics ought to conform, see *On Liberty*, Chapter 1; Berlin, inconsistently with his avowed pluralism, says at the end of "Two Concepts of Liberty" that "only rights can be regarded as absolute"; Rawls claims in *A Theory of Justice*, Chapter 1 that "justice is the first virtue of social institutions"; Dworkin calls equality "the sovereign virtue" in his book, *Sovereign Virtue*; Nozick holds that rights are morally inviolable, see *Anarchy, State, and Utopia*, Preface.

CHAPTER TWO: REASON AS PRUDENCE

The kidnappings, tortures, imprisonments, case histories, and the victims' experiences are cataloged in mind-numbing detail in A Report by Argentina's National Commission on Disappeared People, *Nunca Más* (*Never Again*), (London & Boston: Faber and Faber, 1984). A detailed chronology of events and the reasoning of those directing the transition are given by one of the chief participants, Carlos Santiago Nino, *Radical Evil on Trial*, (New Haven: Yale University Press, 1996). For general reflections and details on truth commissions, see Robert I. Rotberg & Dennis Thompson, eds. *Truth v. Justice: The Morality of Truth Commissions*, (Princeton: Princeton University Press, 2000). On the evil that was done and psychological motivation leading to it, see John Kekes, *The Roots of Evil*, (Ithaca: Cornell University Press, 2005), especially Chapter 6.

This chapter is indebted to Michael Oakeshott's "Rationalism in Politics" in *Rationalism in Politics*, op. cit. What Oakeshott means by rationalism is very close to what I mean by ideology. The literature on ideology is vast. Two useful surveys of it are Mostafa Rejai, "Ideology" in *Dictionary of the History of Ideas*, ed. Philip P. Wiener, (New York: Scribner's, 1973) and Michael Freeden, "Ideology, Political Theory and Political Philosophy" in *Handbook of Political Theory*, eds. Gerald F. Gaus & Chandran Kukathas, (London: Sage, 2004). Both essays have informative bibliographies.

The classic distinction between theoretical and practical reason is in Aristotle's *Nicomachean Ethics,* trans. W. D. Ross, rev. J. O. Urmson, in *The Complete Works of Aristotle,* ed. Jonathan Barnes, (Princeton: Princeton University Press, 1984) and in Immanuel Kant's *Critique of Practical Reason,* trans. Lewis White Beck, (Chicago: University of Chicago Press, 1788/1949) and *Groundwork of the Metaphysics of Morals,* op. cit. A good recent anthology and bibliography of contemporary approaches is *Ethics and Practical Reason,* eds. Garrett Cullity & Berys Gaut, (Oxford: Clarendon Press, 1997). A recent work also with a full bibliography is Henry S. Richardson's *Practical Reasoning about Final Ends,* (Cambridge: Cambridge University Press, 1994).

The distinction between what reason requires and allows is Bernard Gert's in *The Moral Rules,* (New York: Harper & Row, 1966/1973). The distinction between deliberation and justification is discussed, although not under these names, by Christine M. Korsgaard in *Creating the Kingdom of Ends,* (New York: Cambridge University Press, 1996) and *The Sources of Normativity,* (New York: Cambridge University Press, 1996).

Political judgment is discussed by Aristotle in *Politics, Complete Works,* op. cit.; by David Hume in *Essays,* op. cit.; by Hannah Arendt in practically everything she wrote; by John Dunn in *Interpreting Political Responsibility,* (Princeton: Princeton University Press, 1990), and by Ronald Beiner in *Political Judgment,* (Chicago: University of Chicago Press, 1983). The last two works have extensive bibliographies.

CHAPTER THREE: THE PLURALITY OF GOODS

For a survey of the current state of pluralism and an up-to-date bibliography, see Elinor Mason, "Value Pluralism" in the *Stanford Encyclopedia of Philosophy.* Book-length treatments of the subject are Isaiah Berlin, *Four Essays on Liberty,* (Oxford: Oxford University Press, 1969), Stuart Hampshire, *Morality and Conflict,* (Cambridge:

Harvard University Press, 1983), John Kekes, *The Morality of Pluralism*, (Princeton: Princeton University Press, 1993), Joseph Raz, *The Morality of Freedom*, (Oxford: Clarendon Press, 1986), Michael Stocker, *Plural and Conflicting Values*, (Oxford: Clarendon Press, 1990), and Michael Walzer, *Spheres of Justice*, (New York: Basic Books, 1983).

The passage from Hume is in *Enquiries concerning the Human Understanding and the Principles of Morals*, (Oxford: Clarendon Press, 1777/1902), 83. And the passage from Berlin is in "John Stuart Mill and the Ends of Life" in *Four Essays on Liberty*, (Oxford: Oxford University Press, 1969), 188.

For a survey of theories of human nature see Leslie Stevenson's *Seven Theories of Human Nature*, (Oxford: Clarendon Press, 1974) and *The Study of Human Nature*, (Oxford: Oxford University Press, 1981). For the political relevance of theories of human nature, see Ian Forbes and Steve Smith, eds. *Politics and Human Nature*, (London: Frances Pinter Publishers, 1983) and Christopher J. Berry, *Human Nature*, (London: Macmillan, 1986).

Recent defenses of natural law theories are John Finnis's *Natural Law and Natural Rights*, (Oxford: Clarendon Press, 1980) and Robert P. George's *In Defense of Natural Law*, (New York: Oxford University Press, 1999).

There is an enormous number of books on Kantian liberalism. The most influential contemporary work is John Rawls's *The Theory of Justice*, (Cambridge: Harvard University Press, 1974) and *Political Liberalism*, (New York: Columbia University Press, 1993).

Relativism has many versions, many defenders, and many critics. Useful collections of essays defending or criticizing relativism, and providing bibliographies are Michael Krausz & Jack W. Meiland, eds. *Relativism: Cognitive and Moral*, (Notre Dame: University of Notre Dame Press, 1982) and Michael Krausz, ed. *Relativism: Interpretation and Confrontation*, (Notre Dame: University of Notre Dame Press, 1989).

+   +   +

CHAPTER FOUR: NECESSARY LIMITS

I have used Michael Jameson's translation of Sophocles' "The Women of Trachis." See Sophocles II in *The Complete Greek Tragedies*, (Chicago: University of Chicago Press, 1957). Parenthetical references are to the lines of this translation.

On the simplicity of the ideological views of the good, see the references above in the last paragraph of notes to Chapter One.

On the realistic view of human nature, see any of Euripides' tragedies, especially *Bacchea*; Machiavelli's *The Prince*; Hobbes's *Leviathan*, "Of Man"; Bradley's *Ethical Studies*, Essay 7; Freud's *Civilization and Its Discontents* and *Beyond the Pleasure Principle*. Excellent historical studies are Richard Bernstein, *Radical Evil*, (Cambridge: Polity, 2002) and Susan Neiman, *Evil in Modern Thought*, (Princeton: Princeton University Press, 2002). See also, John Kekes, *The Roots of Evil*, (Ithaca: Cornell University Press, 2005).

Here are some highly influential views on the basic goodness of human nature: "the fundamental principle of all morality, about which I have reasoned in all my works . . . is that man is a naturally good creature, who loves justice and order; that there is no original perversity in the human heart." Jean-Jacques Rousseau, *Letter to Beaumont* in *Œuvres complètes*, 5 vols. (Paris: Gallimard, 1959–95), 935. The translation is Timothy O'Hagan's in *Rousseau*, (London: Routledge, 1999), 15.; "man (even the most wicked) does not, under any maxim whatsoever, repudiate the moral law in the manner of a rebel (renouncing obedience to it). The law, rather, forces itself upon him irresistibly by virtue of his moral predisposition." Immanuel Kant, *Religion within the Bounds of Reason Alone*, trans. Theodore M. Greene & Hoyt H. Hudson, (New York: Harper & Row, 1960), 31; the "leading department of our nature . . . this powerful natural sentiment . . . the social feeling of mankind—the desire to be in unity with our fellow creatures, which is already a powerful principle in human nature, and happily one of those which tend to become stronger, even without inculcation, from the influences of advancing civilization." John Stuart Mill, *Utilitarianism*, (Indianapolis: Hackett, 1979), Chapter 3; "the capacity for moral personality ... no race or recognized group of human beings ... lacks" and "moral personality is characterized by two capacities: one for a conception of the good, the other for a sense of justice." John Rawls, *A Theory of Justice*, (Cambridge: Harvard University Press, 1971), 506.

CHAPTER FIVE: LIMITED LIBERTY

This chapter is a revised version of an article published in *Social Philosophy and Policy* 23 (2006): 88–108.

Classic defenses of liberty are John Locke's *Second Treatise of Government*, Benjamin Constant's *The Liberty of the Ancients Compared with that of The Moderns*, Adam Smith's *An Inquiry into the Wealth of Nations*, and John Stuart Mill's *On Liberty*. An excellent anthology containing many of the most important contemporary works on liberty is David Miller's *Liberty*, (New York: Oxford University Press, 1991). Perhaps the most influential contemporary work on liberty is Isaiah Berlin's Inaugural Lecture in 1958, "Two Concepts of Liberty" reprinted in his *Four Essays on Liberty*, (Oxford: Oxford University Press, 1969).

An overview with an excellent bibliography of the libertarian conception is co-authored by Eric Mack and Gerald F. Gaus, "Classical Liberalism and Libertarianism: The Liberty Tradition" in *Handbook of Political Theory*, Gerald F. Gaus and Chandran Kukathas, eds. (London: Sage, 2004). Important statement and defense of this conception is in Friedrich A. Hayek's *The Constitution of Liberty*, (Chicago: University of Chicago Press, 1960). Good and sympathetic discussion of Hayek's work are John Gray's *Hayek on Liberty*, (Oxford: Blackwell, 1984) and Chandran Kukathas's *Hayek and Modern Liberalism*, (Oxford: Clarendon Press, 1989). See also

Jan Narveson, *The Libertarian Idea*, (Philadelphia: Temple University Press, 1988). The passages cited from Mill are in *On Liberty*, (Indianapolis: Bobbs-Merrill, 1956), pp. 17, 82, 93.

I have used the term, "eudaimonist conception", to cover a considerable variety of views. The term is my invention, and as far as I know it does not appear either in classical or contemporary works on liberty. The increasingly influential communitarian-civic republican views of liberty are among those covered by the term. The classic work on monist eudaimonism is Jean-Jacques Rousseau's *Social Contract*. The history of the civic republican view is most illuminatingly discussed by J.G.A. Pocock in *The Machiavellian Moment: Florentine Political Thought and the Atlantic Republican Tradition*, (Princeton, NJ: Princeton University Press, 1975) and Quentin Skinner in *Liberty Before Liberalism*, (Cambridge: Cambridge University Press, 1998). For an excellent survey and bibliography see Richard Dagger's "Communitarism and Republicanism" in *Handbook of Political Theory, op. cit.*

Contemporary versions of pluralist eudaimonism are Hannah Arendt, "What is Freedom?" in *Between Past and Future*, (New York: World Publishing, 1963), William Galston, *Liberal Purposes: Goods, Virtues, and Diversity in the Liberal State*, (Cambridge: Cambridge University Press, 1991), Philip Pettit, *Republicanism: A Theory of Freedom and Government*, (Oxford: Clarendon Press, 1997), and Charles Taylor, *Philosophical Papers 2*, see especially essays 7-12, (New York: Cambridge University Press, 1985).

Classic defenses of limited liberty are in Edmund Burke's *Reflections on the Revolution in France*, Baron de Montesquieu's *The Spirit of the Laws*, Alexis de Tocqueville's *Democracy in America*, and James Fitzjames Stephen's *Liberty, Equality, Fraternity*. Contemporary versions are Shirley Robin Letwin, *The Pursuit of Certainty*, (Cambridge: Cambridge University Press, 1965), Robert Nisbet, *The Twilight of Authority*, (New York: Oxford University Press, 1975), Michael Oakeshott's *Rationalism in Politics*, (Indianapolis: LibertyPress, 1991) and *On Human Conduct*, (Oxford: Clarendon

Press, 1975), Edward Shils, *The Virtue of Civility*, ed. Steven Grosby, (Indianapolis: Liberty Fund, 1997), and Leo Strauss, *What is Political Philosophy?* (Glencoe, IL: Free Press, 1958) and *Liberalism Ancient and Modern*, (New York: Basic Books, 1968).

CHAPTER SIX: TOLERATION WITHIN REASON

For a general survey of the issues involved in toleration and a bibliography of relevant works, see Rainer Forst, "Toleration" *Stanford Encyclopedia of Philosophy*, http://plato.stanford.edu. For the Communist Control Act of 1954, see U.S. Statutes at Large, Public Law 637. Good anthologies of essays with bibliographies are David Heyd, ed. *Toleration*, (Princeton: Princeton University Press, 1996); John Horton & Susan Mendus, eds. *Aspects of Toleration*, (London: Methuen, 1985); and Susan Mendus, *Justifying Toleration*, (Cambridge: Cambridge University Press, 1988). Two booklength works are Susan Mendus, *Toleration and the Limits of Liberalism*, (London: Macmillan, 1989) and Catriona McKinnon, *Toleration: A Critical Introduction*, (London: Routledge, 2006).

I discuss the problem of double-mindedness in "Liberal Double-Mindedness" in *Morality, Reflection and Ideology*, E.R.F. Harcourt, ed. (Oxford: Oxford University Press, 2000).

The parable about the porcupines is in Arthur Schopenhauer, *Parerga and Paralipomena*, vol. 2, trans. E. F. J. Payne, (Oxford: Clarendon Press, 1974/1851), 651–52.

The quotation about the clamor and dogmatism of ideologues is from David Hume, "Of the Protestant Succession" in *Essays Moral Political and Literary*, (Indianapolis: LibertyClassics, 1985/1777), 507.

For the expropriation of toleration by liberals, see e.g. "At the heart of the liberal position stand two ideas . . . pluralism . . . and toleration, or the idea that because reasonable persons disagree about the value of various conceptions of the good life, we must learn to live with those who do not share our ideals." Charles Larmore, *Pat-*

terns of Moral Complexity, (New York: Cambridge University Press, 1987), 23. "The success of liberal constitutionalism came as a discovery of a new social possibility; the possibility of a reasonably harmonious and stable pluralist society. Before the successful and peaceful practice of toleration in societies with liberal institutions there was no way of knowing of that possibility." John Rawls, *Political Liberalism*, (New York: Columbia University Press, 1993), xxv.

CHAPTER SEVEN: JUSTICE AS HAVING WHAT ONE DESERVES

The first thing that must be said about this chapter is that the nature of justice is at the center of contemporary political thought. Most contemporary approaches to justice are liberal and egalitarian. The account given in this chapter, therefore, is a controversial minority view.

Reliable surveys of the state of contemporary discussions are "Justice, distributive" in Lawrence C. Becker & Charlotte B. Becker, eds. *Encyclopedia of Ethics*, second edition, (New York: Routledge, 2001) and Julian Lamont, "Distributive Justice" in *Handbook of Political Theory*, Gerald F. Gaus & Chandran Kukathas, eds. (London: Sage Publications, 2004). A useful anthology of historical and contemporary accounts of justice is Robert C. Solomon & Mark C. Murphy, eds. *What is Justice?* (New York: Oxford University Press, 2000).

Contemporary discussions in one way or another, critically or otherwise, focus on John Rawls's egalitarian theory in *A Theory of Justice*, (Cambridge: Harvard University Press, 1974). An excellent discussion of justice is David Miller, *Principles of Social Justice*, (Cambridge: Harvard University Press, 1999). I discuss and criticize egalitarian views of justice in some details in *The Illusions of Egalitarianism*, (Ithaca: Cornell University Press, 2003).

In discussing what people deserve, I draw on the rapidly growing body of work including e.g. Joel Feinberg, "Justice and Personal Desert," *Nomos VI: Justice,* eds. Carl J. Friedrich and John W. Chapman. (New York: Atherton, 1963); William Galston, *Justice and the Human Good,* (Chicago: University of Chicago Press, 1980); John Kekes, *Against Liberalism,* (Ithaca: Cornell University Press, 1997), Chapter 6; David Miller, *Social Justice,* (Oxford: Clarendon Press, 1976); Michael J. Sandel, *Liberalism and the Limits of Justice,* (Cambridge: Cambridge University Press, 1982); and George Sher, *Desert,* (Princeton: Princeton University Press, 1987).

A good anthology is Louis Pojman & Owen McLeod, eds. *What Do We Deserve?* (New York: Oxford University Press, 1999).

For the moralistic tone of egalitarian ideologues, see for instance, "All humans have an equal basic moral status. They possess the same fundamental rights, and the comparable interests of each person should count the same in calculations that determine social policy. . . . These platitudes are virtually universally affirmed. A white supremacist or an admirer of Adolf Hitler who denies them is rightly regarded as beyond the pale of civilized dialogue." Richard Arneson, "What, If Anything Renders All Humans Morally Equal?" in *Singer and His Critics,* ed. Dale Jamieson, (Oxford: Blackwell, 1999), p. 103. "We cannot reject the egalitarian principle outright, because it is . . . immoral that [the government] should show more concern for the lives of some than of others." Ronald Dworkin, *Sovereign Virtue,* (Cambridge: Harvard University Press, 2000), p. 1. And "a distribution of wealth that dooms some citizens to a less fulfilling life than others, no matter what choices they make, is unacceptable, and the neglect of equality in contemporary politics is therefore shameful." Ronald Dworkin, "Equality—An Exchange," *Times Literary Supplement,* (December 1, 2000), p. 16. "Some theories, like Nazism, deny that each person matters equally. But such theories do not merit serious consideration." Will Kymlicka, *Liberalism, Community, and Culture,* (Oxford: Clarendon Press, 1989), p. 40. "Any political theory that aspires to moral decency must try to devise and justify a form of institutional life which answers to the real strength of impersonal values" and "impersonal values" commit one to "egalitarian impartiality." Thomas Nagel, *Mortal Questions*, (Cambridge: Cambridge University Press, 1979).

CHAPTER EIGHT: THE RIGHT TO PRIVATE PROPERTY

For surveys and bibliographies see, Lawrence C. Becker's "Property" *Encyclopedia of Ethics*, 2nd ed. Lawrence C. Becker & Charlotte B. Becker, eds. (New York: Routledge, 2001); Stephen R. Munser, "Property" *Routledge Encyclopedia of Philosophy*, E. Craig, ed. (London: Routledge, 1998); J. Roland Pennock & John W. Chapman, eds. *Property*, Nomos XXII, (New York: New York University Press, 1980), and Jeremy Waldron "Property" *Stanford Encyclopedia of Philosophy*, [http:/plato.stanford.edu/entries/property/].

The source of thinking of the right to private property as conventional, rather than natural, is David Hume's *Treatise of Human Nature*, Book III, Part II, Chapters II–III.

Understanding the right to private property as a bundle of rights is indebted to A. M. Honore's now classic "Ownership" in *Oxford Essays in Jurisprudence*, ed. A.G. Guest, (Oxford: Oxford University Press, 1961).

The discussion of the importance of the right to private property owes much to H. L. A. Hart's "Are There Any Natural Rights?" *Philosophical Review* 64 (1955): 175–91 and "Utilitarianism and Natural Rights" in *Essays in Jurisprudence and Philosophy*, (Oxford: Clarendon Press, 1983).

For an excellent discussion of the complexities of how property should be understood, see Jeremy Waldron, *The Right to Private Property*, (Oxford: Clarendon Press, 1988), Part One.

Some interest-based attempts at justification are R. M. Dworkin's *Taking Rights Seriously*, (Cambridge: Harvard University Press, 1977) and Neil MacCormick's *Legal Rights and Social Democracy*, (Oxford: Clarendon Press, 1982).

The classical account of the right to private property deriving from mixing one's labor with some freely available resource is John Locke's theory in *The Second Treatise of Government,* Chapter V.

Perhaps the best known contemporary version of the entitlement-based justification is Robert Nozick's *Anarchy, State, and Utopia,* (New York: Basic Books, 1974). The Wilt Chamberlain case is his.

There are numerous defenders of the utility-based justification. Perhaps the best known representative is Friedrich A. Hayek, *The Constitution of Liberty,* (Chicago: University of Chicago Press, 1960) and *The Mirage of Social Justice,* Volume II of *Law, Legislation and Liberty,* (Chicago: University of Chicago Press, 1976).

CHAPTER NINE: EQUALITY AS THE EXCLUSION OF ARBITRARINESS

This chapter uses parts of "Against Egalitarianism," a lecture I gave in 2006 to The Royal Institute of Philosophy and subsequently published in *Political Philosophy,* Anthony O'Hear, ed. (Cambridge: Cambridge University Press, 2007).

For further information on the Texas Rose Rustlers see Robin Chotzinoff, *People with Dirty Hands,* (New York: Macmillan, 1996). The passage about the dire consequences of egalitarianism is from Alexis de Tocqueville, *Democracy in America,* trans. Henry Reeve, (New York: Schocken, 1961), Vol II, 381.

Contemporary work on equality is voluminous and confusing. The source of the confusion is that egalitarians speak of distributive justice, when they mean equality. This reflects their view that justice consists in the equal distribution of resources. Part of my concern in this chapter is to contest this view.

A survey and bibliography of historical and contemporary works on equality is *Equality,* Louis Pojman & Robert Westmoreland, eds. (New York: Oxford University Press, 1997). For surveys of various views on equality, see Richard Arneson, "Equality" in *A Companion to Contemporary Political Philosophy,* Robert Goodin & Phillip Pettit, eds. (Oxford: Blackwell, 1993); and Brian Barry, "Equality" in *Encyclopedia of Ethics*, second edition, Lawrence C. Becker & Charlotte B. Becker, eds. (New York: Routledge, 2001); and Julian Lamont, "Distributive Justice" in *Handbook of Political Theory*, Gerald F. Gaus & Chandran Kukathas, (London: Sage Publications, 2004).

Egalitarians often rely on arguments derived from Locke and Kant, but their arguments actually support the balanced view that limits equality to the legal and political spheres. Both Locke and Kant explicitly deny that their arguments for equality extend to resources. Locke says: "Though I have said . . . that all men by nature are equal, I cannot be supposed to understand all sorts of equality . . . the equality I there spoke of . . . being equal right, every man hath, to his natural freedom without being subject to the will of any other man." *Second Treatise of Government*, Chapter VI, par. 54. As for Kant, he says: "This thoroughgoing equality of individuals within a state, as its subjects, is quite consistent with the greatest inequality in terms of the quantity and degree of their possessions, whether in physical or mental superiority over others or in external goods." "On the common saying: That may be correct in theory, but it is of no use in practice" in *Practical Philosophy* in *The Cambridge Edition of the Works of Immanuel Kant*, trans. ed. Mary J. Gregor, (Cambridge: Cambridge University Press, 1996), 292–293.

The most influential contemporary works defending egalitarianism are John Rawls's *A Theory of Justice*, (Cambridge: Harvard University Press, 1971), Ronald Dworkin's *Sovereign Virtue: The Theory and Practice of Equality*, (Cambridge: Harvard University Press, 2000), and Thomas Nagel's *Equality and Partiality*, (New York: Oxford University Press, 1991).

The passage quoted on p. 180 is from Ronald Dworkin, *Times Literary Supplement*, (December 1, 2000), p. 16. Here are some further examples of egalitarians who really hold the view I attribute to them: "Every nation of the world is divided into haves and have-nots. . . . The gap is enormous. Confronting these disparities, the egalitarian holds that it would be a morally better state of affairs if everyone enjoyed the same level of social and economic benefits." Arneson, "Equality," *op. cit.* p. 489. "Any political theory that aspires to moral decency must try to devise and justify a form of institutional life which answers to . . . egalitarian impartiality." Thomas Nagel, *Equality and Partiality*, op. cit. p. 20. "Undeserved inequalities call for redress . . . in order to treat all persons equally . . . society must . . . redress the bias of contingencies in the direction of equality . . . natural talents [should be treated] as common asset" and "distribution according to effort [is arbitrary because] the better endowed are more likely . . . to strive conscientiously, and there seems to be no way to discount for their greater good fortune. The idea of rewarding desert is impracticable." John Rawls, *Theory of Justice*, op. cit. pp. 100–101 and 311–312. "We want equalization of benefits . . . [because] in all cases where human beings are capable of enjoying the same goods . . . the intrinsic value of their enjoyment is the same." Gregory Vlastos, "Justice and Equality," in *Social Justice*, (Englewood Cliffs: Prentice-Hall, 1962), pp. 50–51.

The promised documentation on p. 182 that egalitarians admit that their view rests on a rationally unjustified act of faith are as follows: "Non-utilitarian moralities with robust substantive equality ideals cannot be made coherent." Richard Arneson, "What, If Anything, Renders All Humans Morally Equal?" in *Singer and His Critics*, Dale Jamieson, ed. (Oxford: Blackwell, 1999), p. 126; "The justification of the claim of fundamental equality has been held to be impossible because it is a rock-bottom ethical premise and so cannot be derived from anything else." Brian Barry, "Equality," *op. cit.* p. 324; "Equality is one of the oldest and deepest elements in liberal thought and it is neither more nor less 'natural' or 'rational' than any other constituent in them. Like all human ends it cannot be defended or justified, for it is itself which justifies other acts." Isaiah Berlin, "Equality" in *Concepts and Categories*, Henry Hardy, ed. (London: Hogarth, 1978), 102; egalitarianism "is not grounded on anything more ultimate than itself, and it is not demonstrably justifiable." Joel Feinberg, *Social Philosophy*, (Englewood Cliffs, N.J.: Prentice-Hall, 1973), p. 94; "I have tried to show the appeal of equality of resources. . . . I have not tried to defend it. . . . So the question arises whether the sort of defense could be provided. . . . I hope it is clear that I have not presented any such argument here." Dworkin, *Sovereign Virtue*, p. 1; another author says that he is going to explore a "type of argument that I think is likely to succeed. It would provide a moral basis for the kind of liberal egalitarianism that seems to me plausible. I do not have such an argument." This does not stop him, however, from claiming that "moral equality, [the] attempt to give equal weight, in essential respects, to each persons' point of view . . . might even be described as the mark of an enlightened ethic." Thomas Nagel, "Equality" in *Mortal Questions*, (Cambridge: Cambridge University Press, 1979), pp. 108, 112; another concludes his discussion of "The Basis of Equality" by saying that "essential equality is . . . equality of consideration," and goes on: "of course none of this is literally an argument. I have not set out the premises from which this conclusion follows." Rawls, *A Theory of Justice*, pp. 507 and 509; "We believe . . . that in some sense every citizen . . . deserves equal consideration. . . . We know that most people in the past have not shared [this belief]. . . . But for us, it is simply there." Bernard Williams, "Philosophy as a Humanistic Discipline," *Philosophy* 75 (2000), p. 492.

The example of abuse is quoted from Ronald Dworkin, *Sovereign Virtue, op. cit.* p. 130, and "Equality—An Exchange," *op. cit.* p. 16. Further examples are "All humans have an equal basic moral status. They possess the same fundamental rights, and the comparable interests of each person should count the same in calculations that determine social policy. . . . These platitudes are virtually universally affirmed. A white supremacist or an admirer of Adolf Hitler who denies them is rightly regarded as beyond the pale of civilized dialogue." Arneson, "What, If Anything, Renders All Humans Morally Equal?" *op. cit.* p. 103; "some theories, like Nazism, deny that each person matters equally. But such theories do not merit serious consideration." Will Kymlicka, *Liberalism, Community, and Culture*, (Oxford: Clarendon Press, 1989), p. 40; "any political theory that aspires to moral decency must try to devise and justify a form of institutional life which answers to the real strength of impersonal values" and "impersonal values" commit one to "egalitarian impartiality." Nagel, *Equality and Partiality*, op. cit. p. 20.

Just for the record, here are some of the abused critics of egalitarianism. John Charvet, *A Critique of Freedom and Equality*, (Cambridge: Cambridge University Press, 1981); Antony Flew, *The Politics of Procrustes*, (Buffalo: Prometheus Books, 1981); Harry G. Frankfurt, "Equality as a Moral Ideal" in *The Importance of What We Care About*, (Cambridge: Cambridge University Press, 1988) and "Equality and Respect" in *Necessity, Volition, and Love*, (Cambridge: Cambridge University Press, 1999); Friedrich A. Hayek, *The Constitution of Liberty*, (Chicago: University of Chicago Press, 1960); John Kekes, *Against Liberalism*, (Ithaca: Cornell University Press, 1997) and *The Illusions of Egalitarianism*, (Ithaca: Cornell University Press, 2003); J. R. Lucas, "Against Equality," *Philosophy* 40 (1965): 296–307 and "Against Equality Again," *Philosophy* 42 (1967): 255–280; Alasdair MacIntyre, After Virtue, (Notre Dame: University of Notre Dame Press, 1984); Wallace Matson, "What Rawls Calls Justice," *Occasional Review* 89 (1978): 45–57; and "Justice: A Funeral Oration," *Social Philosophy and Policy* 1 (1983): 94–113; Jan Narveson, *Respecting Persons in Theory and Practice*, (Lanham, MD: Rowman & Littlefield, 2002); Louis P. Pojman, "A Critique of Contemporary Egalitarianism," *Faith and Philosophy* 8 (1991): 481–504; and George Sher, *Desert*, (Princeton: Princeton University Press, 1987).

CHAPTER TEN: POLITICAL DEMOCRACY

Much has been written about democracy. Two useful surveys with representative bibliographies are Thomas Christiano's "Democracy"

in *Stanford Encyclopedia of Philosophy*, http://plato.stanford.edu/
entries/democracy/ and John S. Dryzek's "Democratic Political
Theory" in *Handbook of Political Theory*, eds. Gerald F. Gaus &
Chandran Kukathas, (London: Sage, 2004): 143–154.

The classic work that still dominates the field is Alexis de Tocqueville's *Democracy in America*, vols. 1–2, trans. Henry Reeve, rev.
Francis Bowen, (New York: Knopf, 1985). Both passages I have
cited from Tocqueville are from these volumes. For more contemporary reflections, see Friedrich A. Hayek's *The Constitution of Liberty*, (Chicago: University of Chicago Press, 1960); Robert A. Dahl,
Democracy and Its Critics, (New Haven: Yale University Press, 1989);
and John Dunn's *Rethinking Modern Political Theory*, (Cambridge:
Cambridge University Press, 1985).

On the dangers of politicization, see Kenneth S. Templeton, Jr.
ed. *The Politicization of Society*, (Indianapolis: LibertyPress, 1979).
This anthology contains significant articles on the subject, each
with references to further works.

The quotation from Dunn is from John Dunn's *The Cunning of
Unreason*, (New York: Basic Books, 2000). And the one from
Churchill is in *The Official Report, House of Commons*, (5th Series), 11
November 1947, vol. 444, cc. 206–207.

CHAPTER ELEVEN: LEGITIMATE AUTHORITY

This chapter is a much revised version of Chapter 7 of my *A Case
for Conservatism*, (Ithaca: Cornell University Press, 1998).

It is a peculiarity of contemporary work on authority that with
rare exceptions the authors ignore moral authority and concentrate
exclusively on political authority. The result is that political authority is discussed extensively and moral authority hardly at all.

For a survey of current work on political authority and good
bibliography, see Thomas Christiano, "Authority" in *Stanford Encyclopedia of Philosophy*. Two very good anthologies of important
articles on political authority are Carl J. Friedrich, ed. *Nomos I:*

Authority, (Cambridge: Harvard University Press, 1958) and Joseph Raz, ed. *Authority*, (New York: New York University Press, 1990).

For moral authority, see Hannah Arendt, "What is Authority?" in *Between Past and Future*, (Cleveland, Ohio: Meridian, 1968), John Kekes, "Moral Authority" in *A Case for Conservatism*, (Ithaca: Cornell University Press, 1998), and the exchange between R. S. Peters and Peter Winch in "Authority" in *Proceedings of the Aristotelian Society*, Supp. Vol. 32 (1958): 207–240.

The passage cited from Confucius is in *The Analects*, Book III, Chapters XVII and XVIII, trans. and exegetical notes by James Legge, (Oxford: Clarendon Press, 1893), see also Confucius, *The Analects*, trans. Raymond Dawson, (Oxford: Oxford University Press, 1993).

CHAPTER TWELVE: CIVILITY AS A SOCIAL CONDITION

Santayana's description is in George Santayana, *Character and Opinion in the United States*, (New York: Norton, 1967/1920), 195–200. The description of *skloka* is from Eliot Mossman, trans. ed. *The Correspondence of Boris Pasternak and Olga Friedenberg, 1910–1954*, (New York: Harcourt, 1982), 303–304.

My account of civility is deeply indebted to Michael Oakeshott's "On the Civil Condition" in his *Human Conduct*, (Oxford: Clarendon Press, 1975) and to Edward Shils, *The Virtue of Civility*, ed. Steven Grosby, (Indianapolis: Liberty Fund, 1997). My debt to them notwithstanding, there are some basic differences between their own quite different accounts and the account I have given. Oakeshott's view is that civility is a political, formal, and a law-governed procedural condition, whereas I think that it is nonpolitical, substantive, and conventional. Oakeshott concentrates on what I have called the relationship of civility and mentions the attitude involved in it only in passing, whereas I think that the attitude is also essential. Shils account is largely descriptive and sociological. I have only small disagreements with it as far as it goes but I do

not think that it goes far enough. I have found it insufficiently ana-
lytical and, in my opinion, it is insufficiently concerned with the
justification of civility. I have, therefore, tried to go beyond it on
these points.

The sources of the quotations illustrating the ideological criti-
cism of participation in particular forms of civility as immoral are,
in the order of citation in the text, as follows: the egalitarians are
Richard J. Arneson, "What, If Anything, Renders All Humans
Morally Equal?" in *Singer and His Critics*, ed. Dale Jamieson, (Oxford:
Blackwell, 1999), 103; Ronald Dworkin, Sovereign Virtue, (Cambridge: Harvard University Press, 2000), 130 and "Equality—An
Exchange," *Times Literary Supplement*, (December 1, 2000), 16; and
Will Kymlicka, *Liberalism, Community, and Culture*, (Oxford: Clarendon Press, 1989), 40; the utilitarian is Peter Singer, *Practical Ethics*,
2nd ed. (Cambridge: Cambridge University Press, 1993), 232; the
do-gooder is Martha Nussbaum, *Upheavals of Thought*, (Cambridge: Cambridge University Press, 2001), 309; the feminist is
Elizabeth Gross, "What is Feminist Theory?" in *Feminist Challenges*,
eds. Carole Pateman & Elizabeth Gross, (London: Allen & Unwin,
1986), 177; and the radical is cited in Jerry Martin, "The University
as Agent of Social Transformation" *Academic Questions*, 6 (1993):
55–72/61.

The historically shifting distinction between the public and the
private is well described by Hannah Arendt, "The Public and the
Private Realm" in *The Human Condition*, (Chicago: University of
Chicago Press, 1958) and Raymond Geuss, *Public Goods, Private
Goods*, (Princeton: Princeton University Press, 2001).

The best history I know of the gradual erosion of the distinction
between the private and the public in American life is Rochelle
Gurstein's *The Repeal of Reticence*, (New York: Hill and Wang,
1996). See also Roger Kimball's review in *The New Criterion* (Janu-
ary 1997): 20–25. For an outstanding contemporary account, see
Thomas Nagel, "Concealment and Exposure" in *Concealment and
Exposure*, (New York: Oxford University Press, 2002).

Notes

The abuse of the Supreme Court and of the Chief Justice is by Ronald Dworkin in "The Supreme Court Phalanx," *New York Review of Books*, 54 (September 27, 2007): 92 and 101.

The quotation about the barbarian is George Santayana's in "The Poetry of Barbarism" in *Interpretations of Poetry and Religion*, (New York: Harper, 1957/1924), 176–177.

INDEX

A NOTE ON THE TYPE

THE ART OF POLITICS *has been set in Monotype Columbus, a type designed by Patricia Saunders. A designer whose career spans the late years of hot-metal composition, the heyday of filmsetting, and the advent of digital typesetting, Saunders participated in the adaptation of a number of essential book faces for digital composition. Designed in 1992 in commemoration of Columbus's first voyage, the present type is based loosely on types used in Spain in the fifteenth and sixteenth centuries. No simplistic pastiche, Columbus has the lively rhythm most often found in types derived from hand-drawn characters, yet few of the quirks that impair the readability of a strict revival.*

DESIGN & COMPOSITION BY CARL W. SCARBROUGH